POLITICS AND ECONOMICS OF THE MIDDLE EAST

ECONOMIC AND SOCIAL ISSUES IN THE MIDDLE EAST AND NORTH AFRICAN COUNTRIES

Politics and Economics of the Middle East

Additional books in this series can be found on Nova's website under the Series tab.

Additional e-books in this series can be found on Nova's website under the e-book tab.

African Political, Economic and Security Issues

Additional books in this series can be found on Nova's website under the Series tab.

Additional e-books in this series can be found on Nova's website under the e-book tab.

POLITICS AND ECONOMICS OF THE MIDDLE EAST

ECONOMIC AND SOCIAL ISSUES IN THE MIDDLE EAST AND NORTH AFRICAN COUNTRIES

NILGÜN ÇIL YAVUZ, M.D.
EDITOR

nova publishers
New York

For permission to use material from this book please contact us:
Telephone 631-231-7269; Fax 631-231-8175
Web Site: http://www.novapublishers.com

Library of Congress Cataloging-in-Publication Data

Economic and social issues in the Middle East and North African countries / editors: Nilg|n Cil Yavuz (Istanbul University, Faculty of Economics, Department of Econometrics, Beyazit, Fatih, Istanbul, Turkey).
pages cm
Includes index.
ISBN: 978-1-62948-152-4 (hardcover)
1. Middle East--Economic conditions--1979- 2. Middle East--Social conditions--21st century. 3. Africa, North--Economic conditions--21st century. 4. Africa, North--Social conditions--21st century. I. Cil Yavuz, Nilg|n, editor of compilation. II. Cil Yavuz, Nilg|n. Purchasing power parity in selected MENA countries.
HC415.15.E26 2013
330.95605--dc23

2013034681

Published by Nova Science Publishers, Inc. † New York

CONTENTS

PREFACE

The Middle East and North Africa (MENA) countries have witnessed important complex economic, social and political changes and transition recently. These changes resulted from not only social and political reasons called "the Arab spring" but also economic reasons from the global economic crisis. External and internal dynamics of the MENA region force governments for a important transformation in terms of better democratic mechanisms, better governance and better social, political and economic environment. It is vital for MENA region to establish a modern and world class social, political and economic structure in order to increase sustainable improvements of the welfare of the society as soon as possible.

MENA economies have a great degree of heterogeneity across countries. Main source of economic growth is natural resources especially oil, natural gas and primary goods for many MENA economies. For this reason, the fluctuations in energy prices in the global economy deeply affect the economic performance and macroeconomic indicators of the economies. Therefore, MENA economies are exposed to macroeconomic vulnerability in the case of internal and external economic and political shocks because of the structural economic problems low productivity and global competitiveness level and foreign dependency in intermediate goods and finance.

In this perspective, main aim of this book is to shed light on the main economic, social and political problems and characteristics of MENA economies by considering the latest the global and regional turmoil. In this context, main contributions of the studies in the book can be summarized as follows:

Çil Yavuz investigates the validity of the purchasing power parity theory for MENA countries by using univariate and panel unit root tests with and without structural breaks over the period from 1990:01 through 2008:12. Çil Yavuz finds the evidence of purchasing power parity for Jordan and Turkey by allowing structural breaks in LM testing strategy, on the other hand Çil Yavuz finds that PPP is not valid only for Egypt by employing the Carrion-i-Silvestre et al. (2005) unit root tests.

Yılancı and Bilen test export led growth hypothesis for four countries namely; Algeria, Egypt, Morocco and Tunisia by using time varying causality test by obtaining critical values via bootstrap simulations over the period 1960 -2011. The results of the analysis show the instability of the export led growth and also growth led export for the interested countries.

Güloğlu and Sarıdoğan investigate the sources of economic growth in the selected MENA countries for the period 1988-2011 by using growth accounting methodology based on the Solow Growth Model and the panel DSUR methodology. Main finding of the study is that the average annual growth rate of GDP per capita for the selected MENA countries and the 1988-2011 period is 1.21 %. Based on the DSUR results, the contribution of capital stock per capita is 43% and the contribution of total factor productivity (TFP)is 57%.

Kıran investigates the validity of the Gibson paradox and Fisher hypothesis for selected MENA countries by using recently developed econometric methods. According to the results, Kıran finds that there is a long run relationship between price level and interest rate of Israel and Turkey, giving validity of the Gibson paradox. And also, there is a long run relationship between inflation and interest rate of Morocco and Turkey, meaning that Fisher hypothesis is valid.

Şener analyses the effects of the global economic crisis on the MENA countries. Şener finds that MENA countries has faced important changes because of the global economic crisis and the Arab Spring. The global financial crisis had important negative impact in MENA region through the decline in oil prices and turmoil in international financial markets. MENA was also hit by the secondary effects of the crisis on trade, remittances, and FDI. As a result, Şener states that MENA countries were affected importantly by the global economic crisis by the channels of declining international prices of the oil, decreasing export, deteriorating expectations and financial markets.

Metin investigates whether the economic freedom depends on the property rights, the freedom from corruption, the political rights and the civil liberties with the linear balanced pooled least squares models, the country specific fixed and random effects models and the country and period specific fixed and random effects models in the Middle East and North Africa from 1999 to

2012. Metin finds that the property rights, the freedom from corruption and the political rights from the significant variables have positive effects on the economic freedom, while the civil liberties has negative effect on the economic freedom. Metin suggests that various government policies should be regulated by considering these factors.

Zeren and Yaraşır Tülümce analyze regional convergence of human capital in Turkey in the period of 2002–2009 by using spatial dynamic panel data analysis. Zeren and Yaraşır Tülümce find that convergence of human capital was not achieved in the regions. Regions initially having low human capital did not achieve faster growth rates than wealthy regions. This result conforms to the expectations because the study does not take into consideration the unique aspects of those regions. Disparities between regions of Turkey cause this result

Metin in the her second study examines the effects of the fiscal freedom, the government spending, the business freedom, the monetary freedom, the trade freedom, the investment freedom and the financial freedom on the rule of law (the property rights and the freedom from corruption) with the linear balanced pooled least squares models, the country specific fixed and random effects models and the country and period specific fixed and random effects models in the Middle East and North Africa from 1999 to 2012. Metin finds that the business freedom, the monetary freedom, the financial freedom, the fiscal freedom and the government spending are the important determinants of rule of law.

Harakat investigates the historical, social, economic and political dynamics of the Arab Spring in MENA region. Harakat states that The Arab Spring constitutes perhaps the most far-reaching political and transition since the end communism in Europe. Indeed, the year 2011 started with stunning news from North Africa: the overthrows of the regime of Tunisia and Egypt. Tunisia in a month and Egypt after seventeen days. Such uprisings are an unprecedented event in the Arab word. New aspirations have been developing, with communication among the demonstrators greatly facilitated through the social media such as Facebook and Twitter. Harakat claims that The Arab people have become so energized and hopeful that they continue bravely making demands despite sometimes brutal government reprisals. Regardless of the final outcomes, the Arab people want change. The Arab spring rebellions occurred seemingly all at once; this was a social, economic, and political problems just waiting to boil over. It is a watershed even, and the surface stability imposed by repressive governments will never be the same.

As a result main economic policy recommendations for the sustainable long-run growth and welfare of the society for MENA countries are that it is vital to establish a modern and world class social, political, social and economic structure and stability in order to increase sustainable improvements of the welfare of the society and economic growth in the long run by improving democratic mechanisms, better governance and better social, political and economic environment and by increasing global competitiveness level via triggering science-technology and innovation oriented development policies such as research and development, education, improving qualified human capital.

Nilgün Çil Yavuz

In: Economic and Social Issues …
Editor: Nilgün Çil Yavuz
ISBN: 978-1-62948-152-4

Chapter 1

PURCHASING POWER PARITY IN SELECTED MENA COUNTRIES

Nilgün Çil Yavuz*
Department of Econometrics Istanbul University, Turkey

ABSTRACT

This chapter investigates the validity of the purchasing power parity theory for MENA countries by using univariate and panel unit root tests with and without structural breaks over the period from 1990:01 through 2008:12.

The results of the unit root tests not allowing structural breaks show the importance of the breaks and each of the real exchange rates of selected MENA countries are non-stationary. Furthermore, the panel LM test supports these results. By allowing structural breaks in LM testing strategy, we find the evidence of purchasing power parity for Jordan and Turkey.

In this chapter, we also employ the Carrion-i-Silvestre et al. (2005) unit root tests that show PPP is not valid for Egypt only. In the panel framework, we find the panel set as non-stationary only by using the panel LM test, which does not allow structural breaks.

---

* Email: yavuznc@istanbul.edu.tr.

1. INTRODUCTION

The purchasing power parity (PPP) theory is one of the oldest and most controversial theories in the determination of the exchange rate. First articulated by scholars of the Salamanca School in the sixteenth century, the simple empirical proposition of the purchasing power parity is that, once converted to a common currency, national price levels should be equal. The modern origins of purchasing power parity trace to the debate on how to restore the world financial system after its collapse during World War I. The Swedish economist Gustav Cassel promoted the use of PPP as a means for setting relative gold parities and treated PPP as a practical empirical theory. In essence, he used inflation differentials to calculate the exchange rate changes needed to maintain PPP (Rogoff, 1996).

Purchasing Power Parity asserts that the exchange rate change between two currencies over any period is determined by the change in the two countries' relative price levels. Because the theory singles out price level changes as the overriding determinant of exchange rate movements, it has also been called the "inflation theory of exchange rates" (Dornbusch, 1985).

The purchasing power parity doctrine has different versions; its "absolute version" states that the equilibrium exchange rate between domestic and foreign currencies equals the ratio between domestic and foreign prices. The "relative version" of the doctrine relates equilibrium changes in the exchange rate to changes in the ratio of domestic and foreign prices (Frenkel, 1978).

The basic building block for any variation of purchasing power parity is the so-called "law of one price" (LOP). Simply put, LOP states that once prices are converted to a common currency, the same good should sell for the same price in different countries. Clearly, the law of one price holds mainly in the breach. Tariffs, transportation costs, and nontariff barriers drive a wedge between prices in different countries with the size of the wedge depending on the tradability of the good. While few empirically literate economists take PPP seriously as a short-term proposition, most instinctively believe in some variant of purchasing power parity as an anchor for long-run, real exchange rates (Rogoff, 1996).

The purchasing-power parity doctrine has had its ebbs and flows over the years. Interest in the doctrine arose whenever existing exchange rates were considered unrealistic and the search began for the elusive concept of equilibrium rates (Balassa, 1964).

Taylor (2000) stated that empirical support for PPP has waxed and waned. From a historical standpoint, there have been numerous studies of PPP for various countries over the period in question, some covering a particular era or monetary regime.

Because of the importance and popularity of the PPP, there is a large and growing body of empirical literature testing the validity of PPP, particularly for the post-Bretton Woods floating period. The literature covers various approaches, especially based on the unit roots and cointegration techniques and their extensions.

In this study, we primarily focused on the validity of the PPP for selected Middle Eastern and North African (MENA) countries. MENA countries are characterized as small, open economies. The size indicates the vulnerability of these economies in terms of trade fluctuations, necessitating the transmission of external shocks to the domestic economy. The degree of openness further exacerbates the transmission channel because many of the MENA countries are highly dependent on the outside world for exports and imports (Bahmani-Oskooee and Kandil, 1997).

MENA countries are prone to high volatility in economic activity, and most of the MENA economies are dependent on their natural resources (mainly oil) and primary goods. The fluctuations in the world markets directly reflect on the economic performance of the region's economies (Abu-Qarn and Abu-Bader, 2007).

Although there are enormous bodies of literature that test the validity of the PPP, there are limited numbers of studies that test the validity of the PPP for the MENA countries.

Bahmani-Oskooee (1998) tested the purchasing power parity theory by testing for the stationarity of the real effective exchange rates of 11 countries in the Middle East. Bahmani-Oskooee (1998) found that, in eight countries, the real effective exchange rates were stationary, supporting the purchasing power parity theory.

Achy (2003) investigated purchasing power parity by examining the specific case of middle income countries. Achy (2003) stated that the ADF test suggests that the null of real exchange rate behaving as a unit root cannot be rejected in 32 of 38 cases. The PPP test provides evidence of parity reversion in eight of the 38 cases.

Narayana and Prasad (2005) examined the validity of the PPP for 11 Middle Eastern countries. Narayana and Prasad (2005) found evidence for PPP in only seven countries (Lebanon, Saudi Arabia, Egypt, Iran, Syria, Tunisia, and Sudan).

Bahmani-Oskooee and Kandil (2007) examined the validity of the PPP for 14 MENA countries by constructing the real effective exchange rates using annual data from 1970–2004. Bahmani-Oskooee and Kandil (2007) found that the standard ADF test supports the PPP only in three countries. However, when nonlinearity in the real effective exchange rates is incorporated into the testing procedure, the number of countries in which the PPP is validated increases to eight: Egypt, Jordan, Morocco, Oman, Qatar, Syria, Tunisia, and Turkey.

Drine and Rault (2008) examined the robustness of the PPP concept for a sample of 80 developed and developing countries. Drine and Rault (2008) found that strong a PPP is verified for OECD countries and a weak PPP for Middle Eastern and North African countries.

Kula et al. (2011) examined the Purchasing Power Parity hypothesis in 13 major MENA countries between 1970 and 1998 by using the Lagrange Multiplier unit root test that endogenously determines structural breaks in the level. They found evidence of PPP for eight of the 13 countries.

2. Econometric Methodology

In this section, a brief explanation of the univariate and panel unit root tests, with and without structural break(s), that were used in the empirical analysis of this study are presented.

2.1. Univariate LM Unit Root Tests

Because the panel LM unit root tests are applied by combining cross-sectional test statistics, we first employed univariate unit root tests. To make a basis for the unit root tests that allow structural breaks, we first describe standard unit root tests and then mention the remaining tests.

At the first step of the study, we apply the univariate LM unit root tests, with and without structural breaks, for testing stationarity of the real exchange rate series.

The LM unit root test is introduced by Schmidt and Phillips (1992, hereafter SP) and can be explained using the following data generating process (DGP) for y_t:

$$\begin{aligned} y_t &= \delta' Z_t + e_t, \\ e_t - \beta e_{t-1} &= \varepsilon_t \end{aligned} \qquad (1)$$

where is the real exchange rate (RER), is a vector of exogenous variables contained in the data generating process, and is an error term with classical properties $\varepsilon_t \sim iid\, N(0, \sigma^2)$. The test for the null hypothesis of the unit root is based on the parameter in Equation (1). Under the null hypothesis of $\beta = 1$, the maximum likelihood estimators (MLE) of can be obtained by estimation of the following equation with the ordinary least squares (OLS) method:

$$\Delta y_t = \delta \Delta Z_t + u_t, \tag{2}$$

where and ΔZ_t show the first differences of the and Z_t, respectively. Now we can obtain a detrended series by using the coefficients which are estimated from Equation (2), as follows:

t=2,…,T (3)

where is the restricted MLE of and equals $\tilde{\psi}_x = y_1 - Z_1\tilde{\delta}$. and Z_1 indicate the first observations of y_t and Z_t, respectively. are coefficients in the regression of on ΔZ_t, as stated above.

The LM-type unit root test statistic can be estimated from the following regression:

$$\Delta y_t = \delta' \Delta Z_t + \phi \tilde{S}_{t-1} + u_t \tag{4}$$

The unit root null hypothesis is described by and the LM t- test statistic is given by t- statistic testing the null hypothesis.

In the existence of autocorrelation in errors, augmentation terms $\Delta \tilde{S}_{t-j}$, j=1,…,k. are included in Equation (4) as suggested by Amsler and Lee (1995). Therefore, the LM test statistic is estimated by augmented regression, which is specified as:

$$\Delta y_t = \delta' \Delta Z_t + \phi \tilde{S}_{t-1} + \sum_1^k \gamma_j \Delta \tilde{S}_{t-j} + u_t \tag{5}$$

where k can be chosen based on the information criteria such as Akaike, Schwarz, etc.

Ever since the seminal work of Perron (1989), there has been a consensus that in the presence of structural breaks, the traditional unit root tests tend to under-reject the null of unit root. Since the introduction of structural breaks in unit root testing, several new unit root tests that consider structural breaks have been introduced into the literature. Though Zivot and Andrews (1992) (ZA) and Lumsdaine and Papell (1997) (LP) are among the most employed tests, because of their simplicity of implementation they are criticized for only allowing structural breaks under the alternative hypothesis. As also mentioned by Lee and Strazicich (2003, 2004), the rejection of the null hypothesis in Zivot and Andrews (1992) and Lumsdaine and Papell (1997) tests does not indicate the acceptance of stationarity with structural breaks. Instead, it indicates the acceptance of stationarity without structural breaks. Nunes et al. (1997) showed that this assumption leads to size distortions in the presence of a unit root with structural breaks. As a result, when utilizing ADF-type endogenous break unit root tests, one might conclude that a time series is trend stationary when, in fact, it is nonstationary with break(s), meaning that spurionus rejections might occur. In contrast to the ADF-type endogenous break tests, the LM unit root test is unaffected by structural breaks under the null hypothesis.

Lee and Strazicich (2003, 2004) suggested two LM unit root tests that allow one and two structural breaks by criticizing the studies of Zivot and Andrews (1992) and Lumsdaine and Papell (1997). These new unit root tests allow structural breaks under both the null and alternative hypotheses and based on Model A and Model C.

Although Perron (1989) employed three models to explain the dynamics of the process with structural breaks, Lee and Strazicich (2003), omitted this model because most economic time-series can be adequately described with Models A and C.

Model A is known as the "crash" model classification of Perron (1989), and it allows for a one-time change in the intercept under the alternative hypothesis. This model can be defined by replacing with in Model 1 where D_t =1 for and zero otherwise. is the date of the structural break and Model C is the second model of the one-break LM unit root test and is known as the "crash-cum-growth" model. It allows for a shift in the intercept and a change in the trend slope under the alternative hypothesis. Model C can be described by $Z_t = [1, t, D_t, DT_t]'$, where for $t \geq T_B + 1$ and zero otherwise.

We can define the models employed in the unit root test of Lee and Strazicich (2004) that allow two breaks as Model AA and Model CC. Model

AA, as an extension of Model A, allows for two shifts in the intercept and is described by where $D_{jt} = 1$ for $t \geq T_{Bj} + 1$, j = 1,2 and 0 otherwise. T_{Bj} denotes the date when the breaks occur. for $t \geq T_{Bj} + 1$, j = 1,2 and 0 otherwise. The Model CC, as an extension of Model C, includes two changes in the intercept and the slope. The Model CC is described by where $DT_{jt} = t - T_{Bj}$ for $t \geq T_{Bj} + 1$, j=1,2 and 0 otherwise. for $t \geq T_{Bj} + 1$, j = 1,2 and 0 otherwise.

One and two break LM-type unit root test statistics are obtained from the Equation (4). However, we redefine the to allow for structural breaks as for Model A and for the Model C, where and $D_t = \Delta DT_t$. B_t and D_t stand for a change in intercept and trend under the alternative and a one period jump and permanent change in drift under the null hypothesis, respectively. Similarly, while is for Model AA, it equals to for Model CC.

The LM test statistics that allow one and two breaks are given by $\tilde{\tau}$ = *t*-statistic for testing the unit root null hypothesis expressed as $\phi = 0$.

We determine the location of the break(s) (T_B) by selecting all possible break points for the minimum unit root test *t*-statistic as follows:

$$\text{Inf}\,\tilde{\tau}(\tilde{\lambda}_i) = \underset{\lambda}{Inf}\,\tilde{\tau}(\lambda),$$

where $\lambda = T_B / T$ and T is the sample size. The search is carried out over the trimming region (0.15*T*, 0.85*T*). Critical values for the one break case are tabulated in Lee and Strazicich (2003) while the two break cases are tabulated in Lee and Strazicich (2004).

2.2. Panel LM Unit Root Tests

In this section, we provide an overview of panel versions of the LM unit root tests, as mentioned in the previous section. The major reason for using panel data is that it increases the power of the tests.

Im et al. (2005) derive panel version of the LM unit root test proposed by SP (1992). They prove that the unit root test based on the Lagrange Multiplier (LM) principle is more powerful than Im, Pesaran, and Shin's (2003, IPS) unit root test that is based on the Dickey-Fuller test.

Another advantage of using the panel LM unit root test is that it is not affected by the presence of structural shifts. To illustrate the underlying model and testing procedure, we consider the following data generating process (DGP) for to test for stationarity in the panel data series:

$$
\begin{aligned}
y_{it} &= Z_{it} + e_{it}, \\
Z_{it} &= \gamma_{1i} + \gamma_{2i} t, \\
e_{it} - \beta_i e_{i,t-1} &= \varepsilon_{it}
\end{aligned}
\tag{6}
$$

where shows the RER again, *i* represents the cross-section of countries (*i* = *1, …, N*), *t* represents the time period (*t* = *1, …, T*), is a vector of exogenous variables. The parameter is used to test the unit root null hypothesis. is a zero-mean error term that allows for heterogeneous variance structure across cross-section units but assumes no cross-correlations. The parameter allows for heterogeneous measures of persistence. The panel LM unit root test statistic is obtained from the following regression:

$$\Delta y_{it} = \delta_i' \Delta Z_{it} + \phi_i \tilde{S}_{i,t-1} + u_{it} \tag{7}$$

where and are the first differenced values of y_{it} and Z_{it}, respectively, $\phi_i = -(1-\beta_i)$, is the detrended value of and is stochastic disturbance term of model. The univariate LM test statistics can be computed using the t–test that for all i (implying non-stationary) versus for some i (implying stationary). The presence of a unit root in Δy_{it} for country "i", in other words implies that the real exchange rate has a unit root for country i, thus PPP is not valid.

First, the optimal *t*-test statistic of the univariate LM unit root test, denoted as LM_i^{τ}, is estimated for the i th cross-section unit (e.g., individual countries). The panel LM unit root test statistic is computed by averaging the univariate LM statistics for each cross-section unit as follows:

$$LM_{\text{barNT}} = \frac{1}{N} \sum_{i=1}^{N} LM_i^{\tau}$$

where LM_i^τ represents either $MinLM$ or $Max|tb|$ of the *i*th cross-section unit, and *N* stands for the number of cross-section units. Im et al. (2005) constructed a standardized panel LM unit root test statistic that is defined as

$$\psi_{Lm} = \frac{\sqrt{N}\left[LM_{\text{barNT}} - E(L_T)\right]}{\sqrt{V(L_T)}}$$

where and are mean and variance of the univariate LM test statistic under the null hypothesis. Im et al. (2005) provide the numerical values for and $V(L_T)$ by computing for various combinations of *T* and *k*. The asymptotic distribution is unaffected by the presence of structural breaks, and the panel LM test statistic converges to a standard normal distribution asymptotically.

A structural break in the model can be incorporated by specifying as $[1, t, D_{it}, T_{it}]'$, where D_{it} is a dummy variable that denotes a mean shift while denotes a trend shift. If a structural break for country *i* occurs at TB_i, then the dummy variable if $t > TB_i$, zero otherwise, and if $t > TB_i$, zero otherwise. Two structural breaks are incorporated by specifying Z_{it} as $[1, t, D1_{it}, D2_{it}, T1_{it}, T2_{it}]'$, where $D1_{it}$ and are dummy variables that capture the first and second structural break, respectively. if $t > TB1$, zero otherwise; if $t > TB2$, zero otherwise and if $t > TB1$, zero otherwise; if $t > TB2$, zero otherwise.

2.3. Panel Unit Root Test with Multiple Structural Breaks

The unit root tests that allow for structural breaks and that are described in the previous section predetermine the number of structural breaks. Because this predetermination can cause loss of power, in this section, we mention a panel unit root test in which we specify the number of breaks endogeunsly.

Carrion-i- Silvestre et al. (2005) developed a test statistic for the null hypothesis of panel stationarity that allows for the presence of multiple structural breaks.

The procedure is based on the panel data version of the Kwiatkowski et al. (1992, KPSS hereafter) univariate stationarity test of Hadri (2000) for the case of multiple changes in level and slope.

The data generation process under the null hypothesis of stationarity is indicated as follows:

$$y_{i,t} = \alpha_i + \sum_{k=1}^{m_i} \theta_{i,k} DU_{i,k,t} + \beta_i t + \sum_{k=1}^{m_i} \gamma_{i,k} DT^*_{i,k,t} + \varepsilon_{i,t} \tag{8}$$

where represents real exchange rate in country i at time t; subscript time periods; shows members of individual countries in the panel; and error term. and are dummy variables and are defined as shown below:

$$DT^*_{i,k,t} == \begin{cases} t - T^i_{b,k} & t > T^i_{b,k} \\ 0 & \text{elsewhere} \end{cases}$$

$T^i_{b,k}$ denotes the kth date of the break for the ith cross section, and $m_i \geq 1$. The model in (1) includes individual effects, individual structural break effects, that is, shifts in the mean caused by the structural break—temporal effects—if $\beta_i \neq 0$, and temporal structural break effects—if $\gamma_{i,k} \neq 0$, that is, when there are shifts in the individual time trend.

The model in (1) includes individual effects and structural break effects.

This specification of the panel data model is, indeed, a counterpart of models with breaks proposed in the univariate framework. And so, when $\beta_i = \gamma_{i,k} = 0$, model in (8) the counterpart of the one proposed by Perron and Vogelsang (1992), whereas when $\beta_i \neq \gamma_{i,k} \neq 0$, we have the specification given by Perron's (1989) Model C.

According to Carrion-i- Silvestre et al. (2005), the important characteristics of the Model (1) are:

I. Individuals may have different numbers of structural breaks: $m_i \neq m_j$

,

II. The structural breaks may have different effects that are measured by $\theta_{i,k}$ and $\gamma_{i,k}$ on each individual time series

III. The structural breaks may be located at different dates. The dates of the breaks are not restricted to satisfy $T_{b,k}^{i} = T_{b,k}, \forall i = 1,\ldots,N$.

The test of the null hypothesis of a stationary panel follows the proposal of Hadri (2000), who designed a test statistic that is simply the average of the univariate stationarity test of Kwiatkowski et al. (1992). The LM test statistic ($\hat{\omega}^2 = N^{-1}\sum_{i=1}^{N}\hat{\omega}_i^2$) for panel stationary is calculated as the average of univariate KPSS tests as shown below:

$$LM(\lambda) = N^{-1}\sum_{i=1}^{N}\left(\hat{\omega}_i^{-2}T^{-2}\sum_{t=1}^{T}\hat{S}_{i,t}^{2}\right) \tag{9}$$

where $LM_i(\lambda_i) = \hat{\omega}^{-2}T^{-2}\sum_{t=1}^{T}\hat{S}_{i,t}^{2}$ is the univariate KPSS test for individual *i*. And $\hat{S}_{i,t} = \sum_{j=1}^{t}\hat{\varepsilon}_{i,j}$ denotes the partial sum process that is obtained using the estimated OLS residuals of Eq. (8), represents a heteroskedasticity and autocorrelation consistent (HAC) estimate of the long-run variance of $\varepsilon_{i,j}$, $\hat{\omega}_i^2 = \lim_{T\to\infty} T^{-1}E\left(S_{i,T}^{2}\right), i = 1,\ldots,N$. This allows the disturbances to be across the cross-sectional dimension. In this study, we estimate the long-run variance by employing the Bartlett kernel with automatic spectral window bandwidth selection as suggested by Sul et al. (2005). The test statistic in Equation (9) can also be used by assuming the homogeneity of the long-run variance across individuals. But in this case, it is formulated as with $\hat{\omega}^2 = N^{-1}\sum_{i=1}^{N}\hat{\omega}_i^2$. On the other hand, λ, in Equation (9) denotes the dependence of the test on the dates of the break. For each individual *i,* it is defined as the vector $\lambda_i = (\lambda_{i,1},\ldots\lambda_{i,m_i})' = (T_{b,1}^{i}/T,\ldots,T_{b,m_i}^{i}/T)'$, which indicates the relative positions of the dates of the breaks on the entire period, *T*.

The test statistic for the null hypothesis of a stationary panel with multiple shifts under the assumption of cross-section independence and the distribution of the statistic by means of bootstrap techniques is:

$$Z(\lambda) = \frac{\sqrt{N}\left(LM(\lambda) - \xi\right)}{\overline{\varsigma}} \sim N(0,1)$$

where and $\bar{\varsigma}^2$ are averages of the individual means and variances of $LM_i(\lambda_i)$, and are formulated as and $\bar{\varsigma}^2 = N^{-1}\sum_{i=1}^{N}\varsigma_i$, respectively. As in the case of the univariate KPSS test statistic, the null hypothesis of stationary in the panel is rejected for large values of $Z(\lambda)$.

The choice of dates of the breaks are based on the argument that minimizes the sequence of an individual *SSR* obtained Eq. (8) as follows:

$$(\hat{T}_{b,1}^{i}, \ldots, \hat{T}_{b,m_i}^{i}) = \arg\min SSR(T_{b,1}^{i}, \ldots, T_{b,m_i}^{i})$$

The dates for all possible for each *i* are estimated, where $m^{\max}$ is the maximum number of breaks. In this paper, the appropriate number of structural breaks is determined by using the modified Schwarz information criterion of Liu, Wu, and Zidek (LWZ, 1997) because Bai and Perron (2006) emphasized that the Modified Information Criterion performs better than the Bayesian Information Criterion in deciding the number of structural breaks. We have performed 10,000 bootstrap simulations to obtain the critical values.

3. Empirical Results

Having outlined the methodology behind the testing procedures employed in the analysis, we begin the empirical exercise with the application of univariate and panel unit root tests (LM-Panel LM), with and without structural breaks. We then submit the results from the panel stationarity test of Carrion-i- Silvestre et al. (2005) that allows for multiple level and slope shifts in the real exchange rate.

The real exchange rate data obtained from the International Financial Statistics (IFS) database of the IMF are used in our empirical analysis for the selected MENA countries of Algeria, Egypt, Iran, Israel, Jordan, Morocco, Saudi Arabia, Tunisia, and Turkey. The analysis covers the period from 1990:01 through 2008:12. Before undertaking the empirical analysis, the data are transformed into logarithmic form.

We first apply individual and panel LM unit root tests for the benchmark and to provide a basis for the unit root tests that allow structural breaks in the data. We report univariate and panel LM unit root tests in Table 1. We determine the maximum lag length by following the suggestion of Schwert (1989) and select the optimal lag length by using the t-significance method as suggested by Campbell and Perron (1992). In this lag selection method, we first estimate the relevant regression with the maximum lag length and test the significance of the last length. We continue this method by dropping the last lag until we find it significant.

The second column of Table 1 shows the LM test statistics. As we compare the calculated individual test statistics with the critical values, we conclude that the real exchange rates of these countries are not stationary at the conventional levels for statistical significance.

Table 1. Individual and Panel LM Unit Root Tests Without Structural Breaks

	Univariate	*k*
	LM test statistic	
Algeria	-2.556	8
Egypt	-2.31	8
Iran	-2.357	0
Israel	-1.587	8
Jordan	-1.631	2
Morocco	-1.488	4
Saudi Arabia	-1.075	1
Tunisia	-1.921	1
Turkey	-2.461	1
Panel LM test statistic = 0.115		

Notes: k shows the optimal lag length. The critical values for univariate LM test without structural break are −3.63, −3.06 and −2.77 at the 1%, 5% and 10% levels, respectively. The critical values for the panel LM test are: −2.326, −1.645 and −1.282 at the 1%, 5% and 10% levels, respectively.

Analysis of the panel LM test statistic, which is normally distributed, also leads us to reach the same result as the individual LM test. The panel data set, which is composed of the selected MENA countries, has a unit root because the test statistic, 0.115, is smaller than the critical values at the convention levels.

Taken together, these results from the LM unit root tests without structural breaks indicate that RERs for the selected MENA countries are nonstationary.

Perron (1989)'s pioneering study showed that ignoring possible structural breaks can lead to incorrect inferences while employing the unit root tests. Since this study was completed, many other studies have been introduced into the literature that consider structural breaks (see Zivot & Andrews, Lumsdaine

& Papell and Perron, for example). In this area, every new study was conducted by eliminating the drawbacks of the previous ones. The individual LM unit root tests that allow for structural breaks and that were used in this paper were developed by criticizing the Zivot & Andrews and Lumsdaine & Papell studies, mostly because those studies disallow structural breaks at the null hypotheses as discussed in the econometric methodology of this study.

We reported the test results of individual and panel LM tests allow for one structural break in Table 2. We prefer to use Model C for the unit root tests that allow structural breaks by following the suggestion of Sen (2003), who proved that when the dates of structural breaks are unknown, Model C is preferable to Model A. Because the critical values of the LM test depend on the location of the structural breaks, we also reported these locations in the fifth column of Table 2.

Indeed, the results confirm Perron's study because we found the real exchange rates of Jordan and Turkey as stationary, but they were found nonstationary by employing the traditional unit root tests. For the mentioned countries, we reject the null of unit root with one structural break against the alternative of stationarity with a structural break. Thus, we can conclude that PPP is valid for these countries.

In the fourth column of Table 2, we present the structural break dates. These structural break dates can also be informative. By analyzing the economic and politic history of the relevant countries in the sample period, we can show which events caused the structural breaks. For example, the election in April 2004, and also the relationship with the United States that was improving in 2004, could have caused the structural break in June 2004. However, the analysis of the results of the panel LM unit root test with a structural break show that the panel is stationary because the test statistic, -7.273, is greater than the critical values are, which leads us to accept the PPP hypothesis for the panel of selected MENA countries.

To consider only one structural break in the case of multiple breaks can cause the non-rejection of the null hypothesis of the unit root, and it could also lead to loss of information as expressed by Lumsdaine and Papell (1997) and Ben-David et al. (2003). Hence, at this step, we employ the unit root tests that allow two structural breaks to see whether allowing one more structural break changes the results. The test results are reported in Table 3.Because the critical values depend on the location of structural breaks, we also presented these locations to obtain the relevant critical values that we placed in the lower part of Table 2. Here, we find the real exchange rate of Jordan as stationary, which indicates the PPP is valid for this country.

Table 2. Panel and Individual LM Unit Root Tests with One Structural Break

	Test statistic	*k*	TB	λ
Algeria	-4.167	8	Jun-2004	0.763
Egypt	-2.497	8	Apr-2002	0.649
Iran	-2.546	0	Jan-1993	0.162
Israel	-2.772	8	Jun-2001	0.605
Jordan	-4.925	1	Jun-2005	0.816
Morocco	-3.025	1	Nov-2000	0.575
Saudi Arabia	-2.639	1	Jun-2005	0.816
Tunisia	-3.349	1	Mar-2000	0.539
Turkey	-4.359	1	Oct-2002	0.675
Panel LM Test Statistic with one structural break:	-7.273			
Critical Values				
λ		1%	5%	10%
0.1		-5.11	-4.50	-4.21
0.2		-5.07	-4.47	-4.20
0.3		-5.15	-4.45	-4.18
0.4		–5.05	-4.50	-4.18
0.5		-5.11	-4.51	-4.17

Notes: The critical values for the panel LM test with one break are −2.326, −1.645 and −1.282at the 1%, 5% and 10% levels, respectively.

The main difference between the last two results seems to be the break dates. While the structural break occurs in June 2004 for Algeria, allowance for two structural breaks changes these dates to March 1992 and March 2000, which are far from June 2004.

The underlying reason for this change can be the way that we obtain the test statistics. Certainly, these break dates can also be indicators of important economic or political events. At the bottom of Table 3, we also present the panel version of this unit root test. We previously mentioned in the econometric methodology section that the structural breaks do not change the distribution of the panel LM test, so by comparing the panel LM test statistic, -10. 377, with the critical values, we can conclude that the panel is stationary.

Table 3. Panel and Individual LM Unit Root Tests with Two Structural Breaks

	Test statistic	*k*	TB1	TB2	λ1	λ2
Algeria	-5.2009	8	Mar-1992	Mar-2000	0.118421	0.539474
Egypt	-3.8596	8	Jun-1994	Nov-2002	0.236842	0.679825
Iran	-3.9247	8	May-1993	Feb-2002	0.179825	0.640351
Israel	-4.0385	4	Jul-1997	Sep-2006	0.399123	0.881579
Jordan	-6.324	1	Apr-2000	Jun-2006	0.54386	0.868421
Morocco	-4.7702	1	Feb-1995	Apr-2002	0.27193	0.649123
Saudi Arabia	-4.7887	1	Dec-1999	Dec-2006	0.526316	0.894737
Tunisia	-4.0103	1	Sep-1996	May-2002	0.355263	0.653509
Turkey	-5.2191	3	Nov-1993	Feb-2003	0.20614	0.692982
Panel LM Test Statistic with two structural breaks: -10.377						
Critical Values						

	λ2								
λ1	0.4			0.6			0.8		
0.2	-6.16	-5.59	-5.27	-6.41	-5.74	-5.32	-6.33	-5.71	-5.33
0.4	-	-	-	-6.45	-5.67	-5.31	-6.42	-5.65	-5.32
0.6	-	-	-	-	-	-	-6.32	-5.73	-5.32

Notes: Critical values for the panel LM test are: −2.326, −1.645 and −1.282 at the1%, 5% and 10% levels, respectively.

A drawback of the LM unit root tests is the determination of the number of structural breaks a priori. By employing panel stationarity tests, we can overcome this deficiency because the number of structural breaks is determined endogenously. Another difference between the CS test and the LM test is testing the null of stationarity against the alternative of the unit root. Table 4 shows both the KPSS stationarity test with structural breaks and the panel stationarity test of Carrion Silvestre. We determine the number of structural breaks with the LWZ method. Necessary critical values were obtained by using 10,000 bootstrap simulations. For each of the series, the number of structural breaks found was two. Thus, when we can compare break dates with the LM unit root test with two structural breaks, we observe that different break dates are found by using these two tests. The main reason underlying this difference is the different estimation methods used.

Table 4. CS Stationarity Tests and Individual Tests with Structural Breaks

					Finite Sample Critical Values (%)		
	KPSS	m	TB1	TB2	10%	5%	1%
Algeria	0.013	2	Oct-1992	Mar-2000	0.043	0.050	0.065
Egypt	0.072	2	Oct-1992	Dec-2002	0.046	0.054	0.070
Iran	0.060	2	Feb-1993	Feb-1995	0.044	0.050	0.064
Israel	0.025	2	Nov-1994	Nov-2001	0.052	0.061	0.078
Jordan	0.033	2	May-2000	Feb-2006	0.047	0.054	0.074
Morocco	0.017	2	Jan-1995	Mar-2000	0.037	0.041	0.051
Saudi Arabia	0.029	2	Dec-1994	Feb-2006	0.050	0.062	0.094
Tunisia	0.014	2	Mar-1995	Feb-2000	0.037	0.042	0.051
Turkey	0.046	2	Dec-1993	Mar-2003	0.040	0.045	0.057
Panel Data Stationarity Tests							
Homogeneity	8.732				4.504	6.206	9.698
Heterogeneity	2.1				2.23	2.818	3.8

As can easily be observed from Table 4, not only are the break dates different, but so are the conclusions about the stationarity properties of the series. We find the real exchange rates of the countries, except Egypt, as stationary, which provides strong evidence for PPP. We also presented the panel CS test results at the bottom of Table 4, which shows these results of the panel as stationary.

Consequently, all the panel unit root tests employed, except the panel LM unit root test that does not allow any structural breaks, provide evidence of PPP that also shows the importance of considering possible structural breaks in unit root testing.

CONCLUSION

In recent years, the purchasing power parity hypothesis has been among the most popular tested theories. Several different econometric methodologies have been employed for different countries and regions, and they show different results. In this study, we focus on the MENA region that has been rarely investigated. By employing unit root tests that allow structural breaks, we aim to analyze the effects of the events, such as economic crises and oil shocks. The results of the unit root tests that do not allow structural breaks show the importance of the breaks because these results show that each of the real exchange rates of selected MENA countries are non-stationary. Furthermore, the panel LM test supports these results. By allowing structural breaks in the LM testing strategy, we find evidence of PPP for Jordan and Turkey. Because the LM tests predetermine the number of breaks, we also employ the Carrion-i-Silvestre et al. (2005) unit root tests that show the PPP is not valid, except for Egypt. In the panel framework, we find this panel set as non-stationary by using the panel LM test that does not allow structural breaks.

References

Abu-Qarn, A.S. & Abu-Bader, S. (2007). Sources of Growth Revisited: Evidence from Selected MENA Countries. *World Development*, 35, 5, 752–771.

Achy, L. (2003). Parity Reversion Persistence in Real Exchange Rates: Middle Income Country Case. *Applied Economics*, 35, 5, 541-553.

Amsler, C. & Lee, J. (1995). An LM Test for a Unit Root in the Presence of a Structural Change. *Econometric Theory: Cambridge University Press*, 11(02), 359-368.

Bahmani-Oskooee, M. (1998). Do Exchange Rates Follow a Random Walk Process in Middle Eastern Countries?. *Economics Letters*, 58, 339–344.

Bahmani-Oskooee, M. & Kandil, M. (2007). Testing the PPP in the Non-linear STAR Framework: Evidence from MENA Countries. *Scientific Journal of Administrative Development*, 5, 19-33.

Bai, J. & Perron, P. (2006). Multiple Structural Change Models: A simulation Analysis. in D. Corbae, S. N. Durlauf, and B. E. Hansen (eds.), Econometric Theory and Practice: Frontiers of Analysis and Applied Research, 212- 237. Cambridge University Press, New York.

Balassa, B. (1964). The Purchasing Power Parity Doctrine: A Reappraisal. *Journal of Political Economy*, 72, 6, 584-596.

Ben-David, D., Lumsdaine, R. & Papell, D.H. (2003). Unit Root, Postwar Slowdowns and Long-Run Growth: Evidence from Two Structural Breaks. *Empirical Economics,* 28(2), 303-319.

Campbell, J.Y. & Perron, P. (1992). Pitfalls and Oppurtunities: What Macroeconomists should Know about Unit Roots. in O.J. Blanchard and J. Fisher (eds.), NBER Economics Annual, Cambridge, MA: MIT Press.

Carrion-i-Silvestre, J.L., Barrio-Castro, T. & Lopez-Bazo, E. (2005). Breaking the Panels. An Application to the GDP per capita. *Econometrics Journal*, 8, 159-175.

Dornbusch, R. (1985). Purchasing Power Parity. *NBER Working Paper Series*, 1591.

Drine, I. & Rault, C. (2008). Purchasing Power Parity for Developing and Developed Countries. What Can We Learn From Non-Stationary Panel Data Models?. *Journal of Economic Surveys*, 22, 4, 752–773.

Frenkel, J.A. (1978). Purchasing Power Parity: Doctrinal Perspective and Evidence from the 1920s. *Journal of International Economics*, 8, 2, 169–191.

Hadri, K. (2000). Testing for Stationarity in Heterogeneous Panel Data. *The Econometrics Journal*, 3, 148–161. doi: 10.1111/1368-423X.00043.

Im, K.S., Lee, J. & Tieslau, M. (2005). Panel LM Unit Root Tests with Level Shifts. *Oxford Bulletin of Economics and Statistics*, 67, 393–419.

Im, K.S., Pesaran, M.H. & Shin, Y. (2003). Testing for Unit Roots in Heterogeneous Panels. *Journal of Economics*, 115, 53-74.

Kula, F., Aslan A. & Feridun M. (2011). Purchasing Power Parity in Mena Revisited: Empirical Evidence in the Presence of Endogenously Determined Break Points. *Ekonomska istraživanja*, 24, 1, 1-12.

Kwiatkowski, D., Phillips, P.C.B., Schmidt, P. & Shin, Y. (1992). Testing the Null Hypothesis of Stationarity against the Alternative of a Unit Root: How sure are we that Economic Time Series Have a Unit Root?. *Journal of Econometrics*, 54, 159–178.

Lee, J. & Strazicich, M.C. (2004). Minimum LM Unit Root Test with One Structural Break. *Appalachian State University Working Papers*, 04-17, 1-15.

Lee, J. & Strazicich, M.C. (2003). Minimum Lagrange Multiplier Unit Root Test With Two Structural Breaks. *The Review of Economics and Statistics*, 85, 4, 1082-1089.

Liu, J., Wu, S. & Zidek, J.V. (1997). On Segmented Multivariate Regressions. *Statistica Sinica*, 7, 497–525.

Lumsdaine, R.L. & Papell, D.H. (1997). Multiple Trend Breaks and the Unit Root Hypothesis. *The Review of Economics and Statistics*, 79, 2, 212-218.

Narayana, P. K. & Prasad, B.C. (2005). The Validity of Purchasing Power Parity Hypothesis for

Eleven Middle Eastern Countries. *Review of Middle East Economics and Finance*, 3, 2, 135-149.

Nunes, L., Newbold, P. & Kuan, C. (1997). Testing for Unit Roots with Breaks: Evidence on the Great Crash and the Unit Root Hypothesis Reconsidered. *Oxford Bulletin of Economics and Statistics*, 59, 435-448.

Perron, P. & Vogelsang, T. J. (1992). Nonstationarity and Level Shifts with an Application to

Purchasing Power Parity. *Journal of Business and Economic Statistics*, 10, 301–320.

Perron, P. (1989). The Great Crash, the Oil Price Shock and the Unit Root Hypothesis. *Econometrica,* 57(6), 1361-1401.

Rogoff, K. (1996). The Purchasing Power Parity Puzzle. *Journal of Economic Literature*, 34, 2, 647-668.

Schmidt, P. & Phillips, P.C.B. (1992). LM Tests For A Unit Root In The Presence Of Deterministic Trends. *Oxford Bulletin of Economics and Statistics*, 54, 257–287. doi: 10.1111/j.1468-0084.1992.tb00002.x

Schwert, G.W. (1989). Tests for Unit Roots: A Monte Carlo Investigation. J*ournal of Business and Economic* Statistics, 7, 147-159.

Sen, A. (2003). On Unit Root Tests when the Alternative is a Trend-Break Stationary Process. *Journal of Business and Economic Statistics*, 21(1), 174-184.

Sul, D., Phillips, P.C.B. & Choi, C.Y. (2005). Prewhitening Bias in HAC Estimations. *Oxford Bulletin of Economics and Statistics*, 67, 517–546.

Taylor, A. (2000). A Century of Purchasing Parity. *NBER Working Paper*, 8012.

Zivot, E. & Andrews, D.W.K. (1992). Further Evidence on the Great Crash, the Oil-Price Shock, and the Unit-Root Hypothesis. *Journal of Business & Economic Statistics, American Statistical Association*, 10(3), 251-270.

In: Economic and Social Issues …
Editor: Nilgün Çil Yavuz

ISBN: 978-1-62948-152-4

Chapter 2

Is Export-Led Growth Hypothesis Stable? Evidence from Time Varying Causality Test

***Veli Yilanci*[1,*] *and Mahmut Bilen*[2,†]**
[1]Sakarya University, Faculty of Economics and Administrative Sciences, Department of Financial Econometrics, Turkey
[2]Sakarya University, Faculty of Economics and Administrative Sciences, Department of Economics, Turkey

Abstract

One of the important tools of emerging markets for accelerating economic growth is increasing exports since an increase in exports also stimulates the production of goods and services. This situation is known as export led growth hypothesis. In this study we test this hypothesis in four countries; Algeria, Egypt, Morocco and Tunisia by using time varying causality test by obtaining critical values via bootstrap simulations over the period 1960 -2011. The results of the analysis show the instability of both export led growth and also growth led export hypotheses for the interested countries.

---

* Assist. Prof. Dr. Sakarya University, Faculty of Economics and Administrative Sciences, Department of Financial Econometrics, yilanci@sakarya.edu.tr.
† Assoc. Prof. Dr. Sakarya University, Faculty of Economics and Administrative Sciences, Department of Economics, bilen@sakarya.edu.tr.

1. INTRODUCTION

Developing countries aim to accelerate their economic growth and one of the ways to achieve this objective is to increase the exports. Hence, to investigate the possible relationship between exports and economic growth has been one of the popular issues in the economic literature to answer the question that of whether a country can stimulate economic growth by promoting exports or not.

There are four types of relationships between exports and economic growth. First of them is known as export led growth (ELG) hypothesis that suppose exports lead economic growth. The main underlying reason for this statement is; introducing of new technologies to the exporting countries and also diffusion of technological knowledge which reduces production costs. On the other hand, the increasing exports also lead to economic growth by increasing the production of goods and services directly. Another explanation for the ELG hypothesis that, increasing foreign exchange rates decrease the pressure on the balance of payments and also provides imports of high quality goods and services that enchance production opportunities.

Second; the finding of the direction of the causality relationship from economic growth to exports known as growth-led export hypothesis that is based on the idea that; economic growth leads the increased efficiency and usage of new technologies that creates a comparative advantage for the country exporting goods and services (Krugman, 1984).

Third; there can be bidirectional causality between exports and output. As Bhagwati (1988) argues; increasing trade may stimulate economic growth which leads to more trade and these consecutive increases continues. Lastly, there can be no causal relationship between the variables. Giles and Williams (2000) states that this case can occur if the growth paths of these two variables are determined by unrelated variables.

There are numerous studies in the literature on the export led growth hypothesis for both developing and developed countries. Panas and Vamvoukas (2002) attempt to deal with the ELG hypothesis for Greece employing annual data which covers the time period 1948-1997 and cannot find supportive evidence. By using cointegration and causality tests, Simsek (2003) tests the validity of the ELG hypothesis in Turkish economy, employing the data over the period 1960-2002 and conclude that the ELG hypothesis is not valid for the analysis period. Abual- Foul (2004) tests the ELG hypothesis for Jordan by using annual data for 1976-1997. Abual-Foul employs three specification of alternative bivariate models as vector autoregressive model (VAR) in levels, VAR in first differences and error correction models. The findings of this study lend support to the ELG hypothesis in the analysis period.

In their studies Mamun and Nath (2005), investigate the same issue for Bangladesh. They employ quarterly data from 1976 to 2003 and use industrial production for the economic growth indicator. Since the results of Engle-Granger cointegration test show there is a long run relationship between the variables, they test the causality relationship in the vector error correction model framework. While they claim there is no evidence of short run causality between the variables, there is a unidirectional causality from exports to industrial production in the long run, which shows the validity of ELG hypothesis only in the long run. Narayan et al. (2007) examine the ELG hypothesis for Papua New Guinea and Fiji using bounds approach to the cointegration and Granger causality tests. The results of this paper show that the ELG hypothesis cannot be rejected for Fiji in the long run and for Papua New Guinea in the short run. Jordaan and Eita (2009) find that both export led growth and growth led export hypotheses are valid in Botswana by using quarterly data for the period 1996 to 2007. In his study, Tastan (2010) investigates export led growth hypothesis for Turkey over the period 1989:01 – 2009:05 employing spectral causality test and the results of the paper support evidence of export led growth and growth led export hypothesis. Seabra and Galimberti (2012) examine the export led growth for 72 countries using panel threshold regression over the period 1974-2003. They found the positive effects of exports on growth in transition and for countries with lower human capital levels. Sandalcilar (2012) investigates the relationship between economic growth and exports in the Brazil, China, India and Russia from 1993 to 2010 employing panel cointegration and causality tests and finds strong evidences to the export oriented growth strategy.

2. Econometric Methodology

To test the Export-Led Growth hypothesis, we need to employ Granger causality test. But, to use non-stationary variables in Granger causality test, we need to take differences of the relevant variables, besides, we should pretest the existence of cointegration relationship. We can overcome these problems by adding extra lags of the series by following the study of Toda and Yamamoto (1995) (TY).

We employ the following VAR$\left(p+d\max\right)$ model to test the causality relationship:

$$y_t = \alpha_0 + \sum_{i=1}^{p+d\max} \beta_i y_{t-i} + \sum_{i=1}^{p+d\max} \delta_i x_{t-i} + e_{1t} \tag{1}$$

$$x_t = \alpha_0 + \sum_{i=1}^{p+d\max} \beta_i y_{t-i} + \sum_{i=1}^{p+d\max} \delta_i x_{t-i} + e_{1t} \tag{2}$$

Where p is the lag order of Vector Autoregressive model and $d\max$ shows the maximum integration order of the variables. The only difference of this test from the Granger causality test is the extra lags, so in the case of the stationary variables, TY causality test become as the same as Granger causality test. The null hypothesis of no-Granger causality for the first and second models, can be defined as follows respectively:

$$\begin{aligned} H_{01} &: \beta_1 = \ldots = \beta_p = 0 \\ H_{02} &: \delta_1 = \ldots = \delta_p = 0 \end{aligned} \tag{3}$$

Thus, indeed we test the significance of the first p lags of right hand variables in the VAR model to test the null hypothesis.

To implement the TY test, we first determine the maximum lag order of the variables ($d\max$). Then we choose the optimal lag length (p) by using Hatemi-J Information Criterion (2003) and estimate the VAR$\left(p+d\max\right)$. In this study, instead of using $d\max$, we will employ one extra lag by following the suggestions of Dolado and Lütkepohl (1996). We test the restrictions which are presented in (3) by using Wald test which is distributed as Chi-Square with number of degrees of freedom p .

Dolado and Lütkepohl (1996) causality test allows testing the existence of the causality relationship for the whole analysis period but we cannot determine whether the test results are stable or not. For example, the causality relationship can be existing for only short time periods. Therefore, we employ the causality test in the time varying framework.

For the time-varying causality test we first determine a fixed sample size (S). Then we apply the test to the following samples, respectively:

$$W_1 = 1,...,S$$
$$W_2 = 1,...,S+1$$
$$W_3 = 1,...,S+2$$
.
.
$$W_{T-S-1} = (T-S-1),...,T$$

That is, we continue to test till using the last observation. After obtaining all the test statistics, we normalize them with the %10 bootstrap critical values which is obtained by following Hacker and Hatemi-J (2006) to consider possible non-normal errors and then draw the figure with the normalized test statistics and the threshold value which equals to 1. The line which is above of the threshold line shows the rejection of the null hypothesis.

3. Data and Empirical Results

This study employs yearly data of exports of goods and services and Gross Domestic for Algeria, Egypt, Morocco, and Tunisia which obtained from World Bank Data service. All data in constant 2000 U.S. dollars and expressed in logarithms. The selection of these countries is mainly because of the lack of data. The dataset covers 1960-2011 period for Egypt and Morocco, 1961-2011 for Tunisia and 1960-2009 for Algeria.

We first compute test statistics for the whole sample and present the test results in Table 1.

As can be seen in Table 1, we cannot reject the null hypothesis that there is no causality from GDP to export only for Algeria and Egypt on the other hand; we cannot reject the reverse relationship only for Algeria. That is, there is bidirectional Granger causality only for Algeria, and there is a unidirectional Granger causality which runs from GDP to exports only for Egypt. In other words, ELG hypothesis is valid only for Algeria.

By employing the test results in Table 1, we only come to a conclusion for the whole of analysis period. However, it is quite possible that the test results can be instable. That is, while ELG hypothesis can be valid in a short subsample periods, it can be invalid for the remaining subsamples. To determine whether the rejection or acceptance of the ELG hypothesis instable;

and also to see in which years ELG hypothesis is valid for the interested economies, we now investigate the ELG hypothesis in a time varying framework. By choosing 30 observations as the fixed subsample length, we present the test results of time varying causality tests in Figure 1 and 2.

Table 1. Results of Causality Test with Bootstrap Simulations

	Wald Statistics	Critical Values		
		1%	5%	10%
H_0:	GDP does not Granger causal Export			
Algeria	22.058*	8.263	4.409	2.857
Egypt	9.323**	10.638	6.961	5.264
Morocco	0.074	7.45	4.264	2.979
Tunisia	0.389	7.567	4.24	2.997
H_0:	Export does not Granger causal GDP			
Algeria	30.023*	10.35	4.475	2.92
Egypt	1.19	10.705	6.764	5.145
Morocco	0.034	7.249	4.215	2.938
Tunisia	0.011	7.398	4.16	2.948

Note: * and ** show the rejection of the null hypothesis at the 1% and 5% levels respectively.

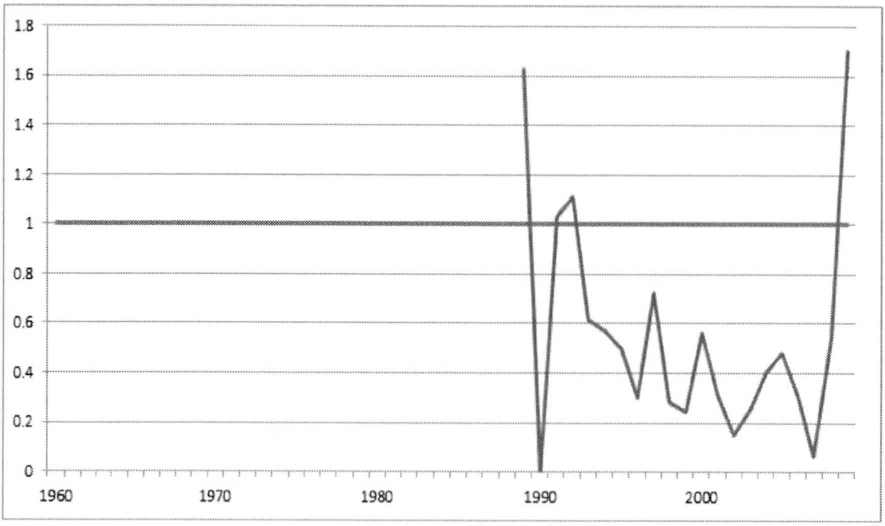

(1.a.) Algeria

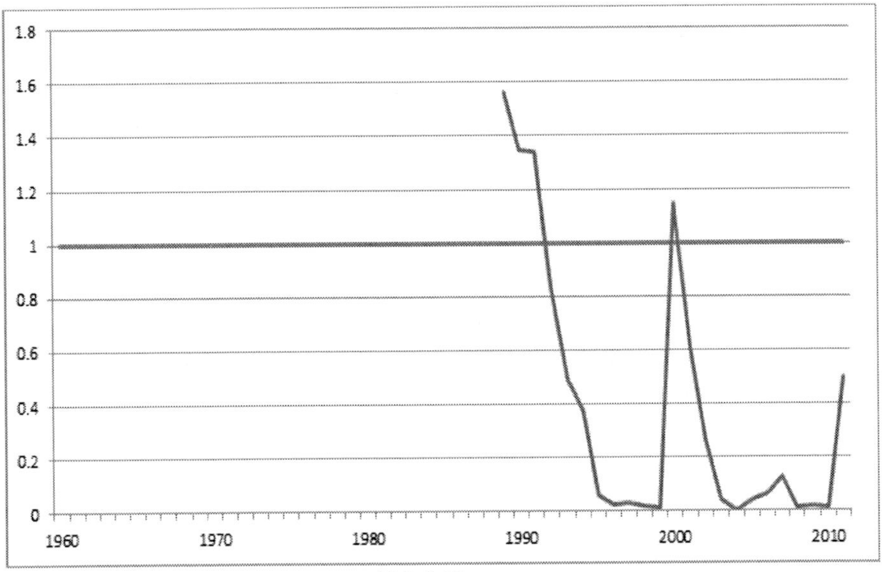

(1.b.) Egypt

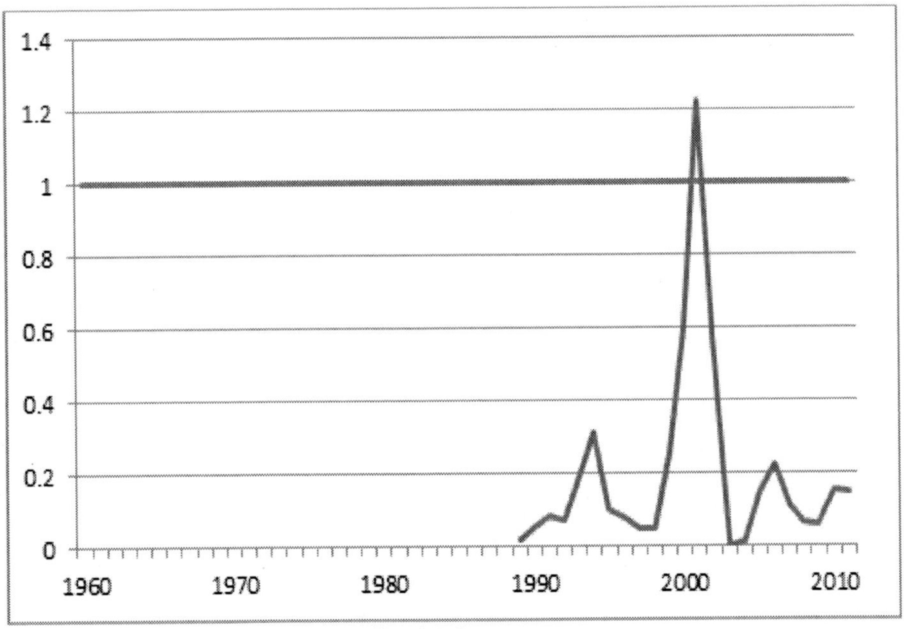

(1.c.) Morocco

Figure 1. (Continued)

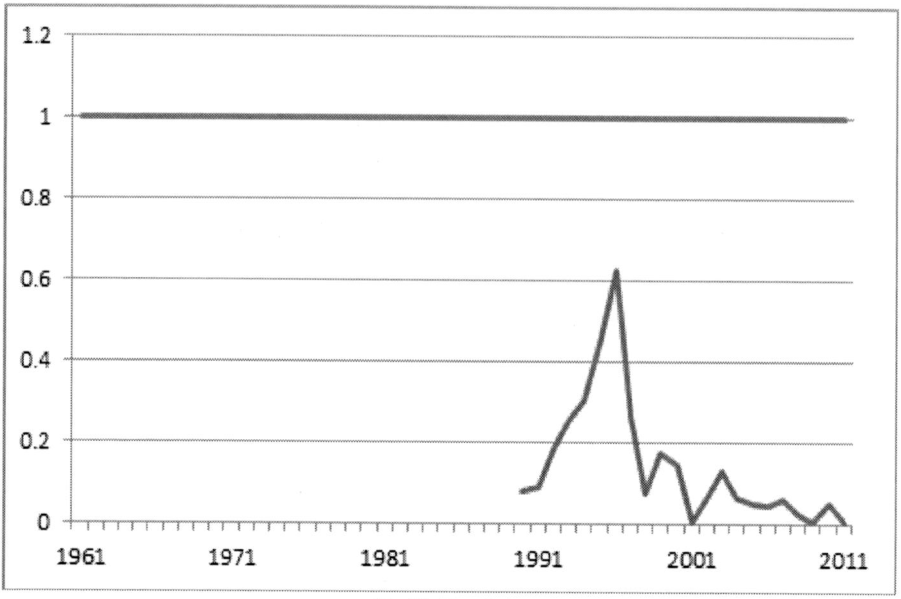

(1.d.) Tunisia

Figure 1. Results of Causality Test from Growth to Export.

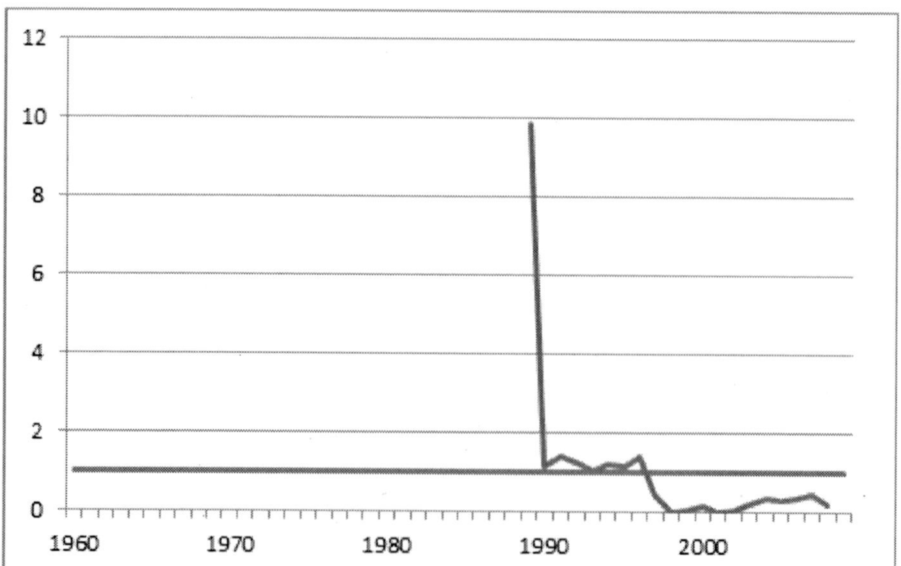

(2.a.) Algeria

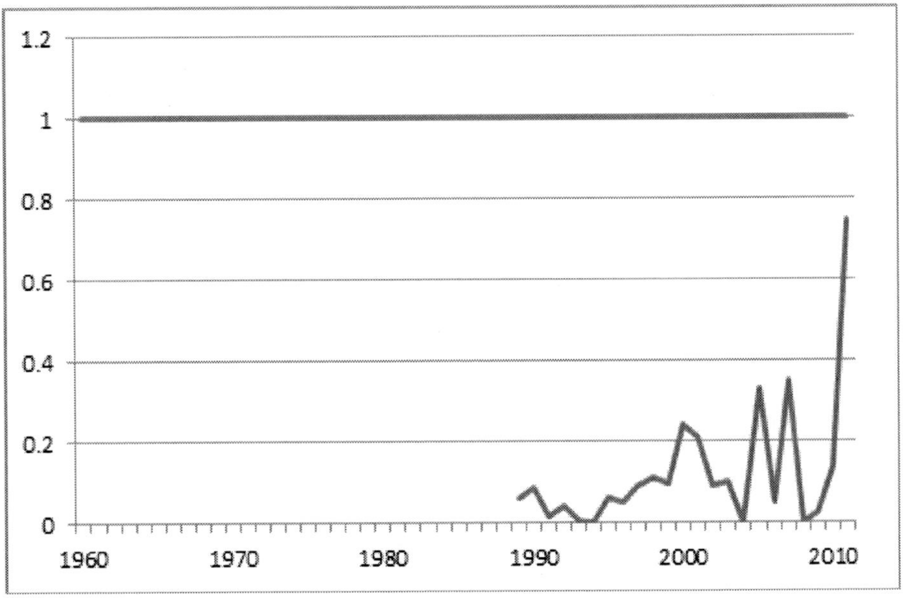

(2.b.) Egypt

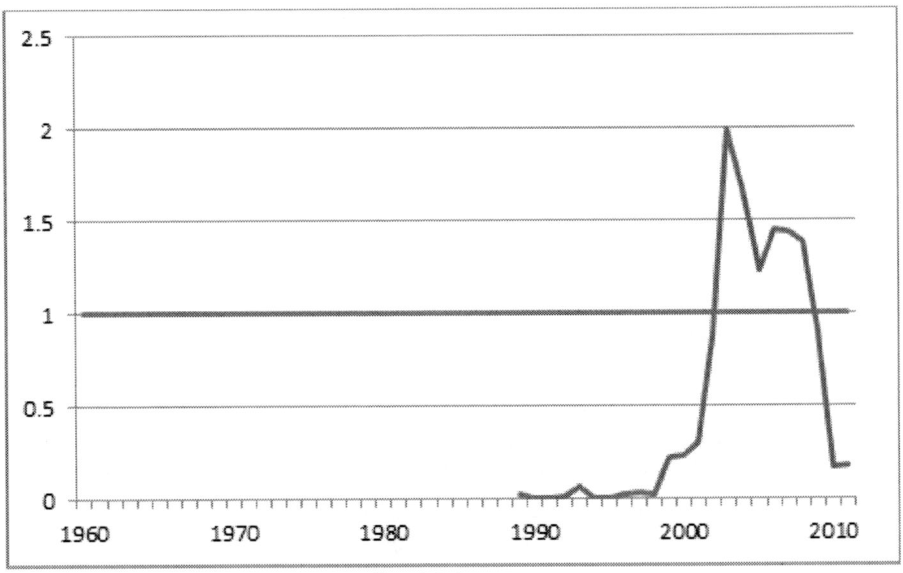

(2.c.) Morocco

Figure 2. (Continued)

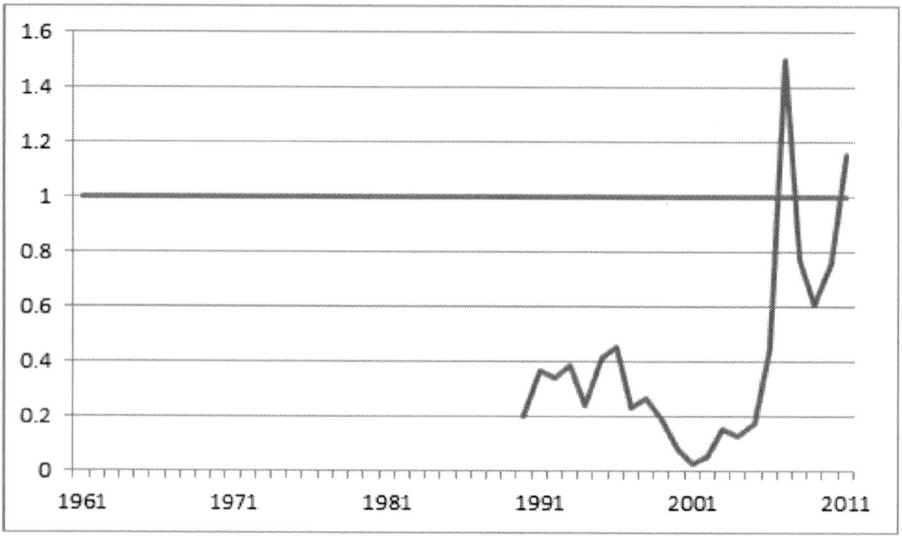

(2.d.) Tunisia

Figure 2. Results of Causality Test from Export to Growth.

Although we could not reject the null hypothesis for the whole sample for Algeria, the results of the time varying causality test in Figure 1.a. show that the non-rejection of the null hypothesis is episodic. We can make same interpretation for Egypt. For Morocco, we can reject the null only, one subsample; 1972-2001. On the other hand the results verify the results in Table 1 for Tunisia.

The inspection of the Figure 2 shows that there exists Granger causality from exports to growth for Algeria until 1996. After this year this causality relationship diminishes. Hence, the rejection of the null hypothesis of non-causality for Algeria arises from the high test statistics which occur till 1996. Figure 2.b. shows the invalidity of ELG hypothesis for the all subsamples for Egypt. On the other hand, Figure 2.c. and 2.d. show the instability of the causality test results since we can reject the null for some subsamples which indeed also shows the importance of the time varying methods. For Morocco, ELG hypothesis is valid for the 1974-2008 period and for Tunisia, this hypothesis valid for only 1978-2007 and 1982-2011 periods.

The reason for the rejection of ELG hypothesis for Algeria after 1996 is the change in the components of exports of Algeria. Petroleum, natural gas forms nearly %97 of export goods of Algeria. While petroleum oils (crude) and gases constitute 70% of total export in 1995, this share increases to 81% in 2010. On the other hand, the share of petroleum oils (refined) decreased from

23% in 1995 to 14% in 2010. The export of crude oil does not allow for introduction of new technologies in the production process to the exporting countries and the increase of this share does not accelerate economic growth.

CONCLUSION

Increasing exports of goods and services is one of the objectives of the developing countries to stimulate their economic growth. In this study, by using Dolado and Lütkepohl (1996) causality test in the time varying framework, we analyzed whether export-led growth hypothesis is valid in four MENA countries. While the results of Dolado and Lütkepohl (1996) causality test show that there is a bidirectional causality for Algeria and a unidirectional causality runs from Gross Domestic Product to exports for Egypt, the results of time varying version of the test show that the results are instable. The reason for the rejection of ELG hypothesis is that for the production of the most of the export components (such as crude oil), the countries do not need to learn new technologies to help increase capacity of the economy and stimulate economic growth.

REFERENCES

Abual-Foul, B. (2004), "Testing the Export-Led Growth Hypothesis: Evidence from Jordan", *Applied Economics Letters,* 11, 393–396.

Bhagwati, J.N. (1988), *Protectionism.* Cambridge, MA: MIT Press.

Dolado, J. J. and Lütkepohl, H. (1996), "Making Wald Tests Work for Cointegrated VAR Systems", *Econometric Theory,* 15(4), 369-386.

Grossman, G.M. and E. Helpman (1991), *Innovation and growth in the global economy,* Cambridge, MA: MIT Press.

Hacker, R. S. and Hatemi-J, A. (2006) "Tests for Causality between Integrated Variables Using Asymptotic and Bootstrap Distributions: Theory and Application" Applied Economics, 38(13), 1489-1500.

Hatemi-J, A. (2003), "A New Method to Choose Optimal Lag Order in Stable and Unstable VAR Models", *Applied Economics Letters*, 10(3), 135-137.

Jordaan, A.C. and Eita, J.H. (2009), "Testing the Export-Led Growth Hypothesis for Botswana: A Causality Analysis", *Botswana Journal of Economics,* 6(10), 2-14.

Judith A. Giles & Cara L. Williams (2000), "Export-Led Growth: A Survey of the Empirical Literature and Some Non-Causality Results. Part 1", *The Journal of International Trade & Economic Development: An International and Comparative Review,* 9:3, 261-337.

Krugman, P.R. (1984), "Import Protection as Export Promotion". In H. Kierzkowski (ed.) *Monopolistic Competition in International Trade.* Oxford: Oxford University Press.

Mamun, K. A. and Nath, H. K. (2005), "Export-Led Growth in Bangladesh: A Time Series Analysis", *Applied Economics Letters,* 12(6), 361-364.

Narayan, P. K., Narayan, S., Prasad, B.C. and Prasad, A. (2007), "Export-Led Growth Hypothesis: Evidence from Papua New Guinea and Fiji", *Journal of Economic Studies,* 34(4), 341-351.

Panas, E. and Vamvoukas, G. (2002), "Further Evidence on the Export-Led Growth Hypothesis", *Applied Economics Letters,* 9:11, 731-735.

Sandalcılar, A.R. (2012), "Bric Ülkelerinde Ekonomik Büyüme Ve İhracat Arasindaki İlişki: Panel Eşbütünleşme ve Panel Nedensellik", *Süleyman Demirel Üniversitesi İktisadi ve İdari Bilimler Fakültesi Dergisi,* 17 (1) : 161-179.

Seabra, F. and Galimberti, J.K. (2012), "Conditioned Export-Led Growth Hypothesis: A Panel Threshold Regressions Approach", *Revista de Economia,* 38(2), 7-24.

Şimşek, M. (2003), "İhracata Dayalı-Büyüme Hipotezinin Türkiye Ekonomisi Verileri ile Analizi, 1960-2002", *Dokuz Eylül Üniversitesi İktisadi ve İdari Bilimler Fakültesi Dergisi,* 18 (2), 43-63.

Taştan, H. (2010), "Türkiye'de İhracat, İthalat ve Ekonomik Büyüme Arasındaki Nedensellik İlişkilerinin Spektral Analizi", *Ekonomi Bilimleri Dergisi,* 2 (1), 87-98.

Toda, H.Y. and Yamamoto, T. (1995), "Statistical Inference in Vector Autoregressions with Possibly Integrated Processes", *Journal of Econometrics,* 66, 225-250.

In: Economic and Social Issues …
Editor: Nilgün Çil Yavuz

ISBN: 978-1-62948-152-4

Chapter 3

AN ECONOMETRIC ANALYSIS OF THE SOURCES OF ECONOMIC GROWTH FOR SELECTED MENA COUNTRIES UNDER THE GLOBAL AND REGIONAL TURMOIL

***Bülent Güloğlu**[*1] **and Ercan Saridoğan**[2†]*
[1]Pamukkale University, Department of Econometrics, Denizli, Turkey
[2]Istanbul University, Department of Econometrics, Istanbul, Turkey

ABSTRACT

The Middle East and North Africa (MENA) *countries have witnessed important political changes recently. These changes resulted from not only political reasons but also* economic reasons. In this context, main aim of this study is to investigate the sources of economic growth in the selected MENA countries for the period 1988-2011by using growth accounting methodology based on the Solow Growth Model and the panel DSUR methodology. Main finding of the study is that the average annual growth rate of GDP per capita for the selected MENA countries and the 1988-2011 period is 1.21 %. Based on the DSUR results, the contribution of capital stock per capita is 43% and the contribution of total factor productivity (TFP) is 57%.

[*] bguloglu@pau.edu.tr.
[†] ercan.saridogan@istanbul.edu.tr.

Main economic policy recommendations for the sustainable long-run growth of the MENA countries are that it is vital to establish economic and political stability, increasing global competitiveness by triggering science-technology and innovation oriented development policies such as research and development, education, improving qualified human capital.

1. INTRODUCTION

MENA region has a population of 355 million, with 85 percent living in middle-income countries, eight percent in high-income countries and seven percent in low-income countries. The MENA region came into the Arab Spring with multiple strengths: a young and educated population; a strong resource base and an economic resilience that helped it weather the 2008/9 global financial crisis. Economies across the region were rebounding. Tunisia and Egypt had strong reserve cushions and had benefited from tourism and flows of foreign direct investment. Absolute poverty was low with approximately four percent of the population living under US$1.25 a day. But the benefits of growth were not shared equally, and systems in which economic opportunities were monopolized by a privileged few led to social frustration and widespread protests (World Bank, 2013).

The Middle East and North Africa (MENA) region is going through a period of unprecedented change. In the 'Arab Spring' countries, political transition, pressing social demands, and an adverse external environment have combined to increase the near-term risks to macroeconomic stability. Arab Spring countries need to set out on their own paths toward economic modernization and transformation (International Monetary Fund (2012). This transformation deeply affects the economic, political and social fundamentals.

Bisat et al. (1997) stated that sustaining a high rate of economic growth is the major policy issue facing the Arab economies. Bisat et al. (1997) claimed that in the 1960s and 1970s, the Arab countries' growth performance was bolstered by the discovery of natural resources and, at a later stage, favorable external terms of trade shocks. Growth during the boom period was associated with a high level of investment. The sharp decline in energy prices (starting in the mid 1980s) contributed to a fall in both growth and investment rates. Bisat et al. (1997) found that increasing long-run growth requires improvements in both investment and domestic savings. Bisat et al. (1997) argue that in the past, the Arab region's growth was overly reliant on volatile external sources of funding, and total factor productivity growth was too low.

Qarn and Abu-Bader (2007) stated that the Middle East and North Africa (MENA) countries have high volatility characteristics in economic activity. Most of the MENA economies are dependent on their natural resources (mainly oil) and primary goods. The fluctuations in the world markets directly reflect on the economic performance of the region's economies. Sound policies that are based on understanding the principal determinants of economic growth are, thus, essential to alleviate the impact of the exogenous shocks.

Habibi (2009) stated that the global crisis was transmitted to Arab economies through several distinct channels: the financial markets, the crude oil market, Arab investments in global asset markets, tourism, the remittance income of Arab workers, and the region's non-oil exports, originating primarily in North Africa and destined for Europe.

Reinikka (2010) stated that the impact of the 2008–09 global financial and economic crisis varied substantially among the countries in the MENA region. Oil exporters were hardest hit because the crisis affected them directly through two different channels: (a) a negative terms-of-trade shock associated with the drop in oil prices; and (b) a financial shock, which destabilized overextended domestic banks and led to the bursting of a real estate bubble. Oil-importing MENA countries were hurt mostly by the secondary effects of the crisis on trade, remittances, and foreign direct investment (FDI).

Doa and Doaa (2010) stated that financial systems in the MENA region have not been highly vulnerable to the crisis so far due to their limited integration with global financial institutions, the impact of the global recession on the real economy can be significant in many MENA countries; these impacts differs according to the characteristic per group of countries.

Neaime Simon (2012) argue that the spillover effects of the recent global financial crisis on MENA countries and its effects on their stock markets varied according to their degree of financial integration with the more mature financial markets. Given their strong linkages with global stock markets, the stock markets of Egypt, Jordan, Kuwait, Morocco, and the United Arab Emirates (UAE) were the most affected by the global financial crisis, with insignificant impacts on Saudi Arabia, which was not that affected by the crisis due to the fact that its financial market has remained relatively closed to foreign investors and its degree of financial integration has remained low.

World Bank (2013) stated that the process of political change and transition across much of the MENA region continued into 2013, with a great degree of heterogeneity across countries. Creating the right environment for growth will be critical as only growth can drive job creation for the large numbers of unemployed, especially young people. Recent political changes will only be meaningful if they lead to concrete social and economic improvements.

2. Theoretical Framework

Economic growth and its determinants are the cornerstone of the economics because the welfare of the society mainly depends on the economic growth. In the economic growth models, critical factor determining economic growth is the technological change. Exogenous growth models assume that technological change is exogenous. After 1960s, economic growth models evolved from exogenous growth models into endogenous growth models accepting technological changes triggered by the appropriate economic policies. Technological change in the growth model is represented by total factor productivity or as called "Solow Residual".

Growth accounting methodology introduced by Solow (1957) aims to decompose the sources of economic growth by considering the equation 1:

$$Q = F(K, L, t) \tag{1}$$

Where, Q is output; K, capital and L, labour are inputs. The variable *t* for time appears in *F* to allow for technical change. Technical change is represented by any kind of shift in the production function. In the Solow model, shifts in the production function are defined as neutral if they leave marginal rates of substitution untouched but simply increase or decrease the output attainable from given inputs. In that case the production function takes the special form

$$Q = A(t)\, f(K, L) \tag{2}$$

where the multiplicative factor *A (t)* measures the cumulated effect of shifts over time. Differentiate (Eq.2) totally with respect to time and divide by Q,

$$\frac{\dot{Q}}{Q} = \frac{\dot{A}}{A} + A\frac{\delta f}{\delta K}\frac{\dot{K}}{Q} + A\frac{\delta f}{\delta L}\frac{\dot{L}}{Q} \tag{3}$$

where dots indicate time derivatives

$$if\ define\ w_k = \frac{\delta Q}{\delta K}\frac{K}{Q}\quad, w_L = \frac{\delta Q}{\delta L}\frac{L}{Q},\quad we\ obtain,\ \frac{\dot{Q}}{Q} = \frac{\dot{A}}{A} + w_k\frac{\dot{K}}{K} + w_L\frac{\dot{L}}{L}$$

Solow (1957) stated that $\dot{A}/A$ and thence *A(t)* can be estimated by time series. Assuming factors are paid their marginal products and F is homogeneous of degree one. This has the advantage of making everything come out neatly in terms of intensive magnitudes as follows:

$$\frac{\dot{q}}{q} = \frac{\dot{A}}{A} + w_k\frac{\dot{k}}{k} \tag{4}$$

where $q = \frac{Q}{L}$;$k = \frac{K}{L}$; $w_L = 1 - w_K$ and $\dot{q}/q = \dot{Q}/Q - \dot{L}/L$, Equation.4 expresses output per worker as the sum of weighted average growth rates of inputs and the growth of TFP.

In order to estimate share of the inputs, there are different methodologies. Abu-Qarn and Abu-Bader (2007) stated that since input shares are very crucial in the debates of convergence and the relative importance of input accumulation versus productivity, it is of great significance to estimate them accurately. However, many methods of estimating the shares of inputs in income have been used and none have been found to be adequate. The intensive form of the production function by assuming constant returns to scale to estimate the share of the inputs has some advantages such as reducing heteroskedasticity and eliminating multicollinearity. Intensive form of the Cobb-douglas production function is written as follows:

$$\left(\frac{Y}{L}\right)_t = a\left(\frac{K}{L}\right)_t^{\alpha}\quad, 0 < a < 1$$

$$Ln\left(\frac{Y}{L}\right)_t = a + \alpha Ln\left(\frac{K}{L}\right)_t + \varepsilon_t$$

$$Ln(y_t) = a + \alpha Ln(k_t) + \varepsilon_t \tag{5}$$

Following Ismihan and Metin-Ozcan (2008) and Senhadji (2000) we obtain contribution of the inputs by utilizing Equation (Eq.5).

Growth in output per worker (g_y) can be decomposed as follows:

$$g_y = \alpha g_k + g_a , \qquad (6)$$

where g_y, growth in y ; g_k , growth in k and g_a, TFP growth.

Equation (Eq.5) identifies the two sources of growth in output per worker (g_y): contribution of growth in capital per worker [αg_k] and contribution of growth in TFP. TFP growth (g_a) can be calculated as a *residual* ($g_a = g_y - \alpha g_k$).

It is vital to estimate capital stock series for the model estimation in Eq.5. The stock of capital is the accumulation of the stream of past investments in the perpetual inventory method. Capital stock is measured by following (Harberger, 1978; Nehru and Dhareshwar, 1993) as follows :

$$\left(K_t - K_{t\text{-}1}\right)/K_{t\text{-}1} = -\delta + \left(I_t/K_{t\text{-}1}\right) \quad \Rightarrow \quad K_{t\text{-}1} = I_t/\left(\delta + g\right)$$

where K, capital stock, I, gross fixed capital formation, δ, depreciation rate (0.05) and g, average growth rate of real GDP.

3. Literature

Nehru and Dhareshwar (1993) analysed total factor productivity growth rates for a selected group of 92 developing and industrial countries from 1960 to 1990 (of which 68 are from developing countries) by derivation of a new database of physical capital stock and by using a constant returns to scale Cobb-Douglas production function with imposed factor shares. Nehru and Dhareshwar (1993) calculated total factor productivity growth for MENA countries by using the residual between output growth and the weighted sum of labor and capital growth. Nehru and Dhareshwar (1993) found that the capital stock grew faster in the 1973-90 period following the oil price shock, but the growth of TFP turned negative during the period for MENA countries. Nehru and Dhareshwar (1993) found that the growth of TFP for MENA countries are as follows 0.4 for 1960-90 period, 2.3 for 1960-73 period, -0.5 for 1973-90 period and -0.7 for 1980-90 period.

Collins and Bosworth (1996) analysed the sources of growth in output for East Asia countries and MENA region as well by using growth accounts that decompose the growth in output per worker from 1960 to 1994 into the contributions from the accumulation of physical and human capital and a residual measure of the change in total factor productivity (TFP). Collins and Bosworth (1996) found that growth of output per worker for MENA countries are 1.6 for 1960-94 period, 4.7 for 1960-73 period, -0.3 for 1973-94 period, 0.5 for 1973-84 period and -1.1 for 1984-94 period. Contribution of total factor productivity on growth of output per worker for MENA countries are -0.3 for 1960-94 period, 2.3 for 1960-73 period, -1.9 for 1973-94 period, -2.2 for 1973-84 period and -1.5 for 1984-94 period

Bisat et al. (1997) explained the historical experience of the region—specifically, why the high growth/high investment period of the 1970s and early 1980s proved unsustainable, thus giving way to a period of low growth/low investment? Bisat et al. (1997) claimed that three factors are important for the answer. First, that the investment process throughout the two periods was not accompanied by sufficient improvements in total factor productivity. Second, the disappointing evolution of total factor productivity was compounded in the second half of the period by declining investment rates. Third, that the funding of investment activities was overly dependent on volatile external sources.

Senhadji (1999) analysed the source of cross-country differences in total factor productivity for 88 countries for 1960-94 by using growth accounting exercise. Their estimates of value of the share of physical capital vary significantly across regions, both in levels and first differences. They found that the mean value of the share of physical capital the for Middle East and North Africa is (0.63) in levels and 0.54 when the production function is estimated in first difference. They also found the value of the share of physical capital with human capital (0.65) and without human capital (0.62). Senhadji (1999) found that the contribution of TFP on the economic growth in Mena for the analysis sub-periods is too low or negative.

Makdisi et al. (2007) stated that the overall growth performance of the MENA region over the period 1960–2000 has been both mixed and characterized by a higher degree of volatility compared to the other regions in the world. They found that capital is less efficient; trade openness less beneficial to growth and the impact of adverse external shocks more pronounced, in addition, total factor productivity growth in the MENA region, was not an important source of growth in comparison to the other regions owing to among other things, the lower quality of its institutions, modest stock of human capital and its educational system that focused on preparing students for public sector employment. Within the MENA region, non-oil and diversified economies have fared much better than the oil-exporting countries both in terms of output growth and total factor productivity growth. Finally, they claimed that the degree of exposure to internal and external shocks, the extent of economic diversification and international competitiveness were important factors explaining variations in growth performance within the MENA region.

Qarn and Abu-Bader (2007) analysed the growth accounting analysis for 10 Middle Eastern and North African (MENA) countries over the period 1960-98. Qarn and Abu-Bader (2007) estimated the long-run share of capital in income by using cointegration (country-specific) and panel data (region-specific) methods. They obtain share of physical capital (α) in the range of 0.37–0.70 when including quality-adjusted labor,, while it ranges between 0.49 and 0.73 when no human capital is included. Qarn and Abu-Bader (2007) concluded that the analysis of the sources of growth shows that for the selected MENA countries, the role of TFP in determining economic growth is insignificant and often detrimental. Most of the growth is due to the accumulation of physical capital and improvements in the quality of labour.

Bhattacharya and Wolde (2010) analysed main constraints on growth in the MENA region by attempting to quantify the impact of the various constraints faced by local businesses highlighted by the World Bank's Business Enterprise surveys. Bhattacharya and Wolde (2010) found that the key direct constraints to growth in the MENA region are difficulties in access to finance, labor skill mismatches and shortages, and electricity constraints.

Serranito (2013) analysed catching-up dynamics for MENA countries towards the level of income in Europe. Serranito (2013) found that the periods of divergence outnumber the periods of convergence and since the year 2000 all countries but Syria have been converging toward the European per-capita income level. Serranito (2013) concluded that technological diffusion is a major determinant of the convergence process.

Andreano et al. (2013) analysed the convergence in per capita output across MENA countries. They found that the empirical analysis confirms the hypothesis of conditional convergence. They also state that the long-term growth in this highly heterogeneous area is the result of a set of socio-economic, technological, and governance factors. The degree of international openness and the government intervention and expenditure are important economic control variables. The improvement of governance factors, such as actions to reduce corruption, the greater reliability and efficiency of government, political stability and violence reduction, play a role in stimulating the long-run behavior and moving up the development path of the steady-state. Technological development and human capital are both highly relevant for the growth.

4. ECONOMETRIC ANALYSIS

4.1. Model and Data

In panel data form, the model can be written as:

$$y_{it} = x'_{it}\beta + u^*_{it} \text{ where} \quad \text{(Eq.1)}$$

$$x_{it} = x_{i,t-1} + \varepsilon_{it} \text{ and } u^*_{it} = D'_{lt}\delta_{lt} + u_{it}$$

$$u_{it} = \rho_i u_{i,t-1} + \sum_{j=1}^{k-1} \gamma_{ij} \Delta u_{i,t-j} + \eta_{it}$$

$$\eta_{it} = \lambda_i f_t + e_{it}$$

i=1,2,…N and t=1,2,…T

In the equation Eq.1, y_{it} represents the ith country's GDP per worker at time t, x_{it} represents the ith country's Capital Stock per worker at time t, and the subscripts t and i denote time and individuals (sectors).

All variables are expressed logarithmically so that the coefficients show the elasticities. In equation 1 the term f_t stands for unobserved common effects and its presence induces cross sectional dependence in the model. As the coefficient of this unobserved common factor (λ_I) makes it clear, the effect of an observed shock varies across countries. The term D represent the leads and lags of explanatory variables and included in the model to take into account the correlations between u^*_{it} and e_{it}. To obtain consistent and efficient[1] estimate of the above model we use Dynamic Seemingly Unrelated Regression technique(DSUR) advanced by Mark et al.(2005).

1 As stated by Mark et al.(2005) DSUR is asymptotically efficient compared to the single equation methods.

Data source for the all variables is the World Bank, GDP and capital stock per capita are constant 2000 US$. MENA countries considered in the model are Algeria, Egypt, Iran, Israel, Jordan, Malta, Morocco, Tunisia, Yemen for the period 1988-2011

4.2. THE METHODOLOGY AND EMPIRICAL RESULTS

Before proceeding to DSUR panel regressions we investigate stationarity properties of the variables under study. The CIPS test (Pesaran, 2007) and the Z_A^{SPC} and Z_A^{LA} tests (Hadri and Kurozumi, 2012) are used to test stationarity. The main advantage of these tests is that they allow for cross sectional dependence. Thus, before implementing panel unit root tests, we test the absence of cross-section correlations using the bias-adjusted LM (LM_AD) test developed by Pesaran et al. (2008). The test results are shown in Table 1. As can be seen the LM_AD test results show strong evidence for the significance of the cross correlations across the MENA countries. As a result we use the CIPS and the Z_A^{SPC} and Z_A^{LA} tests to check the stationarity of series considered in the study[2]. It should be noted that in the CIPS test the null hypothesis is "non-stationarity" while in the Z_A^{SPC} and the Z_A^{LA} tests it is "stationarity" As can be seen from Table 1, the variable y seems nonstationary according the CIPS test regardless of tests equations including only intercept or both intercept and trend. As for the Z_A tests, except for test with intercept the others do not reject the stationarity hypothesis. Thus the tests show contradictory results. The test results for the variable x is more stable. Except for the Z_A^{SPC} test intercept with trend all tests reject the stationarity. It seems that the series are integrated of different order. In this study we use the Durbin-Hausman cointegration test developed by Westerlund (2008) which allows us to test for cointegration among series of different order of integration.

[2] Unit root test results for the series in first difference are not reported to save space.

Table 1. Panel Unit Root Tests Results (Series in Level)

	LM_AD* Intercept	LM_AD* Intercept +trend	CIPS Intercept	CIPS Intercept + trend	Z_A^{SPC} Intercept	Z_A^{LA} Intercept	Z_A^{SPC} Intercept + trend	Z_A^{LA} Intercept +trend
y	30.056***	54.291***	-1.4219	-1.2478	-0.875	**5.013*****	-1.654	-2.062
x	28.933***	29.216***	-1.2767	-1.9564	**10.48*****	**22.12*****	-0.662	**4.901*****

*** indicates that statistics are significant at the 1% level of significance.
LM_AD* statistics test for the absence of cross section dependence.
For the CIPS test the null hypothesis is nonstationarity,
Critical values for the CIPS test are obtained from Pesaran (2007).
The z_A^{SPC} and z_A^{LA} tests the null hypothesis is stationarity.

The distribution of the z_A^{SPC} and z_A^{LA} statistics are asymptotically normal.

Notice that Westerlund (2008) developed two statistics, namely, the group dimension (DH_g) and the panel dimension (DH_p). The Durbin-Hausman panel (DH_p) test makes the assumption that the autoregressive parameter is the same for all cross-sections, both under the null and alternative hypotheses. Under this assumption, if the null hypothesis is rejected, it amounts to accepting the existence of cointegration for all cross-sections. The Durbin-Hausman group (DH_g) test permits the autoregressive parameter to differ accross cross-sections under the alternative hypothesis.

Thus, if the null hypothesis is rejected, it means that it is not valid for at least some sectors; that is, there is co-integration. The Durbin-Hausman test results and the LM* test results are given in Table 2. We can observe that the LM* tests rejects the absence of cross-sectional dependence for the residuals of the model. The (DH_g) and (DH_p) tests both reject the null hypothesis of no-cointegration at a 1% level of significance. On the other hand, we assume slope heterogeneity, and test this assumption using the slope homogeneity tests in Pesaran and Yamagata (2008b). Swamy homogeneity test (1970) and $\mathbf{X}^2$ is standard Wald test for slope homogeneity results are shown in Table 2. All test statistics rejected the null hypothesis of homogeneity.

Table 2. Cross Sectional Dependence, Cointegration and Slope Homogeneity Tests

LM*	44.618***
DH_g	7.874***
DH_p	13.361***
$\hat{S}$	233.80***
X^2	5819.837***

*** indicates that statistics are significant at the 1% level of significance respectively.
LM* :Bias-corrected LM test for cross sectional dependence (Pesaran et al. (2008).
DHg and DHp : test for cointegration Westerlund (2008).

$\hat{S}$ is Swamy homogeneity test (1970) and X^2 is standard Wald test for slope homogeneity.

After confirmed that the variables cointegrated, then we analyse the long run panel cointegration coefficient by using panel DSUR technique and compare the results with different panel regression techniques.

The Pooled OLS Results in Table-3 show the estimation coefficient for the capital stock in the growth accounting equation. The share of capital stock in the growth accounting equation is 0.46 for pooled OLS results in Table-3. On the other hand, the estimated share of capital stock in the growth accounting equation is 0.413 for pooled SUR results in Table-4. The coefficients of share of capital stock are significant statistically and in line with previous studies for MENA region.

Table 3. Pooled OLS Results for MENA Region Common Time Effect

	PDOLS	S.E. Param	*Z* statistics
Lnk (α)	0.460	0.306	1.503 *

S.E. Param : Standard error based on parametric correction.

*, **, *** indicates that statistics are significant at the 10%, 5% and 1% level of significance respectively.

The 1%, 5% and 10% critical values for the standard normal distributed *Z* statistics are 2.326, 1.645 and 1.282.

Table 4. Pooled SUR for MENA Region

	PDSUR	S.E. Param	*Z* statistics
Lnk (α)	0.413	0.010	41.3***

S.E. Param : Standard error based on parametric correction.

*, **, *** indicates that statistics are significant at the 10%, 5% and 1% level of significance respectively.

The 1%, 5% and 10% critical values for the standard normal distributed *Z* statistics are 2.326, 1.645 and 1.282.

Table-5 shows the sources of economic growth selected MENA countries for the period 1988-2011. Average growth of output per worker is 1.21% for this period. Contribution rate of capital per worker is 0.58% and contribution share of capital per worker is 47.9% for the OLS results. Contribution rate of TFP is 0.63% and contribution share of TFP is 52.1 % for the OLS results. On the other hand, contribution rate of capital per worker is 0.52% and contribution share of capital per worker is 43.0% for the SUR results. Contribution rate of TFP is 0.69% and contribution share of TFP is 57 % for the OLS results.

Table-5. Sources of Economic Growth Selected MENA Countries (1988-2011 period)

Methodology	Capital Deepening (α)	Growth of Output per worker	Contribution rate of: (%)		Contribution share of : (%)	
			Capital Per worker	TFP	Capital Per worker	TFP
OLS Results	0.460	1.21	0.58	0.63	47.9	52.1
SUR Results	0.413	1.21	0.52	0.69	43.0	57.0

Note: The growth rate (g) of any variable (y) is obtained from the following regression: ln(y) = c + g*trend.

MENA(9): Algeria, Egypt, Iran, Israel, Jordan, Malta, Morocco, Tunisia, Yemen, Period:1988-2011.

CONCLUSION

It is very important to determine the source of economic growth for the selected Middle East and North Africa (MENA) countries to investigate the sustainability of long-run economic growth policies in those countries. In this study, we investigated the sources of economic growth for the selected MENA countries over the period 1988-2011 by using growth accounting methodology based on the Solow Growth Model and the panel DSUR methodology. Main finding of the study is that average growth of output per worker is 1.21% for the period 1988-2011. Contribution rate of capital per worker is 0.58% and contribution share of capital per worker is 47.9% for the OLS results. Contribution rate of TFP is 0.63% and contribution share of TFP is 52.1 % for the OLS results. On the other hand, contribution rate of capital per worker is 0.52% and contribution share of capital per worker is 43.0% for the SUR results. Contribution rate of TFP is 0.69% and contribution share of TFP is 57 % according to the OLS results. Main economic policy recommendations for the sustainable long-run growth of the MENA countries would be that establishing economic and political stability, increasing global competitiveness by triggering science-technology and innovation oriented development policies through research and development and improving qualified human capital.

REFERENCES

Abu-Qarn A.S., and Abu-Bader S., (2007). "Sources of Growth Revisited: Evidence from Selected MENA Countries" World Development Vol. 35, No. 5, pp. 752-771.

Andreano M.S., Laureti L., Postiglione P., (2013). "Economic growth in MENA countries: Is there convergence of per-capita GDPs?" Journal of Policy Modeling, Available online 13 March 2013, in press.

Bhattacharya, R., Wolde, H., (2010). "Constraints on Growth in the MENA Region". IMF Working Paper, No WP/10/30, February, Washington DC.

Bisat, A., El Erian, M., and Helbling, T. (1997). "Growth, Investment, And Savings In The Arab Economies". IMF Working Paper WP/97/85, IMF, Washington.

Bosworth B., and Collins S.M., (2003) The Empirics of Growth: An Update, Brookings Institution.

Doaa, S.A., Doaa A. (2010). "The Effect Of The Global Financial Crisis On Migrant Workers Among MENA Countries" International Conference on Economic Modelling , pp.1-20.

Habibi Nader., (2009). "The Impact of the Global Economic Crisis on Arab Countries: A Year-End Assessment" Middle East Brief, December 2009, No. 40.

Hadri K., and Kurozumi, E.(2012), "A Simple Panel Stationarity Test İn The Presence Of Serial Correlation And A Common Factor", Economic Letters. Vol. 115, Issue 1, pp. 31–34.

Harberger, A.C.(1978). Perspectives on capital and technology in less developed countries. In M. J. Artis, & R. A. Nobay (Eds.), Contemporary economic analysis. London: Croom Helm.

International Monetary Fund (2012). "Regional Economic Outlook Update: Middle East and Central Asia" International Monetary Fund, Washington, D.C., April.

Ismihan, M.,and Metin-Ozcan K., (2008). "Productivity and Growth in an Unstable Emerging Market Economy: The Case of Turkey, 1960–2004."

Department of Economics Discussion Paper no. 08–01, Bilkent University, Ankara.

Makdisi, S., Fattah, Z., & Liman, I. (2007). Determinants of economic growth in the MENA Countries, explaining growth in the Middle East. In J. B. Nugent, & M. H. Pesaran (Eds.), Contributions to economic analysis, vol. 278 (pp. 31–60). Amsterdam: Elsevier.

Mark N.C., Ogaki M., Sul D., (2005) "Dynamic Seemingly Unrelated Cointegrating Regressions" Review of Economic Studies, Vol.72, Issue 3, pp. 797-820.

Neaime Simon (2012). "The global financial crisis, financial linkages and correlations in returns and volatilities in emerging MENA stock markets" Emerging Markets Review 13, pp. 268–282.

Nehru, V. and Dhareshwar A., (1993) "A New Database on Physical Capital Stock: Sources, Methodology and Resultsé", Revista Analisis de Economico, Vol.8, N.1, pp.37-59.

Pesaran, M. H., (2007), "A Simple Panel Unit Root test in the presence of Cross-section Dependence", Journal of Applied Econometrics, Vol. 22, Issue 2, pp. 265–312.

Pesaran, M. H., Yamagata T.(2008b) "Testing Slope Homogeneity in Large Panels" Journal of Econometrics, Vol. 142, Issue 1, pp. 50–93.

Pesaran,H., Ullah A., Yamagata T., (2008) "A bias-adjusted LM test of error cross-section Independence", Econometrics Journal, Vol. 11, Issue 1, pp. 105–127.

Ritva Reinikka (2010). "The Financial Crisis, Recovery, and ong-Term Growth in the Middle East and North Africa" in "The Day After Tomorrow", Otaviano. Canuto, Marcelo M. Giugale (Edt). World Bank Publications, pp.377-386.

Senhadji, A. (2000) "Sources of Economic Growth: An Extensive Growth Accounting Exercise", IMF Staff Papers, 47, 1, pp.129-157.

Serranito F., (2013). "Heterogeneous technology and the technological catching-up hypothesis: Theory and assessment in the case of MENA countries" Economic Modelling, vol. 30 pp. 685–697.

Solow, R.M. (1957). "Technical Change And The Aggregate Production Function". The Review of Economic Statistics, Vol. 39, No. 3, Aug., pp.312-320.

Swamy P.A.V.B. (1970). "Efficient Inference in a Random Coefficient Regression Model"Econometrica, Vol. 38, No. 2. pp. 311-323.

Westerlund J. (2008), "Panel Cointegration Tests of the Fisher Effect", Journal of Applied Econometrics, Vol. 23, Issue 2, pp.193–233.

World Bank (2013)."Middle East and North Africa: Regional Brief " World Bank, April.

In: Economic and Social Issues …
Editor: Nilgün Çil Yavuz

ISBN: 978-1-62948-152-4

Chapter 4

RE-EXAMINATION OF THE GIBSON PARADOX AND FISHER HYPOTHESIS: EVIDENCE FROM MENA COUNTRIES

Burcu Kiran*
Istanbul University, Faculty of Economics, Beyazit, Istanbul, Turkey

ABSTRACT

Keynes brought attention to the long run relationship between price level and interest rate, called the Gibson paradox. On the other hand, Fisher suggested a long run relationship between inflation rate and interest rate, known as Fisher hypothesis. This chapter investigates the validity of the Gibson paradox and Fisher hypothesis for selected MENA countries by using recently developed econometric methods. In the first step of the analysis, the unit root properties of the series are tested by using traditional unit root tests and inconclusive results are obtained. Two reasons are considered for these inconclusive results: existense of structural breaks in the series and/or fractional integration properties of the series. Since the findings obtained from unit root tests with structural breaks and fractional alternatives give that integration orders of the series are different, we consider to apply bounds testing cointegration procedure which does not require the pre-testing of the series in the model for unit roots. According to the results, there is a long run relationship between price level and interest rate of Israel and Turkey, giving validity of the

* E-mail: kburcu@istanbul.edu.tr; Tel: (212) 440-00-00 /11661.

Gibson paradox. And also, there is a long run relationship between inflation and interest rate of Morocco and Turkey, meaning that Fisher hypothesis is valid.

Introduction

The empirical evidence of strong positive correlation between the price level, as measured by a logarithmic price index, and the long term interest rate, as measured by the yield to maturity of long term bonds, first presented by Gibson (1923). Gibson (1923) pointed out that interest rates rose and fall roughly concurrently with the level of prices in the United Kingdom over 150 years. Since there was no theoretical reason for this relation, Keynes brought attention to the long run relationship between the level of price index and the rate of interest and observed in a well-known quote, "the tendency of prices and interest rates to rise together and to fall together" is one of the most completely established empirical facts within the whole field of quantitative economics (Ram, 1987). This phenomenon is named by Keynes (1930) the "Gibson paradox". Keynes (1930) suggests that increases in the demand for loans raise the interest rates and result in an increased money supply and level of prices, and conversely for decreases in the demand for loans. This explanation is generalized to changes in aggregate supply and demand which result in a positive correlation between interest rates and prices by Sargent (1973). On the other hand, Fisher hypothesis introduced by Irving Fisher(1930) suggested a long run relationship between the inflation rate and the rate of interest.

Fisher(1930) maintains that the expected inflation is reflected in the nominal interest rates and the real interest rates are constant. In other words, there should be a long run relationship in the adjustment of nominal interest rate corresponding to changes in expected inflation. If the Fisher hypothesis holds, then short term interest rates will be an efficient predictor of future inflation (Mishkin 1992). More importantly, since monetary policy changes have an impact on financial markets, the effectiveness of monetary policies in a given period may be determined by investigating the Fisher hypothesis. When the monetary policy is effective, nominal interest rates tend to move in accordance with the expected rate of inflation which can possibly be controlled by a central bank. In this relation, the real interest rates remain constant. Because, the anticipated changes in money supply and inflation do not affect the real interest rates (Ito 2009).

The Gibson paradox and Fisher hypothesis have been frequently investigated in both theoretical and empirical economics due to their importance, using recent advances in the field of applied econometrics. But, there is no clear agreement among researchers in regard to these phenomenons. Sargent (1973) examines the statistical relationships between prices and interest rates to explain the Gibson paradox and finds two main conclusions: The first one is that interest rates are indeed correlated with the price level, i.e., the Gibson paradox does exist. The second is that Fisher's explanation of this phenomenon is inadequate. Shiller and Siegel (1977) analyze the correlation between interest rates and prices and their results from spectral techniques confirm the correlation between long term interest rates and prices for very long term swings, but indicate a significant short cycle correlation only for short term interest rates. Milne and Torous (1984) examine the Canadian evidence on the existence of the Gibson paradox over the period 1870-1981 and find a positive and statistically significant correlation between the long term interest rates and the price levels. Lee and Petruzzi (1986) analyze the Gibson paradox by using a simple model and find that this paradox is significant in the United States. On the other hand, they find that there is a significant correlation between British interest rates and U.S price levels. Ram (1987) investigates the Gibson paradox and Fisher hypothesis for 44 countries over the periods of about 30 years and indicates that the Gibson paradox is widely observed in the post-World War II era. Corbae and Ouliaris (1989) argue that simple linear regression form of nominal interest rate and log of price level gives spurious results. They examine the Gibson paradox by using simple linear regression and cointegration methods and find that interest rate and price level are not cointegrated, thus invalidating the use of standard econometric procedures for testing the significance of the price level variable. Chen and Lee (1990) apply a general vector autoregressive moving average (VARMA) model to examine the dynamic relationship between prices and interest rates and find some evidence of unidirectional relation from prices to interest rates, but they find no evidence of unidirectional relation from interest rates to prices. Klein (1995) examines the empirical correlations for the Gibson and Fisher relationships based on U.S data. The finding correlations reveal a slight preference for the Gibson relationship. Serletis and Zestos (1999) investigate the empirical relationship between nominal interest rates and prices for eight European Union (EU) countries to support the Gibson paradox over the period 1957:01-1994:04 and conclude that Gibson paradox regressions are spurious. Berument and Jelassi (2002) test whether the Fisher hypothesis holds for a sample of 26 countries by assessing the long run relationship between nominal interest rates and inflation rates taking into consideration the short run dynamics of interest rates. The finding results support that there is a one-to-one relationship between the interest rate and inflation for more than half of the countries under study. Atkins and Serletis (2003) examine the empirical relationship between prices and interest rates for Canada, Italy, Norway, Sweden, the United Kingdom and the United States in order to support Gibson paradox and Fisher effect. Their findings from bounds test imply that there is no long run relationship between price level and nominal interest rate and between inflation and nominal interest rate. Lardic and Mignon (2003) and Ghazali and Ramlee (2003) examine the Fisher hypothesis for G7 countries by using fractional cointegration concept and find that it is valid for majority of the countries. Halıcıoglu (2004) tests the existence of Gibson paradox for Turkey by using regression and time series analyses over the period 1950-2002. The results reveal that there is no support of the Gibson paradox. Turgutlu (2004) investigates the cointegration and fractional cointegration relationship between nominal interest rates and inflation for Turkey. His findings indicate that Fisher hypothesis is not valid according to the results of cointegration method. On the other hand, it is found that Fisher hypothesis is valid according to the fractional cointegration method. Şimşek and Kadılar (2006) investigate the Fisher hypothesis for Turkey by using bounds testing approach to cointegration and their results support the Fisher hypothesis. Kasman et. al. (2006) investigate the validity of the Fisher hypothesis using data from 33 developed and developing countries. Their results show that fractional cointegration between nominal interest rates and inflation is found for a large majority of countries, implying the validity of the Fisher hypothesis. Şimsek and Kadılar (2008) examine the Gibson paradox by using Turkish quarterly data over the period from 1987:01 to 2004:04 and support the Gibson's findings for Turkey.

The aim of this chapter is to examine the validity of the Gibson paradox and Fisher hypothesis for 5 selected MENA countries: Armenia, Israel, Kuwait, Morocco and Turkey. These relationships are important for MENA countries because a number of them recently decided to adopt price stability and inflation targeting as their main monetary policy goal. They have been able to contain inflationary pressures of the last two decades by targeting the nominal exchange rate. By pegging their currencies to a relatively low inflation currency such as the Euro or the US dollar, and relying on high interest rate policies to defend their exchange rates, they have succeeded in containing inflation. Even though they reduced inflation substantially, this policy generated persistent real exchange rate appreciations, losses in competitiveness, large trade and budget deficits, the accumulation of sizeable debts and serious currency crises (Neaime, 2008).

This chapter fills the gaps in the literature. To our best knowledge, there exists no previous study examining both Gibson paradox and Fisher hypothesis for MENA countries except Turkey.

The rest of the paper is organized as follows: Section 2 briefly gives the theoretical model of the Gibson paradox and Fisher hypothesis. Section 3 provides a description of the data and contains the empirical results. Finally, Section 4 summarizes and concludes.

2. Theoretical Model of the Gibson Paradox and Fisher Hypothesis

According to the Gibson paradox, the levels of a general price index and interest rate move together (Klein, 1995):

$$p_t = f(ir_t) + e_t \tag{2.1}$$

or more specifically:

$$p_t = \alpha + \beta ir_t + e_t \text{ (linear)} \tag{2.2}$$

$$\ln p_t = \alpha' + \beta' ir_t + e_t \text{ (semi log-linear)} \tag{2.3}$$

where p_t is the price index at time t, ir_t is the interest rate and e_t is random error. This relationship does not need to be linear or linear logarithmic, it is possible to consider different specifications. It needs only a positive relationship. If the relationship between interest rates and price levels does not hold, many other alternatives can be considered. In the literature, the Fisher hypothesis which states a relationship between inflation and interest rate, is an often used alternative. In following relationship, the expected inflation rate (π_t^e) is on the left side instead of price level while the same interest rate variable is on the right side:

$$\frac{\Delta p_t}{p_t} = \pi_t^e = g(ir_t) + u_t \tag{2.4}$$

The linear form of this relationship can be shown as follows:

$$\frac{\Delta p_t}{p_t} \sim \Delta \ln p_t = \pi_t^e = \gamma_t + \delta ir_t + u_t \tag{2.5}$$

More conventionally, the expected inflation rate is subtracted from the nominal interest rate to obtain real interest rate. In other words, the nominal interest rate is equal to the real interest rate plus expected inflation. It is given in a simple form as:

$$ir_t = r_t + \pi_t^e \tag{2.6}$$

where ir_t is the nominal interest rate known at time t, r_t is the real interest rate and π_t^e is the expected inflation rate. This implies that if inflation expectations are accurate, the nominal interest rate will follow the evolution of inflation. The mentioned relation is not estimable. Assuming efficient markets (Fama 1975), the observed inflation (π_t) can be decomposed into its expected component and a forecast error, u_t, orthogonal to all information at time t (Granville and Mallick 2004):

$$\pi_t = \pi_t^e + u_t \tag{2.7}$$

We can rewrite this relationship in a regression framework as below:

$$ir_t = \alpha_1 + \beta_1 \pi_t + \varepsilon_t \tag{2.8}$$

where α_1 and β_1 are parameters to be estimated and ε_t is a composite error term under the rational expectation assumption. The Fisher hypothesis asserts that the β_1 should be unity (or near unity) and the residuals ε_t should be stationary (Million 2004). It is important to note that testing whether $\beta_1 = 1$

using conventional regression methods is valid only if nominal interest rates and inflation are stationary ($I(0)$) since the distribution of the parameters is nonstandard otherwise. If ir_t and π_t are integrated of order one ($I(1)$), the Fisher hypothesis may be tested by examining whether the linear combination of these two variables is stationary ($I(0)$). If ε_t is stationary, Equation (2.8) may be interpreted as a cointegration regression. This means that there is an equilibrium relationship between nominal interest rates and inflation, with the error term ε_t representing short run deviations from a long run equilibrium. Thus, finding a cointegrating relationship between ir_t and π_t supports the Fisher hypothesis. In a similar viewpoint, a significant cointegration relationship between ir_t and p_t (or $\ln p_t$) gives the validity of the Gibson paradox.

3. Data and Empirical Results

To investigate the Gibson paradox and Fisher hypothesis for MENA countries, namely Armenia, Israel, Kuwait, Morocco and Turkey, we use quarterly and seasonally unadjusted series of price level, nominal interest rate and inflation rate. The ***price level is the logarithmic*** consumer price index ($LCPI$), interest rate (IR) is the three-month time ***deposit rate and*** inflation rate (INF) is the logarithmic first difference of the consumer price index. The time periods are different for each countries based on the data availability as shown in Table 1.

Table 1. The time periods for considered countries

Countries	Time period
Armenia	1995:01 - 2012:02
Israel	1985:04 - 2012:02
Kuwait	1991:01 - 2012:02
Morocco	1998:01 - 2012:02
Turkey	1992:04 - 2012:02

The source of the data is International Financial Statistics (IFS) database of IMF.

3.1. Unit Root Properties of the Series

In the first step of the analysis, unit root properties of the series are tested by using Augmented Dickey Fuller (ADF) and Philips-Perron (PP) unit root tests. The results are reported in Table 2.

Table 2. The results of unit root tests

Countries	Series	ADF	PP
Armenia	*IR*	-1.098	-6.107[a]
	ΔIR	-5.798[a]	-
	LCPI	-2.591	-4.320[a]
	ΔLCPI	-3.788[a]	-
	INF	-4.086[b]	-12.952[a]
	ΔINF	-	-
Israel	*IR*	-4.094[a]	-9.788[a]
	ΔIR	-	-
	LCPI	-3.561[b]	-3.237[c]
	ΔLCPI	-	-
	INF	-3.792[b]	-3.565[b]
	ΔINF	-	-
Kuwait	*IR*	-3.324[c]	-2.176
	ΔIR	-	-4.036[a]
	LCPI	-0.743	-0.822
	ΔLCPI	-6.574[a]	-6.578[a]
	INF	-7.146[a]	-7.137[a]
	ΔINF	-	-
Morocco	*IR*	-2.901	-3.173
	ΔIR	-3.827[a]	-6.065[a]
	LCPI	-2.925	-2.776
	ΔLCPI	-9.746[a]	-10.089[a]
	INF	-9.713[a]	-10.324[a]
	ΔINF	-	-
Turkey	*IR*	-3.963[b]	-4.045[b]
	ΔIR	-	-
	LCPI	-1.801	-1.404
	ΔLCPI	-7.631[a]	-7.693[a]
	INF	-7.595[a]	-7.739[a]
	ΔINF	-	-

[a, b] and [c] mean rejection of the null hypothesis at the 1%, 5% and 10% significance levels, respectively.

The unit root test results give that the integration orders of the series do not seem to be clear cut. As expected, INF series are stationary in level for all countries according to the results of both unit root tests. On the other hand, both IR and $LCPI$ series are found stationary in level for Israel and nonstationary for Morocco. Based on the both ADF and PP unit root tests, nonstationarity is found for the $LCPI$ series of Kuwait and Turkey and stationarity is found for the IR series of Turkey. For remaining series (the IR and $LCPI$ series of Armenia and IR series of Kuwait), the ADF and PP unit root tests give contrary results. Depending on these specific unit root test procedures, the series are inconclusive either $I(0)$ or $I(1)$ for some cases. There may be two reasons of inconclusive unit root results: existense of structural breaks in the series and/or fractional integration properties of the series. In our analysis, we examine the existence of structural breaks in the series at first.

3.1.1. Unit Root Properties of the Series under Structural Breaks

Perron (1989) argues that the presence of structural breaks can reduce the power of the tests and the changes in the deterministic components of the time series can lead to biased results. Therefore, in order to capture the effects of any possible structural breaks, we also use the minimum LM unit root test suggested by Lee and Strazicich (2003). This test is not affected by the breaks in examining the stationarity properties and allows for two endogenously determined breaks in the intercept and trend. The data-generating process (DGP) for the minimum LM unit root test suggested by Lee and Strazicich (2004) with two structural breaks is expressed by:

$$y_t = \delta' Z_t + e_t, \quad e_t = \beta e_{t-1} + \varepsilon_t \tag{3.1.1.1}$$

where Z_t consists of deterministic terms and $\varepsilon_t \sim iid\ N(0,\sigma^2)$. According to the LM unit root test with two structural breaks, Model AA allows two structural breaks in the intercept, and is described by $Z_t = [1, t, D_{1t}, D_{2t}]$ where

$$D_{1t} = \begin{cases} 1 & \text{if } t \geq TB_1 + 1 \\ 0 & \text{otherwise} \end{cases}$$

$$D_{2t} = \begin{cases} 1 & \text{if } t \geq TB_2 + 1 \\ 0 & \text{otherwise.} \end{cases}$$

Here, TB_1 and TB_2 denote the break dates. Model CC includes two breaks in the intercept and the trend, and is described by $Z_t = [1, t, D_{1t}, D_{2t}, T_{1t}, T_{2t}]$ where

$$T_{1t} = \begin{cases} t - TB_1 & \text{if } t \geq TB_1 + 1 \\ 0 & \text{otherwise} \end{cases}$$

$$T_{2t} = \begin{cases} t - TB_2 & \text{if } t \geq TB_2 + 1 \\ 0 & \text{otherwise.} \end{cases}$$

The LM unit root test statistic is obtained from the following regression:

$$\Delta y_t = \alpha' \Delta Z_t + \phi \tilde{S}_{t-1} + \sum \gamma_i \Delta \tilde{S}_{t-i} + \mu_t \qquad (3.1.1.2)$$

where $\tilde{S}_t$ is a detrended series such that $\tilde{S}_t = y_t - \tilde{\psi}_x - Z_t \tilde{\delta}_t$, $t = 2,..,T$. $\tilde{\delta}$ is a vector of coefficients in the regression of Δy_t on ΔZ_t; $\tilde{\psi}_x = y_1 - Z_1 \tilde{\delta}$ and y_1 and Z_1 are the first observations of Y_t and Z_t, respectively. Δ is the difference operator. The lagged terms $\Delta \tilde{S}_{t-i}$, $i = 1,..,k$, are inserted to correct for serial correlation in Equation (3.1.1.2). The number of augmentation terms $\Delta \tilde{S}_{t-i}$, $i = 1,..,k$, is determined by following a "general to specific" procedure (starting with max *k*=4 for quarterly data) described in Strazicich et al. (2004). The unit root hypothesis is tested via the *t*-ratio of ϕ, this statistic being denoted as $\tilde{\tau}$.

Table 3. The results of minimum LM unit root test with two structural breaks

Countries	Series	TB_1	TB_2	k	S_{t-1}	D_{1t}	D_{2t}	T_{1t}	T_{2t}
Armenia	* *IR*	1996:03	2003:02	0	-0.729[b] (-6.016)	-3.917 (-1.059)	-0.558 (-0.152)	15.585[a] (7.604)	-1.227 (-1.228)
	LCPI	1997:04	2003:02	4	-0.654[b] (-5.643)	0.111[a] (4.905)	-0.040[c] (-1.767)	-0.087[a] (-6.128)	0.050[a] (5.639)
	INF	1995:04	2005:01	4	-1.004[c] (-5.475)	0.052[c] (1.811)	-0.123[a] (-4.229)	0.093[a] (3.623)	0.086[a] (5.302)
Israel	*IR*	1988:02	2000:02	4	-0.449 (-4.347)	0.466 (0.312)	0.269 (0.188)	3.594[a] (3.202)	-1.568[a] (-3.641)
	* *LCPI*	1990:04	1998:03	4	-0.242 (-4.026)	-0.010 (-0.964)	0.058[a] (5.488)	-0.001 (-0.321)	-0.038[a] (-7.339)
	INF	1990:02	2002:01	4	-0.779[a] (-7.955)	-0.064[b] (-2.019)	0.017 (0.547)	0.089[a] (7.815)	-0.019[a] (-2.805)
Kuwait	*IR*	2000:04	2005:04	4	-0.215 (-4.894)	-0.296 (-1.399)	0.166 (0.790)	-0.263[a] (-3.403)	0.324[a] (3.395)
	LCPI	2006:02	2007:02	4	-0.436[c] (-5.460)	0.004 (0.601)	-0.006 (-0.875)	0.013[a] (3.158)	0.014[a] (3.016)
	INF	1993:03	2007:03	0	-0.889[a] (-7.849)	0.022[a] (2.701)	0.014[c] (1.723)	-0.008[a] (-2.632)	0.006[a] (2.736)
Morocco	*IR*	1999:02	2004:02	2	-0.594 (-5.144)	0.383[a] (2.773)	-0.230[c] (-1.724)	-0.081 (-0.942)	0.414[a] (6.676)
	LCPI	2006:03	2008:02	3	-1.588[a] (-6.404)	0.019[a] (3.060)	-0.002 (-0.331)	0.003 (1.348)	0.007[a] (2.269)
	* *INF*	2002:01	2008:02	0	-1.360[a] (-10.41)	0.002 (0.275)	-0.010 (-1.430)	0.000 (0.336)	0.010[a] (3.875)

Table 3. (Continued)

Countries	Series	TB_1	TB_2	k	S_{t-1}	D_{1t}	D_{2t}	T_{1t}	T_{2t}
Turkey	* *IR*	1997:01	2003:03	3	-1.106[a] (-6.260)	-6.454 (-0.710)	-0.960 (-0.106)	1.716 (0.566)	-11.290[a] (-3.689)
	LCPI	1998:04	2003:01	2	-0.541[c] (-5.385)	-0.005 (-0.179)	0.038 (1.255)	-0.027[b] (-2.460)	-0.108[a] (-10.34)
	INF	1994:04	2003:02	0	-1.165[a] (-10.02)	-0.073[b] (-2.149)	-0.062[c] (-1.835)	0.047[a] (3.318)	-0.002 (-0.294)
Critical Values of the Two Breaks Minimum LM Test									
λ_2	0.4			0.6			0.8		
λ_1	1%	5%	10%	1%	5%	10%	1%	5%	10%
0.2	-6.16	-5.59	-5.27	-6.41	-5.74	-5.32	-6.33	-5.71	-5.33
0.4	-	-	-	-6.45	-5.67	-5.31	-6.42	-5.65	-5.32
0.6	-	-	-	-	-	-	-6.32	-5.73	-5.32

TB_1 and TB_2 are the break dates, k is the lag length, S_{t-1} is the coefficent on the unit root parameter. The figures in parantheses are t-statistics. Critical values for the coefficient on the dummy variables follow the standard normal distribution.

[a, b, c] denote statistical significance at 1%, 5% and 10% significance levels, respectively. For Model CC, critical values depend on the location of the breaks and come from Lee and Strazicich (2004).

* means that the minimum LM test with one structural break is more suitable based on the statistically significance of the breaks.

The null hypothesis of a unit root is tested against the alternative hypothesis of trend stationarity. Structural breaks (TB) are determined by selecting all possible break points for the minimum t-statistic as follows:

$$LM_{\tau} = \inf_{\lambda} \tilde{\tau}(\lambda) \tag{3.1.1.3}$$

where $\lambda = T_B / T$. The critical values are tabulated in Lee and Strazicich (2004) for the two breaks case. The results of the minimum LM unit root test with two structural breaks can be seen in Table 3.

The results of the minimum LM unit root test results reveal mixed results. According to the results for Armenia and Turkey, all IR, $LCPI$ and INF series are found stationary in level. On the other hand, for Kuwait and Morocco, $LCPI$ and INF series are found stationary in level while IR series shows nonstationarity. The results of Israel give that both IR and $LCPI$ series are nonstationary while INF series shows stationarity. In this point, identification of the estimated structural breaks which can be seen under the TB_1 and TB_2 columns of the Table 3 is very important. The breaks for IR series of Armenia occur at the date of 1996:03 and 2003:02. But, it is clear from the t-statistics of these break dates that only first break (1996:03) in the trend (T_{1t}) is statistically significant. It means that the minimum LM test with one structural break is more appropriate for the IR series of Armenia and we need to repeat the analysis by using this version. The results for $LCPI$ series of Armenia give that the structural breaks are identified at 1997:04 and 2003:02 and both breaks in the intercept and trend (D_{1t}, D_{2t}, T_{1t} and T_{2t}) are statistically significant. The identified structural break dates for INF series of Armenia are 1995:04 and 2008:02 and these breaks are statistically significant in both intercept and trend. The results for the case of Israel are as follows: The break dates for IR series are estimated as 1988:02 and 2000:02. The reported t-statistics indicate that first and second breaks are only statistically significant in the trend (T_{1t} and T_{2t}). These dates are found as 1990:04 and 1998:03 for the $LCPI$ series. But, only second break in the intercept and trend (D_{2t}, T_{2t}) is found statistically significant. Here, similar to the Armenia case, the minimum LM test with one structural break is more appropriate. On the other hand, the break dates for INF series of Israel are found as 1990:02

and 2002:01. Based on the *t*-statistics of these breaks, first break is statistically significant in both intercept and trend (D_{1t}, T_{1t}) and second break is significant only in the trend (T_{2t}). In the case of Kuwait, the break dates for *IR* series are 2000:04 and 2005:04, the break dates for *LCPI* series are 2006:02 and 2007:02. These breaks for both *IR* and *LCPI* series are statistically significant only in the trend (T_{1t} and T_{2t}). The results for the *INF* series of Kuwait indicate that the identified structural breaks occur at 1993:03 and 2007:03 and they are statistically significant in both intercept and trend (D_{1t}, D_{2t}, T_{1t} and T_{2t}). The results for the *IR* series of Morocco reveal that first and second breaks are identified at the date of 1999:02 and 2004:02, respectively. Based on the *t*-statistics of these breaks, it is clear that first break is only statistically significant in the intercept (D_{1t}) while the second break is statistically significant in both intercept and trend (D_{2t} and T_{2t}). The identified structural break dates for *LCPI* series of Morocco are 2006:03 and 2008:02. The first break is found statistically significant in the intercept (D_{1t}) while the second break is statistically significant in the trend (T_{2t}). For *INF* series of Morocco, the dates of 2002:01 and 2008:02 are the identified structural breaks and only second break in the trend is statistically significant (T_{2t}). In this case, the minimum LM test with one structural break is more appropriate as reported before. Finally, we need to examine the case of Turkey. The breaks for *IR* series of Turkey occur at 1997:01 and 2003:03. According to the *t*-statistics of the breaks, only second break in the trend (T_{2t}) is found statistically significant. It is necessary to repeat the analysis by using the minimum LM test with one structural break. Identified two structural breaks (1998:04 and 2003:01) are found statistically significant in trend (T_{1t} and T_{2t}) for *LCPI* series. On the other hand, the dates of 1994:04 and 2003:02 are identified for *INF* series of Turkey. First break is statistically significant in the intercept and the trend (D_{1t} and T_{1t}) while second break is statistically significant only in the intercept (T_{1t}). In this point, we apply the minimum LM test with one structural break for the series (*) which only one break case is found more appropriate based on the two breaks case. These are *IR* series of Armenia and Turkey, *LCPI* series of Israel and also *INF* series of Morocco. The obtained results for the mentioned series are reported in Table 4.

Table 4. The results of minimum LM unit root test with one structural break

Countries	Series	TB_1	k	S_{t-1}	D_{1t}	T_{1t}
Armenia	*IR*	1996:03	0	-0.294 (-3.451)	-0.966 (-0.236)	9.231[a] (5.341)
Israel	*LCPI*	1994:04	4	-0.049 (-2.246)	0.003 (0.309)	-0.026[a] (-10.76)
Morocco	*INF*	2007:03	0	-1.299[a] (-10.284)	0.006 (0.813)	0.002[a] (2.974)
Turkey	*IR*	2003:02	3	-0.812[a] (-5.430)	-0.929 (-0.101)	-17.909[a] (-4.607)

Critical Values of the One Break Minimum LM Test			
λ	1%	5%	10%
0.1	-5.11	-4.50	-4.21
0.2	-5.07	-4.47	-4.20
0.3	-5.15	-4.45	-4.18
0.4	-5.05	-4.50	-4.18
0.5	-5.11	-4.51	-4.17

TB_1 is the break date, k is the lag length, S_{t-1} is the coefficent on the unit root parameter. The figures in parantheses are t-statistics. Critical values for the coefficient on the dummy variables follow the standard normal distribution.

[a] denotes statistical significance at 1% significance level. For Model C, critical values depend on the location of the breaks and come from Lee and Strazicich (2003).

The results of the one break minimum LM unit root test indicate that the *IR* series of Armenia and *LCPI* series of Israel are nonstationary while the *INF* series of Morocco and *IR* series of Turkey are stationary. Based on the identified structural breaks, it can be said that the break at 1996:03, the break at 1994:04, the break at 2007:03 and the break at 2003:02 are statistically significant in trend (T_{1t}) for the *IR* series of Armenia, *LCPI* series of Israel, *INF* series of Morocco and *IR* series of Turkey, respectively. In sum, the results of unit root tests with structural breaks give mixed results and there is no consensus on the integration orders of the series as can be seen from Table 5.

Table 5. The results on the integration orders of the series

Countries	Series	Appropriate test type	Decision
Armenia	*IR*	LM test with one break	$I(1)$
	LCPI	LM test with two breaks	$I(0)$
	INF	LM test with two breaks	$I(0)$
Israel	*IR*	LM test with two breaks	$I(1)$
	LCPI	LM test with one break	$I(1)$
	INF	LM test with two breaks	$I(0)$
Kuwait	*IR*	LM test with two breaks	$I(1)$
	LCPI	LM test with two breaks	$I(0)$
	INF	LM test with two breaks	$I(0)$
Morocco	*IR*	LM test with two breaks	$I(1)$
	LCPI	LM test with two breaks	$I(0)$
	INF	LM test with one break	$I(0)$
Turkey	*IR*	LM test with one break	$I(0)$
	LCPI	LM test with two breaks	$I(0)$
	INF	LM test with two breaks	$I(0)$

As reported before, another possibility for traditional unit root tests to give contradictory results is fractional integration properties of the series. In other words, the contradictions may arise because the $I(d)$ concept where d is an integer. Since traditional unit root tests are too restrictive, we also take into account the possible fractional integration properties of the series in our analysis.

3.1.2. Unit Root Properties of the Series under Fractional Alternatives

To examine the time series behavior in the concept of fractional integration, we also apply LM test developed by Robinson (1994) to test unit roots and other forms of nonstationary hypotheses, embedded in fractional alternatives. The main advantage of the Robinson (1994) procedure is that it tests unit and fractional roots with a standard null limit distribution, which is unaffected by inclusion or not of deterministic trends. In the structure of this test, following model is considered:

$$y_t = \beta' z_t + x_t \ , \ t = 1, 2, ... \tag{3.1.2.1}$$

where y_t is the observed time series for $t = 1, 2, ...T$, $\beta = (\beta_1, ..., \beta_k)'$ is a $(k \times 1)$ vector of unknown parameters, and z_t is a $(k \times 1)$ vector of deterministic regressors such as an intercept or a linear trend. The regression errors x_t can be explained as follows:

$$(1 - L)^d x_t = u_t \ , \ t = 1, 2, ... \tag{3.1.2.2}$$

where L is the lag operator and u_t is an $I(0)$ process. Here, d can take any real value. If $d = 0$ in Equation (3.1.2.2), $x_t = u_t$, and a "weakly autocorrelated" x_t is allowed for. When $d > 0$, x_t is said to be "strongly autocorrelated" or "strongly dependent." Clearly, the unit root case corresponds to $d = 1$ in (3.1.2.2). If $d > 0$, x_t is said to be long memory (Granger and Joyeux, 1980; Hosking, 1981). If $0.5 < d < 1$, the process is nonstationary and exhibits long memory, whereas the process is stationary and exhibits long memory, if $0 < d < 0.5$. It is important to note that when $d < 0.5$, the process is stationary and mean reverting with the effect of the shocks dying away in the long run and when $0.5 \leq d$, the process is nonstationary even if the fractional parameter is significantly less than 1. The null hypothesis of the test can be seen below:

$$H_0 : d = d_0 \tag{3.1.2.3}$$

Specifically, the test statistic is given by

$$\hat{r} = \frac{T^{1/2}}{\hat{\sigma}^2} \hat{A}^{-1/2} \hat{a} \tag{3.1.2.4}$$

where T is the sample size and

$$\hat{a} = \frac{-2\pi}{T}\sum_{j=1}^{T-1}\psi(\lambda_j)g(\lambda_j;\hat{\tau})^{-1}I(\lambda_j);$$

$$\hat{\sigma}^2 = \sigma^2(\hat{\tau}) = \frac{2\pi}{T}\sum_{j=1}^{T-1}g(\lambda_j;\hat{\tau})^{-1}I(\lambda_j);$$

$$\hat{A} = \frac{2}{T}\left(\sum_{j=1}^{T-1}\psi(\lambda_j)^2 - \sum_{j=1}^{T-1}\psi(\lambda_j)\hat{\varepsilon}(\lambda_j)' \times \left(\sum_{j=1}^{T-1}\hat{\varepsilon}(\lambda_j)\hat{\varepsilon}(\lambda_j)'\right)^{-1} \times \sum_{j=1}^{T-1}\hat{\varepsilon}(\lambda_j)\psi(\lambda_j)\right)$$

$$\psi(\lambda_j) = \log\left|2\sin\frac{\lambda_j}{2}\right|; \qquad \hat{\varepsilon}(\lambda_j) = \frac{\partial}{\partial\tau}\log g(\lambda_j;\hat{\tau}_j); \qquad \lambda_j = \frac{2\pi j}{T};$$

$$\hat{\tau} = \arg\min_{\tau\in T^*}\sigma^2(\tau)$$

where $I(\lambda_j)$ is the periodogram of u_t, and T^* is a compact subset or the Euclidean space. Under certain regularity conditions, the test statistic is

$$\hat{r} \rightarrow_d N(0,1) \text{ as } T \rightarrow \infty. \qquad (3.1.2.5)$$

Thus, a one-sided $100\alpha\%$ level test of the null hypothesis (3.1.2.3) against the alternative $H_1: d > d_0$ is given by the rule "Reject H_0 if $\hat{r} > z_\alpha$ " where the probability that a standard normal variate exceeds z_α is α, and conversely, a one-sided $100\alpha\%$ level test of the null hypothesis against the alternative $H_1: d < d_0$ is given by the rule "Reject H_0 if $\hat{r} < -z_\alpha$". The results of Robinson(1994) test performed on the individual series for testing the unit root null hypothesis ($d_0 = 1$) under white noise distribution assumption can be seen in Table 6.

The results in the table indicate that the unit root null hypohesis $(d_0 = 1)$ cannot be rejected for IR series of Armenia and Morocco and $LCPI$ series of Israel, Kuwait and Turkey. Since integration orders of the each series are different, it is clear that standard cointegration methods which assume that all the variables are integrated of order one $I(1)$, are not suitable in testing Gibson paradox and Fisher hypothesis for considered countries.

Table 6. The results of Robinson test for unit root

Countries	Series	Test statistic
Armenia	*IR*	-1.52[b]
	LCPI	-2.10
	INF	-3.29
Israel	*IR*	-3.44
	LCPI	0.38[b]
	INF	-2.31
Kuwait	*IR*	6.11
	LCPI	0.19[b]
	INF	-3.81
Morocco	*IR*	-0.96[b]
	LCPI	-2.39
	INF	-4.09
Turkey	*IR*	-2.20
	LCPI	0.69[b]
	INF	-4.37

[b] indicates nonrejection values of the null hypothesis at the 5% significance level. We consider only the test where u_t is assumed to be white noise, for the specification with a linear trend.

3.2. Bounds Testing Cointegration Procedure

In our analysis, to empirically analyse the Gibson paradox and Fisher hypothesis, the bounds testing cointegration procedure developed by Pesaran et al. (2001) is used due to the following reasons: First of all, the bounds testing procedure does not require the pre-testing of the series in the model for unit roots. Similar to our unit root test results, it can be applied irrespective of whether the regressors in the model are purely $I(0)$, purely $I(1)$ and mutually cointegrated. Secondly, the bounds test procedure is simple and it allows the cointegration relationship to be estimated by ordinary least squares (OLS) method once the lag order of the model is identified. Finally, the test is relatively more efficient in small or finite sample data. In the first step of the bounds testing approach, the following regression equation is estimated by using OLS method:

$$\Delta y_t = \alpha + \sum_{i=1}^{k} \beta_i \Delta y_{t-i} + \sum_{i=1}^{k} \gamma_i \Delta x_{t-i} + \delta_1 y_{t-1} + \delta_2 x_{t-1} + \varepsilon_t \qquad (3.2.1)$$

where y and x denote the dependent and independent variables, respectively. Here, δ_i 's are the long run multipliers, α is the drift and ε_t is the white noise error terms. In this equation, we conduct an F test for the joint significance of the coefficients of the lagged levels of the series, i.e., $H_N : \delta_1 = \delta_2 = 0$ against the alternative $H_A : \delta_1 \neq \delta_2 \neq 0$. The null hypothesis suggests that there is no long run relationship between the series. Pesaran et al. (2001) compute two sets of critical values for a given significance level. If the computed F statistic exceeds the upper critical value, the H_0 is rejected irrespective of the orders of integration for the series. If the F statistic is below the lower critical value, it suggests no cointegration between the series. Finally, if the statistic falls between the lower and upper critical values, the result is inconclusive.

Even though the bounds test framework does not require pretesting of the integration order of the series, the unit root tests could convince us whether or not the autoregressive distributed lag (ARDL) model should be used. This is to ensure that the series are not $I(2)$ stationary so as to avoid spurious results. According to Quattara (2004), the computed F statistics are not valid in the presence of $I(2)$ series. Because, the bounds test is based on the assumption that the variables are $I(0)$ or $I(1)$. Therefore, the implementation of the unit root tests in the bounds test procedure might still be necessary in order to ensure that none of the variables is integrated of order 2 or beyond. In this point, our unit root test results confirm that the series are not $I(2)$ stationary in our analysis. Therefore, the bounds testing could be proceeded.

3.2.1. The Cointegration Test Results for Gibson Paradox

As reported in the theoretical model section of the paper, we take into account the long run relationship between IR and $LCPI$ series in order to test Gibson paradox for considered MENA countries. For this purpose, we estimate Equation (3.2.1) as follow in our analysis:

$$\Delta LCPI_t = \alpha + \sum_{i=1}^{k} \beta_i \Delta LCPI_{t-i} + \sum_{i=1}^{k} \gamma_i \Delta IR_{t-i} + \delta_1 LCPI_{t-1} + \delta_2 IR_{t-1} + \varepsilon_t \quad (3.2.1.1)$$

where $LCPI$ and IR are the ***logarithmic*** consumer price index and the interest rate, respectively. Here, the most important stage is to choose appropriate lag orders. The lag orders in the our analysis are selected by using Schwarz (SC) information criterions. We set the maximum lag order at 4 and choose the lag order which minimizes the model selection criteria and ensures that there is no evidence of serial correlation. The values of SC criterion and LM test results for serial correlation are reported in Table 7.

Table 7. Lag length selection results for Gibson paradox

Countries	Lag	SC	Prob. - LM(1)	Prob. - LM(4)
Armenia	1	-3.325	0.115	0.000
	2	-3.747	0.039	0.000
	3	-3.762	0.001	0.002
	4	-3.829	0.217	0.228
Israel	1	-5.813	0.030	0.033
	2	-5.783	0.069	0.023
	3	-5.719	0.564	0.092
	4	-5.728	0.216	0.351
Kuwait	1	-6.438	0.623	0.647
	2	-6.323	0.747	0.147
	3	-6.207	0.592	0.003
	4	-6.347	0.773	0.904
Morocco	1	-6.581	0.596	0.638
	2	-6.424	0.638	0.782
	3	-6.283	0.252	0.085
	4	-6.175	0.059	0.431
Turkey	1	-4.149	0.403	0.209
	2	-4.043	0.200	0.021
	3	-4.081	0.353	0.169
	4	-4.024	0.759	0.229

The numbers under the columns of LM(1) and LM(4) are probability values of the serial correlation LM test for order 1 and 4, respectively.

According to the results in the table, the appropriate lag length which minimizes the SC information criterion and ensures no serial correlation is found as 4 for Armenia and Israel, as 1 for Kuwait, Morocco and Turkey. By using these lags, we estimate Equation (3.2.1.1) and test the null hypothesis

$H_N : \delta_1 = \delta_2 = 0$ against the alternative of $H_A : \delta_1 \neq \delta_2 \neq 0$. The calculated F statistics of bounds cointegration test for Gibson paradox is tabulated in Table 8.

Table 8. Bounds cointegration test results for Gibson paradox

Countries	F-statistic
Armenia	0.574
Israel	5.562[c]
Kuwait	2.874
Morocco	1.361
Turkey	38.861[a]
Critical Values of the Bounds Test	Lower Upper
1 %	6.84 7.84
5 %	4.94 5.73
10 %	4.04 4.78

Critical values are obtained from the Table CI(iii) of Pesaran et al.(2001).

As can be seen from the table, the calculated F statistics for Israel and Turkey (5.562 and 38.861, respectively) are found to exceed the upper critical values. These results support the existence of a long run relationship between $LCPI$ and IR series of Israel and Turkey, hence, the validity of the Gibson paradox.

3.2.2. The Cointegration Test Results for Fisher Hypothesis

In order to test the Fisher hypothesis for MENA countries, the long run relationship between IR and INF series is investigated following the theoretical explanation of Fisher hypothesis. In the concept of bounds test procedure, the Equation (3.2.1) is estimated for IR and INF series as below:

$$\Delta IR_t = \alpha + \sum_{i=1}^{k} \beta_i \Delta IR_{t-i} + \sum_{i=1}^{k} \gamma_i \Delta INF_{t-i} + \delta_1 IR_{t-1} + \delta_2 INF_{t-1} + \varepsilon_t \quad (3.2.1.2)$$

where IR is the interest rate and INF is the inflation rate. Similar to the Gibson paradox case, we again set the maximum lag order at 4 and choose the lag order which minimizes the SC criteria and ensures that there is no evidence of serial correlation. It is important to note that choosing appropriate lag order is an important stage for bounds test cointegration procedure. The lag length selection results for Fisher hypothesis are given in Table 9.

Table 9. Lag length selection results for Fisher hypothesis

Countries	Lag	SC	Prob. - LM(1)	Prob. - LM(4)
Armenia	1	5.631	0.391	0.253
	2	5.727	0.018	0.000
	3	4.910	0.152	0.261
	4	4.835	0.000	0.000
Israel	1	4.147	0.004	0.009
	2	3.867	0.038	0.003
	3	3.898	0.000	0.000
	4	3.662	0.939	0.200
Kuwait	1	0.080	0.006	0.000
	2	0.104	0.000	0.006
	3	0.038	0.328	0.785
	4	0.101	0.742	0.576
Morocco	1	-0.635	0.210	0.521
	2	-0.498	0.769	0.628
	3	-0.360	0.301	0.777
	4	-0.235	0.489	0.027
Turkey	1	7.251	0.032	0.003
	2	7.211	0.426	0.006
	3	7.334	0.001	0.005
	4	7.283	0.578	0.175

The numbers under the columns of LM(1) and LM(4) are probability values of the serial correlation LM test for order 1 and 4, respectively.

The results in the table reveal that the appropriate lag length is 3 for Armenia and Kuwait, 1 for Morocco and 4 for Israel and Turkey when the minimization of the SC information criterion and absence of serial correlation are considered together. By taking account of these lags, we estimate Equation (3.2.1.2) and test the null hypothesis $H_N : \delta_1 = \delta_2 = 0$ against the alternative hypothesis $H_A : \delta_1 \neq \delta_2 \neq 0$. The obtained F statistics can be seen in Table 10.

Since the calculated F statistics exceed the upper critical values for Morocco and Turkey (9.766 and 9.465, respectively) at the 1% significance level, it can be said that there is a long run relationship between IR and INF

series of these countries. These results point out that the Fisher hypothesis is valid for Morocco and Turkey.

Table 10. Bounds cointegration test results for Fisher hypothesis

Countries	F-statistic
Armenia	3.732
Israel	3.126
Kuwait	2.597
Morocco	9.766[a]
Turkey	9.465[a]
Critical Values of the Bounds Test	Lower Upper
1 %	6.84 7.84
5 %	4.94 5.73
10 %	4.04 4.78

Critical values are obtained from the Table CI(iii) of Pesaran et al.(2001).

CONCLUSION

This chapter examines the validity of the Gibson paradox and Fisher hypothesis for selected MENA countries (namely, Armenia, Israel, Kuwait, Morocco and Turkey) by using different econometric methods. These countries are selected based on the data availability. As a first step, we test the unit root properties of the interest rate, price level and inflation series by using traditional unit root tests which do not take into account structural breaks and fractional alternatives. Since obtained results are inconclusive, the unit root properties of the series are re-investigated by using unit root tests with structural breaks and fractional integration alternatives. After finding similar results, we apply bounds testing cointegration procedure in testing long run relationship between interest rate and price level and also between interest rate and inflation rate. The reason is that this test does not require pre-testing of the series in the model. The results give that there is a long run relationship between price level and interest rate of Israel and Turkey, implying validity of the Gibson paradox. On the other hand, a long run relationship between inflation and interest rate is found for Morocco and Turkey, hence, validity of the Fisher hypothesis.

REFERENCES

Atkins, F. J. & Serletis, A. (2003). Bounds Tests of the Gibson Paradox and the Fisher Effect: Evidence from Low-Frequency International Data', *Manchester School*, 71: 673-679.

Berument, H. & Jelassi, M. (2002). The Fisher Hypothesis: A Multi-Country Analysis. *Applied Economics*, 34, 1645-1655.

Chen, C. & Lee, C. J. (1990). A VARMA Test on the Gibson Paradox. *Review of Economics and Statistics*, 72, 96–107.

Corbae, D. & Oualiris, S. (1989). A Random Walk Through the Gibson Paradox. *Journal of Applied Econometrics*, 4, 1-47.

Fama, E.F. (1975). Short Term Interest Rates as Predictors of Inflation. *American Economic Review*, 35, 143–159.

Fisher, I. (1930). *The Theory of Interest*. The Macmillan Company, New York. (http://www.econlib.org/library/YPDBooks/Fisher/fshToI.html)

Ghazali, N. A. & Ramlee, S. (2003). A Long Memory Test of Long-run Fisher Effect in the G7 Countries. *Applied Financial Economics*, 13, 763-769.

Gibson, A. H. (1923). The Future Course of High Class Investment Values. *Banker's Magazine*, 115, 15-34.

Granger, C.W.J. & Joyeux, R. (1980). An Introduction to Long-Memory Time Series Models and Fractional Differencing. *Journal of Time Series Analysis*, 1, 15-29.

Granville, B. & Mallick, S. (2004). Fisher Hypothesis: UK Evidence over a Century. *Applied Economics Letters*, 11, 87-90.

Halicioglu, F. (2004). The Gibson Paradox: An Empirical Investigation for Turkey. *European Research Studies Journal*, 27, 111-119.

Hosking, J. (1981). Fractional Differencing. *Biometrika*, 68, 165-176.

Ito, T. (2009). Fisher Hypothesis in Japan: Analysis of Long-Term Interest Rates under Different Monetary Policy Regimes. *The World Economy*, 32, 1019-1035.

Kasman, S., Kasman, A. & Turgutlu, E. (2006). Fisher Hypothesis Revisited: A Fractional Cointegration Analysis. *Emerging Markets Finance and Trade*, 42, 59-76.

Keynes, J.M. (1930). *Treatise of Money*. Vol. II, New York: Harcourt, Brace and Company.

Klein, L.R. (1995). An Economic Interpretation of the Gibson Relationship. *Atlantic Economic Journal*, 23, 159-176.

Lardic, S. & Mignon, V. (2003). Fractional Cointegration Between Nominal Interest Rates and Inflation: A Re-examination of the Fisher Relationship in the G7 Countries. *Economics Bulletin*, 3, 1-10.

Lee, C. J. & Petruzzi, C.R. (1986). The Gibson Paradox and the Monetary Standard. *The Review Bulletin of Economics and Statistics*, 68, 189-196.

Lee, J. & Strazicich, M.C. (2003). Minimum Lagrange Multiplier Unit Root Test with Two Structural Breaks. *Review of Economics and Statistics*, 85, 1082 – 1089, doi: 10.1162/003465303772815961, http://dx.doi.org/10.1162/003465303772815961

Lee, J. & Strazicich, M.C. (2004). Minimum LM Unit Root Test with One Structural Break. *Working papers*, No. 17, Boone, NC: Appalachian State University, Department of Economics.

Million, N. (2004). Central Bank's Interventions and the Fisher Hypothesis: A Threshold Cointegration Investigation. *Economic Modelling*, 21, 1051-1064.

Milne, W.J. & Torous, W.N. (1984). Long-Term Interest Rates and the Price Level: The Canadian Evidence on the Gibson Paradox. *Canadian Journal of Economics*, 17, 327-339.

Mishkin, F. (1992). Is the Fisher Effect for Real? A Re-examination of the Relationship between Inflation and Interest Rates. *Journal of Monetary Economics*, 30, 195-215.

Neaime, S. (2008). Monetary Policy Transmission and Targeting Mechanisms in the MENA Region. *Economic Research Forum, Working Paper*, 395.

Perron, P. (1989). The Great Crash, The Oil Price Shock, and The Unit Root Hypothesis. *Econometrica*, 57, 1361-1401. http://www.jstor.org/stable/1913712.

Pesaran, M.H., Shin, Y. & Smith, R.J. (2001). Bounds Testing Approaches to the Analysis of Level Relationships. *Journal of Applied Econometrics*, 16, 289-326.

Quattara, B. (2004). Foreign Aid and Fiscal Policy in Senegal. Mimeo University of Manchester.

Ram, R. (1987). A Broader Multicountry Perspective on the Gibson Paradox and Fisher's Hypothesis. *De Economist*, 135, 219-230.

Robinson, P.M. (1994). Efficient Tests of Nonstationary Hypothesis. *Journal of the American Statistical Association*, 89, 1420-1437.

Sargent, T.J. (1973). Interest Rates and Prices in the Long Run: A Study of the Gibson Paradox. *Journal of Money, Credit and Banking*, 4, 385-449.

Serletis, A. & Zestos, G. (1999). On the Gibson Paradox. *Review of International Economics*, 7, 117-125.

Shiller, R.J. & Siegel, J. (1977). The Gibson Paradox and Historical Movements in Real Interest Rates. *Journal of Political Economy*, 85, 891-907.

Strazicich, M.C., Lee, J., & Day, E. (2004). Are Incomes Converging Among OECD Countries? Time Series Evidence With Two Structural Breaks. *Journal of Macroeconomics*, 26, 131-145. doi:10.1016/j.jmacro.2002.11.001, http://dx.doi.org/10.1016/j.jmacro.2002.11.001

Şimşek, M. and Kadılar, C. (2006). Fisher Etkisinin Türkiye Verileri ile Testi. *Doğuş University Journal*, 7, 99-111.

Şimşek, M. & Kadılar, C. (2008). Gibson Çelişkisinin Türkiye Verileri ile Analizi. *Sosyal Bilimler Dergisi*, 20, 115-127.

Turgutlu, E. (2004). Fisher Hipotezinin Tutarlılığının Testi: Parçalı Durağanlık ve Parçalı Koentegrasyon Analizi. *D.E.Ü. İ.İ.B.F. Dergisi*, 19, 55-74.

In: Economic and Social Issues …
Editor: Nilgün Çil Yavuz
ISBN: 978-1-62948-152-4

Chapter 5

THE EFFECTS OF GLOBAL ECONOMIC CRISIS ON MENA COUNTRIES

Sefer Şener*
Department of Economics, Istanbul University, Turkey

ABSTRACT

The main aim of this study is to analyse the effects of the global economic crisis on the MENA countries. The MENA countries have faced important changes because of the global economic crisis and the Arab Spring. Economic growth slowed significantly with the global economic and financial crisis of 2008-2009. More recently, a wave of protests driven by longstanding socio-political and economic issues spread across several countries. The global financial crisis of 2008 had important negative impact in MENA through the decline in oil prices and turmoil in international financial markets. MENA was also hit by the secondary effects of the crisis on trade, remittances, and FDI. As a result, MENA countries were affected substantially by the global economic crisis through the channels of declining international prices of the oil, decreasing exports, deteriorating expectations and financial markets.

Keywords: Global economic crisis, MENA countries

---

* Email: sefersener@istanbul.edu.tr.

1. INTRODUCTION

The Arab world has seen many important shifts over the past decade. The Global Economic and Financial Crisis of 2008-2009 badly affected high economic growth which last nearly ten years. The recent wave of protests caused by longstanding socio-political and economic issues spread across several countries, leading to instability and the fall of the regimes in Tunisia, Egypt, and Libya after months of a violent revolution. These events – commonly known as the "Arab Spring" – have spurred major political changes, notably in Tunisia and Egypt, where new constitutions are being drafted and entirely new governments elected. However to resolve the root causes of the current events in the region, political changes have to be accompanied by structural economic reform.

The arguments on creation of more and better employment opportunities for the 2.8 million young people entering the labor markets every year have intensed awareness of key socio-economic challenges. Reducing unemployment will have to focus on three groups that are disproportionately affected – the young, the educated, and women (World Economic Forum and the OECD, 2011:6)

The young and growing workforce, abundant energy resources, and a growing momentum to look for ways to diversify their economies imply that the growth potential of the region is high. Looking beyond the next couple of years, however, MENA countries continue to face formidable longer term challenges. Becauseincome growth has not been sufficient given MENA's high population growth, standards of living in the region have stagnated. The world's one of the lowest formal employment rate have been brought about by high unemployment rates, particularly youth unemployment, low labor force participation, especially for females, and informality. Private investment rates have not increased commensurately with greater market and private sector orientation in most countries in the region. Among key long term growth challenges are access to finance, which is very low in MENA, competitiveness, and the non-competitive business environment facing enterprises in MENA. (World Bank, 2010:vi).

By the end of 2010, countries in the Middle East and North Africa (MENA) had largely recovered from the global financial crisis, and growth rates were expected to reach pre-crisis levels in 2011. By the beginning of 2011, the prodemocracy movements seen in Tunisia and Egypt, and spread to Bahrain, Libya, Syria and Yemen resulted in swift regime change in the end. The unrest and uncertainty associated with these movements have affected the short-term macroeconomic outlook and the status and speed of economic reforms in the region. The medium-run growth prospects are likely to improve, especially if the political changes are associated with more open and accountable governance and more rapid reforms (World Bank, 2011).

2. The Global Economic Crisis

Breaking out with a financial meltdown in the United States and Europe in early 2008; The Global Financial Crisis had spread to the rest of the world within a short period of time. In the early stages of the crisis, large international banks that had overinvested in risky real estate mortgages suffered severe losses as real estate prices declined in 2007. The insolvency of major financial institutions and the erosion of household wealth in real estate and equity markets in turn led to a sharp decline in investor and consumer confidence. Although the rapid mediation of Western governments prevented their economies from plunging into depression, the acuate decline in consumer and corporate spending pushed the U.S. and European economies into the worst recession since World War II. This worldwide economic slowdown led to a sharp decline in the demand for oil, food, and other commodities (Habibi, 2009:2).

The recovery has suffered new setbacks, and uncertainty weighs heavily on the outlook. A key reason is that policies in the major advanced economies have not rebuilt confidence in medium-term prospects. Tail risks, such as those relating to the viability of the euro area or major U.S. fiscal policy mistakes, continue to preoccupy investors (IMF, 2012:1).

IMF The World Economic Outlook (WEO) forecast thus sees only a gradual strengthening of activity from the relatively disappointing pace of early 2012. As seen on Table 1 Global growth is projected at 3.3 and 3.6 percent in 2012 and 2013, respectively. Output is expected to remain sluggish in advanced economies but still relatively solid in many emerging market and developing economies. Unemployment is likely to stay elevated in many parts of the world, and financial conditions will remain fragile. In many advanced economies, injections of liquidity are having a positive impact on financial stability, output, and employment, but the impact may be diminishing over time (IMF, 2012:1).

Many governments have taken serious steps towards reducing excessive deficits, however because of the high uncertainty, low confidence and weak financial sectors, fiscal achievements have been accompanied by disappointing growth or recessions. In emerging market and developing economies, policymakers are conscious of the need to rebuild fiscal and monetary policy space but are wondering how to calibrate policies in the face of major external downside risks. An effective policy response in the major advanced economies is the key to improving prospects and inspiring more confidence about the future. In the short term, the main tasks are to rule out the tail risk scenarios and adopt concrete plans to bring down public debt over the medium term. Reducing the risks to the medium-term outlook presaged by the public debt overhang in the major advanced economies will require supportive monetary policies and appropriate structural reforms, as well as careful fiscal policy (IMF, 2012:1).

Table-1. Overview of the World Economic Outlook Projections, (Percent change)

	Year-over-Year		
		Projections	
	2011	2012	2013
World output	**3.8**	**3.3**	**3.6**
Advanced economies	1.6	1.3	1.5
Of which: United States	1.8	2.2	2.1
European Union	1.6	–0.2	0.5
Emerging and developing economies	6.2	5.3	5.6
Of which: MENAP	3.3	5.1	3.6
CCA	6.7	5.7	5.5
Commonwealth of Independent States	4.9	4.0	4.1
Of which: Russia	4.3	3.7	3.8
World trade volume (goods and services)	**5.8**	**3.2**	**4.5**
Commodity prices			
Oil[1]	31.6	2.1	–1.0
Nonfuel[2]	17.8	–9.5	–2.9

Sources: IMF, *World Economic Outlook* (October 2012) and *Middle East and Central Asia Regional Economic Outlook* (November 2012).
[1]Simple average of prices of U.K. Brent, Dubai, and West Texas Intermediate crude oil. The average price of oil in U.S. dollars a barrel was $104.01 in 2011; the assumed price based on future markets is $106.18 in 2012 and $105.10 in 2013.
[2]Average (measured in U.S. dollars) based on world commodity export weights.

Source: International Monetary Fund, "Regional economic outlook. Middle East and Central Asia", Washington, D.C., November 2012, p.7.

3. The Effects of Global Economic Crisis on MENA Countries

The Global Financial and Economic Crisis had affected the three country groupings in the Middle East and North Africa (MENA) variously: the Gulf Cooperation Council (GCC), developing oil exporters, and oil importers. Among these three groups, the GCC oil exporters were hardest hit because the crisis affected them directly through two different channels: (a) a negative terms-of-trade shock associated with the drop in oil prices; and (b) a financial shock, which destabilized overextended domestic banks and led to the bursting of a real estate bubble. Growth collapsed for this group of countries from 6 percent in 2008 to less than 1 percent in 2009. Abundant reserves and repatriated funds enabled the GCC governments to respond quickly with monetary and fiscal stimuli and avoid a deeper deceleration in growth. (Reinikka, 2010:377).

The global financial crisis of 2008 is regarded as the worst global recession since World War II, and had a direct, negative impact in MENA through the decline in oil prices and turmoil in international financial markets. Secondary effects of the crisis on trade, remittances, and FDI was the following hit for MENA. Countercyclical policies and financial sector support measures are expected to have limited the decline in output in 2009 by encouraging consumption and investment activity. In addition, a significant adjustment in imports is expected to have occurred between 2008 and 2009 due to compression in investment, private expenditure, and a decline in imports of intermediate inputs used in the production of exports (World Bank, 2010:1)

Some important developments have been seen in the Middle East and North Africa (MENA) region in 2011. A wave of popular protest demanding more social equity and stronger economic development has led to political change at an unprecedented and unexpected scale. Social unrest affected many countries, but the degree of resulting political change varied across the region. Economic, social, and political reforms in a number of countries have been triggered by the protests and culminated in the resignation of ruling presidents in Tunisia and Egypt and in forceful regime change in Libya. While these events have contributed to uncertainty in the short term, and many countries are set to experience a drop in economic output in 2011, they present great promise for the future development of the countries in question and the region as a whole. A political transition is under way in a number of countries, and reforms aimed at enhancing competitiveness are high on the agenda of many governments and supported by the international community. If such reforms are carried out, the region has the potential to rebound and provide better employment opportunities and improved standards of living for its population (World Economic Forum and the OECD, 2011:9).

Arab economies were transmitted by The global crisis through several distinct channels: the financial markets, the crude oil market, Arab investments in global asset markets, tourism, the remittance income of Arab workers, and the region's non-oil exports, originating primarily in North Africa and destined for Europe (Habibi, 2009:2).

It is suggested that transitions from other regions provide medium-run gains from moving to more open and accountable governments are sizable. Income growth tends to stabilize at a higher average rate in the decade after transition, and income volatility at a lower rate, as compared with the previous period. The results will depend on how swiftly and credibly governments can commit to reform. In the meantime, as investors wait for political uncertainty to be resolved in countries affected by political turmoil, it is inevitable that investment will be delayed and economic challenges will emerge. Experiences of earlier transitions show that these difficulties tend to be limited; growth typically dips for only one year and then returns to or exceeds previous levels. These challenges alter the short-term economic outlook and subject it to significant uncertainty in several countries in the region (World Bank, 2011:4).

The financial sector was the initial pathway. Regional stock markets which had traditionally suffered from high degrees of volatility were the first financial shock wave. Between the years 2004-2007, these markets received large volumes of new investment as a result of the inflow of record-high oil revenues and the repatriation of their foreign investments by some Arab private investors after the September 2001 attacks. Some countries such as Egypt and Jordan, which had previously liberalized their financial markets, experienced especially sizeable foreign investment inflows. In the meantime, Arab stock markets remained highly volatile (Habibi, 2009:2).

The movements in financial market indicate a modest tightening of financing conditions for absolute as well as the corporate sector, which is expected to rinsen regional growth. FDI inflows are likely to decline and short-term capital outflows to rise in the countries affected by unrest, putting downward pressure on exchanges rates. The range of the decline in investment will depend on how long it takes for uncertainty to be resolved (World Bank, 2011:5).

The oil market was the second channel for transmission of the global economic crisis to MENA Arab countries. The decline in the demand for crude oil caused by the global recession gave rise to a sharp decline in its price. After reaching a peak of $133 per barrel in July 2008, the price of oil fell more than 70%, to an average of $39 per barrel in February 2009. During this period, OPEC members also implemented a production cut (effective January 1, 2009) to stabilize the price. The combination of lower price and reduced output in Arab oil-exporting countries led to a convincing loss of oil revenues for those countries (Habibi, 2009:3).

The decline in value of the foreign assets of GCC countries and Libya was the third channel for the transmission of the global crisis to the Middle East. The intense increase in oil revenues of these countries during 2003–2008 caught their governments by surprise. Apprehensive of the volatile nature of oil revenues in the previous three decades, they did not increase their fiscal spending at a fast pace; instead, they transferred a sizeable portion of their windfall oil revenues into their Sovereign Wealth Funds (SWF), which in turn invested them in global markets. As the size of these funds grew over time, however, SWF managers concluded that investing these large sums in bank deposits and U.S. government bonds was no longer a sound long-term strategy, because low-risk assets offered very low rates of return. Arab SWFs, along with their Asian counterparts raised their investments in equities and real estate beginning in 2007. Some invested in U.S. and European financial institutions, such as Citigroup and Merrill Lynch, which subsequently suffered heavy losses. As a result, the sharp decline in the stock markets and real estate prices in the U.S. and Europe resulted in large losses for the Arab SWFs (Habibi, 2009:4).

The global financial cirisis of 2008 hit MENA countries however the degree of damage will depend on their degree of economic integration, and their ability to implement certain macroeconomic and structural policies (Doaa and Doaa, 2010:4). Due to the limited integration of their banking sectors into global financial markets, developing oil exporters felt the impact of the crisis mostly through the negative oil price shock. Growth declined only slightly from 2.9 percent in 2008 to 2.2 percent in 2009. These countries pursue procyclical fiscal policies however during the crisis some governments reacted with countercyclical measures, but the extent to which they were able to do so depended on their fiscal space, reserves, and access to external financing. Strong non-oil gross domestic product (GDP) growth—at nearly 5 percent in 2009—helped soften the decline in overall growth (World Bank, 2010:2).

In terms of integration into global financial markets, the Middle East falls behind all other emerging-market regions other than Africa; but although a lower level of financial integration is a disadvantage under normal circumstances, it can protect an emerging region when the global economy sinks into a severe financial crisis. In this case, however, the Middle East and North Africa (MENA) region is affected by global economic conditions through fluctuations in the oil market—and some MENA countries have developed strong economic linkages with the global economy that go beyond oil. North African nations maintain strong trade and investment relations with Europe, while the oil-rich countries of the Gulf Cooperation Council (GCC) have accumulated a large portfolio of financial and equity investments in advanced economies. All these factors increase these economies' exposure to global economic downturns (Habibi, 2009:1).

Oil-importing MENA countries were hurt mostly by the secondary effects of the crisis on trade, remittances, and foreign direct investment (FDI). Growth, which was high before the crisis, decelerated from close to 7 percent in 2008, to a moderate pace of 4.8 percent in 2009. Key nonoil sectors such as services and tourism remained relatively resilient, while the decline in oil and other commodity prices limited the deterioration of their external balances. Stimulus packages in the Arab Republic of Egypt, Jordan, Morocco, and Tunisia also helped soften the deceleration in growth (Reinikka, 2010:378).

Many MENA countries including Egypt, Morocco, Tunisia, Jordan, and Lebanon built heavily upon tourism as an important source of service sector jobs and foreign exchange revenue, and the global recession of the past two years has reduced the number of foreign tourists in the Middle East. Tourism revenues are reported a 9.5% decline in the first half of 2009 as compared with the first half of 2008.6 in Egypt. Hotel occupancy rates in Dubai and Abu Dhabi (capital of the UAE) declined by 16% and 7%, respectively, in the first four months of 2009 vis-à-vis the same interval in 2008.7. However, while the flow of Western and Asian tourists remained below normal, Arab tourist arrivals increased during the summer. This was also owing to the global economic crisis, as many Arab families who usually vacationed in Europe or North America were forced to choose less expensive destinations, within the region. This increase in intraregional tourism has partially offset the decline in international tourism for many Middle Eastern destinations; but at the aggregate level, all Middle East countries have experienced a decline in tourist arrivals and tourism revenue in the first half of 2009 (Habibi, 2009:4).

Higher levels of gainful employment in the region will necessitate more private sector jobs, and enhancing various aspects of competiveness will likely support this process by boosting private sector growth in the region. Improving competitiveness and raising employment levels will clearly be a complex process necessitating simultaneous progress across a number of the interrelated challenges identified in this chapter. Yet, given the present reform momentum and policy reform coordination at the national level, much can be achieved to help Arab economies can meet these employment challenges going into the future. (World Economic Forum and the OECD, 2011:11).

High unemployment has been a problem in MENA for years, and prospects for improvement has been darken by the crisis in the near term. While the impact of the crisis on official unemployment rates has been negligible in most MENA countries, participation rates, which were already low compared to other countries prior to the crisis, have declined as discouraged workers dropped out of the labor force and decided not to seek work in the official labor market. Aggregate labor statistics also hide the negative impact on some sectors. Workers in the manufacturing sectors have been especially vulnerable during this crisis, although job losses in these sectors were offset to some extent by the job creation in the nontradable goods and services industries (Reinikka, 2010:379).

Remittances are an important source of income for several Arab countries. Worker remittances in Jordan, Morocco, Egypt, and Tunisia accounted in 2007 for 22.7%, 9%, 6%, and 5%, respectively, of their GDP. Arab countries enjoyed positive growth in 2008 by their remittance incomes before being adversely impacted by the global crisis in 2009. Job opportunities for North African workers has been reduced by the economic downturn in Europe and as a result, the volume of remittances has diminished. Morocco, for example, reported a 12.5% decline in its remittances between June 2008 and June 2009.9 Though the experience of most MENA countries is similar to Morocco's, Tunisia reported an 8% increase in its remittance revenue over the same period10—owing mainly to the higher skill level of Tunisian migrant workers as compared with workers from other Arab countries (Habibi, 2009:4).

Although FDI significantly increased and economic grew robustly MENA countries continue to suffer from long-term structural unemployment between 2001 and 2008. The high unemployment rate, in particular among youth, women, and the educated, has been exacerbated by the financial crisis and the economic slowdown which followed the Arab Spring. While FDI can have a positive impact on employment, the link between FDI and employment creation is not automatic. It depends on a number of factors, including the type of investment, the objectives of foreign investors, and the sectors that are the investment target. Limited employment creation in the MENA region can be explained in large part by an underdeveloped private sector, which was not able to absorb a rapidly expanding labour force, a workforce which lacks the necessary skills to respond to business needs, and FDI that was focused on capital-intensive sectors such as hydrocarbons. Governments can help increase the impact of FDI on jobs (in terms of volume and quality) by designing and implementing better policies in the areas of skills development, labour policy, further economic integration of women, expansion of linkage programs, and development of sectors with high employment potential (World Economic Forum and the OECD, 2011:11).

The relatively closed financial systems of most MENA countries shielded them from the financial crisis—the first wave of the global crisis. However, these countries were unable to escape the adverse impact of the severe worldwide economic recession that followed—the second wave. The impact of the global slowdown on tourism, oil revenues, and remittances has already been noted. For the North African countries, which have strong economic links with Europe, the economic recession in that region led to a noticeable decline in their merchandise exports. Thus Egypt, Morocco, and Tunisia have reported sharp declines in their exports of agricultural and manufactured products in 2009. (More than 70% of Morocco's total exports go to Europe; the comparable figure for Tunisia is 80%.) As shown in Chart 5, merchandise exports for five Arab oil-importing countries during the first half of 2009 as compared with the first half of 2008. Chart 5 also demonstrates that the exports of Jordan and Lebanon have been more resilient than those of other Arab oil-importers (Habibi, 2009:5).

The Middle East and North Africa region is recovering from the financial crisis along with the global economy. The recovery from the crisis differs by country depending on initial conditions and the intensity of the impact via the three principal channels through which the global financial crisis affected MENA economies—the financial sector, the price of oil, and the balance of payments, reflecting the impact on trade, remittances and FDI flows (World Bank, 2010:v)

The Middle East and North Africa (MENA) countries had largely recovered from the global financial crisis by the end of 2010 and growth rates were expected to reach pre-crisis levels in 2011. In early 2011, a series of prodemocracy movements began that resulted in swift regime change in Tunisia and Egypt, and spread to Bahrain, Libya, Syria and Yemen. The short-term macroeconomic outlook and the status and speed of economic reforms have been affected by the unrest and uncertainty associated with these movements in the region. The medium-run growth prospects are likely to improve, especially if the political changes are associated with more open and accountable governance and more rapid reforms. While short-run challenges will be brought by political change; the transition has the potential to significantly boost economic growth and raise living standards in the medium run. If the political changes lead to greater accountability and transparency in governance, countries could relax a key constraint to growth and steer resources more effectively to productive uses while reducing unproductive rent-seeking behavior. Better rule of law will promote competition and political stability will attract investment, facilitating more rapid growth in a sustainable way. More voice for civil society will prevent the unequal application of regulations, and can lead to more inclusive growth. It will also bring dignity and raise wellbeing. While the challenges are many, the opportunities are more (World Bank, 2011:4).

The Middle East and North Africa region have a mixed economic outlook. Most of the oil exporting countries of the region is growing at healthy rates while the oil importers face subdued economic expectancy. The region's oil exporters are expected to post solid growth in 2012, largely on account of Libya's better than-expected post-war recovery. In the countries of the Gulf Cooperation Council (GCC), growth remains robust, supported by expansionary fiscal policies and accommodative monetary conditions. For these countries, as for the region more broadly, the medium-term challenge is to generate enough jobs for a young and rapidly growing population. The slowdown witnessed in 2011 in the region's oil importers persists. A moderate economic recovery is expected in 2013, but is subject to heightened downside risks. For the Arab countries in transition (ACTs), ongoing political transitions also weigh on growth. With policy buffers largely eroded, the need for action on both macroeconomic stabilization and growth-oriented reforms is becoming increasingly urgent. Countries will need to put in place safety nets to protect the poor and build consensus for some difficult and urgent fiscal choices, while people will need to feel that the burdens of economic reform are being borne equitably (IMF, 2012:5)

Table-2 shows the MENAP Region's selected economic indicators, the global economic crisis affects importantly the main macroeconomic indicators especially for the year 2009.

Figure-1 shows the GDP per capita and population for Middle East, North Africa, Afghanistan, and Pakistan economies. The GDP per capita is higher Qatar, United Arab Emirates, Kuwait, Oman, Saudi Arabia than other countries.

Table-3 shows the selected economic indicators for the MENAP Oil Exporter economies, the global economic crisis affects negatively the real GDP growth except Iran and Algeria especially for the year 2009. Consumer price inflation was affected positively by the global economic crisis. Current account balance and fiscal balance were also affected by the global economic crisis.

Table-4 shows the selected economic indicators for the MENAP Oil Importer economies, the global economic crisis affects negatively the real GDP growth except Afghanistan, Sudan and Syrian especially for the year 2009. Consumer price inflation was affected positively by the global economic crisis except Pakistan. Current account balance and fiscal balance were also affected by the global economic crisis.

Trade channel is the major pass through of the global financial crisis onto the non-oil producing MENA countries of Egypt, Morocco and Tunisia. Another important transmission channel of the global financial crisis on the economies of the MENA region. have also been constituted by the still weak regional trade and financial integration linkages and the heavy dependence on external resources to finance development. As the relatively limited global financial integration of some MENA markets has prevented a complete fallout of those markets as a result of the recent financial crisis, greater MENA trade/financial integration could have helped the region avert the negative effects of the crisis on its economies, and could have dampened the effects of the trade channel pass through (Neaime, 2012).

While the economies of Arab countries were impacted by the global crisis, Arab governments resorted to a variety of measures, similar to those adopted by other governments worldwide, to mitigate the negative consequences. This involved a mix of monetary and fiscal stimulation along with stricter financial regulations in most countries. However the unique circumstances of its economy was reflected by the relative weight of these measures in each country. A recent IMF study offers a detailed breakdown of the financial and monetary policy responses of each MENA country.12 Since

Table 2. MENAP Region: Selected Economic Indicators, 2000–13 (Percent of GDP, unless otherwise indicated, p:projection)

MENAP1								
	2000–06	**2007**	**2008**	**2009**	**2010**	**2011**	**2012p**	**2013p**
Real GDP (annual growth)	5.4	5.8	4.4	2.6	4.8	3.3	5.1	3.6
Current Account Balance	9.2	13.1	13.7	2.0	7.0	13.2	11.2	9.7
Overall Fiscal Balance	3.1	6.2	6.6	–3.0	–0.4	1.5	1.5	0.4
Inflation, p.a. (annual growth)	5.9	9.9	14.3	7.3	7.3	10.3	10.9	9.5
MENAP oil exporters								
	2000–06	**2007**	**2008**	**2009**	**2010**	**2011**	**2012p**	**2013p**
Real GDP (annual growth)	5.8	5.3	4.0	1.7	5.3	3.9	6.6	3.8
Current Account Balance	13.4	18.6	19.7	4.8	11.0	18.7	16.4	14.2
Overall Fiscal Balance	7.4	12.4	13.3	–1.8	2.5	5.9	6.1	4.4
Inflation, p.a. (annual growth)	6.7	11.5	15.0	5.7	6.6	10.4	11.5	9.7
Of which: Gulf Cooperation Council								
	2000–06	**2007**	**2008**	**2009**	**2010**	**2011**	**2012p**	**2013p**
Real GDP (annual growth)	5.7	5.3	6.3	–0.2	5.5	7.5	5.5	3.7

Table 2. (Continued)

Current Account Balance	15.4	19.9	22.7	7.5	14.4	24.1	23.6	21.1
Overall Fiscal Balance	11.5	17.9	24.8	–0.7	4.5	12.7	14.6	11.2
Inflation, p.a. (annual growth)	1.6	6.6	11.0	3.0	3.2	3.6	3.5	3.6
MENAP oil importers								
	2000–06	**2007**	**2008**	**2009**	**2010**	**2011**	**2012p**	**2013p**
Real GDP (annual growth)	4.9	6.8	5.3	4.2	4.0	2.0	2.1	3.3
Current Account Balance	–0.8	–2.5	–4.1	–4.8	–3.1	–3.5	–5.2	–4.4
Overall Fiscal Balance	–4.5	–5.2	–5.6	–5.0	–5.6	–7.0	–7.8	–7.4
Inflation, p.a. (annual growth)	4.5	7.1	13.0	10.2	8.5	9.9	9.7	9.2
MENA1								
	2000–06	**2007**	**2008**	**2009**	**2010**	**2011**	**2012p**	**2013p**
Real GDP (annual growth)	5.5	5.7	4.5	2.6	5.0	3.3	5.3	3.6
Current Account Balance	10.0	14.5	15.3	2.6	7.7	14.2	12.2	10.6
Overall Fiscal Balance	3.9	7.7	8.4	–2.8	0.2	2.5	2.5	1.4
Inflation, p.a. (annual growth)	5.9	10.2	14.6	6.2	7.0	9.8	10.9	9.5

MENA oil importers								
	2000–06	**2007**	**2008**	**2009**	**2010**	**2011**	**2012p**	**2013p**
Real GDP (annual growth)	4.7	6.7	6.1	4.9	4.3	1.4	1.2	3.3
Current Account Balance	–1.3	–1.8	–2.8	–4.6	–3.6	–5.2	–6.9	–5.8
Overall Fiscal Balance	–5.3	–5.1	–4.8	–5.2	–5.6	–7.5	–8.7	–7.7
Inflation, p.a. (annual growth)	4.2	6.7	13.6	7.3	8.0	7.9	9.0	8.8
Memorandum								
Arab countries in transition (excl. Libya)								
	2000–06	**2007**	**2008**	**2009**	**2010**	**2011**	**2012p**	**2013p**
Real GDP (annual growth)	4.6	6.0	6.3	4.5	4.7	1.2	2.0	3.6
Current Account Balance	1.1	–1.1	–2.5	–3.9	–3.3	–4.9	–5.4	–4.6
Overall Fiscal Balance	–5.2	–5.5	–5.2	–5.7	–6.0	–8.0	–9.1	–8.0
Inflation, p.a. (percent)	4.7	7.1	14.0	7.7	8.4	7.9	7.8	8.6

Source: International Monetary Fund, "Regional economic outlook. Middle East and Central Asia", Washington, D.C., November 2012, p.7 [1]2011–13 data exclude Syrian Arab Republic. MENAP: (1) Oil exporters: Algeria, Bahrain, Iran, Iraq, Kuwait, Libya, Oman, Qatar, Saudi Arabia, the United Arab Emirates, and Yemen; (2) Oil importers: Afghanistan, Djibouti,Egypt, Jordan, Lebanon, Mauritania, Morocco, Pakistan, Sudan, Syria, and Tunisia; (3) Arab countries in transition: Egypt, Jordan, Libya, Morocco, Tunisia, and Yemen. MENA: MENAP excluding Afghanistan and Pakistan. Note: Data refer to the fiscal year for the following countries: Afghanistan and Iran (March 21/March 20), Qatar (April/March), and Egypt and Pakistan (July/June).

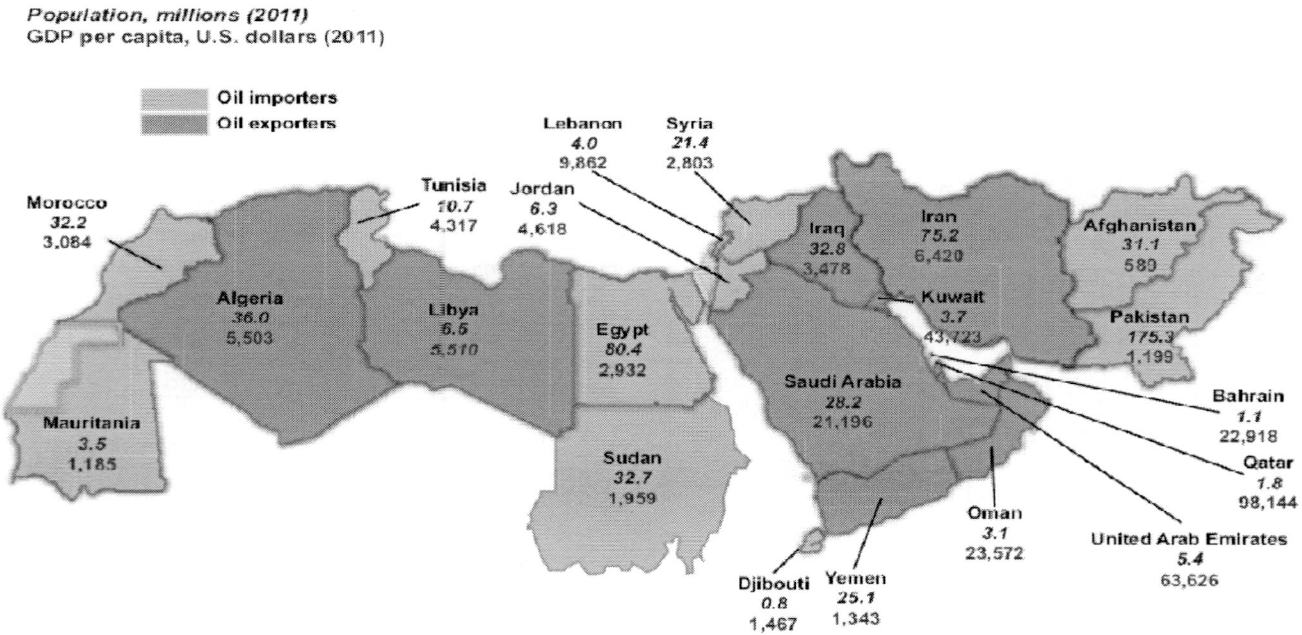

Source: International Monetary Fund, "Regional economic outlook. Middle East and Central Asia", Washington, D.C., November 2012, p.3.

Figure 1. GDP per capita and Population for Middle East, North Africa, Afghanistan, and Pakistan.

Table 3. MENAP Oil Exporters: Selected Economic Indicators

p:projection	Real GDP Growth *(Annual change; percent)*							
	2000–06	**2007**	**2008**	**2009**	**2010**	**2011**	**2012p**	**2013p**
MENAP	5.8	5.3	4.0	1.7	5.3	3.9	6.6	3.8
Algeria	4.1	3.0	2.4	2.4	3.3	2.4	2.6	3.4
Bahrain	6.1	8.4	6.3	3.2	4.7	2.1	2.0	2.8
Iran, I.R. of	6.0	6.4	0.6	3.9	5.9	2.0	–0.9	0.8
Iraq	…	1.5	9.5	2.9	3.0	8.9	10.2	14.7
Kuwait	7.7	6.5	4.2	–7.8	2.5	8.2	6.3	1.9
Libya	5.3	6.4	2.4	–1.4	3.7	–59.7	121.9	16.7
Oman	3.7	6.7	13.1	3.9	5.0	5.4	5.0	3.9
Qatar	11.2	18.0	17.7	12.0	16.7	14.1	6.3	4.9
Saudi Arabia	3.9	2.0	4.2	0.1	5.1	7.1	6.0	4.2
UAE	8.2	6.5	5.3	–4.8	1.3	5.2	4.0	2.6
Yemen	4.3	3.3	3.6	3.9	7.7	–10.5	–1.9	4.1
	Consumer Price Inflation *(Year average; percent)*							
	2000–06	**2007**	**2008**	**2009**	**2010**	**2011**	**2012p**	**2013p**
MENAP	6.7	11.5	15.0	5.7	6.6	10.4	11.5	9.7
Algeria	2.3	3.6	4.9	5.7	3.9	4.5	8.4	5.0
Bahrain	0.9	3.3	3.5	2.8	2.0	–0.4	0.6	2.0
Iran, I.R. of	13.3	18.4	25.4	10.8	12.4	21.5	25.2	21.8
Iraq	…	30.8	2.7	–2.2	2.4	5.6	6.0	5.5
Kuwait	1.9	5.5	10.6	4.0	4.0	4.7	4.3	4.1

Table 3. (Continued)

Libya	…	6.2	10.4	2.4	2.5	15.9	10.0	0.9
Oman	0.5	5.9	12.6	3.5	3.3	4.0	3.2	3.0
Qatar	4.7	13.8	15.0	–4.9	–2.4	1.9	2.0	3.0
Saudi Arabia	0.3	4.1	9.9	5.1	5.4	5.0	4.9	4.6
UAE	4.4	11.1	12.3	1.6	0.9	0.9	0.7	1.6
Yemen	11.5	7.9	19.0	3.7	11.2	19.5	15.0	12.7
	General Gov. Overall Fiscal Balance ***(Percent of GDP)***							
	2000–06	**2007**	**2008**	**2009**	**2010**	**2011**	**2012p**	**2013p**
MENAP	7.4	12.4	13.3	–1.8	2.5	5.9	6.1	4.4
Algeria	7.6	4.4	7.6	–6.4	–2.3	–0.2	–3.9	–1.3
Bahrain1	1.6	1.9	4.9	–6.6	–7.0	–2.4	–3.9	–3.6
Iran, I.R. of1	2.7	7.4	0.7	1.0	1.6	–0.2	–2.9	–3.9
Iraq	…	11.9	–1.3	–20.5	–8.8	7.6	–1.9	3.1
Kuwait1	28.2	39.0	19.8	26.8	25.2	29.1	30.2	26.4
Libya	13.2	24.0	25.1	–3.0	16.7	–27.7	19.4	7.7
Oman1	9.1	11.1	13.7	–2.1	4.0	8.1	7.1	5.8
Qatar	8.7	10.9	9.8	13.4	2.6	12.3	9.6	8.5
Saudi Arabia	10.5	16.3	34.4	–4.7	3.4	14.0	16.6	11.2
UAE	7.3	16.0	16.8	–12.8	–2.2	3.1	7.5	7.5
Yemen	0.2	–7.2	–4.5	–10.2	–4.0	–4.3	–5.7	–6.0

	Current Account Balance ***(Percent of GDP)***							
	2000–06	**2007**	**2008**	**2009**	**2010**	**2011**	**2012p**	**2013p**
MENAP	13.4	18.6	19.7	4.8	11.0	18.7	16.4	14.2
Algeria	15.5	22.8	20.1	0.3	7.5	10.0	6.2	6.1
Bahrain	6.3	15.7	10.2	2.9	3.6	12.6	9.9	10.5
Iran, I.R. of	5.5	10.6	6.5	2.6	6.0	12.5	3.4	1.3
Iraq	…	11.5	18.8	–13.4	–3.0	8.3	0.3	6.1
Kuwait	28.8	36.8	40.9	26.7	31.9	44.0	44.1	39.2
Libya	23.8	43.8	42.3	14.7	19.8	1.3	21.8	10.3
Oman	10.3	5.9	8.3	–1.2	8.6	16.7	14.0	10.0
Qatar	25.0	25.4	28.7	10.2	26.7	30.2	29.6	26.8
Saudi Arabia	15.6	24.3	27.8	5.6	14.6	26.5	26.1	22.7
UAE	9.8	6.9	7.9	3.5	3.2	9.7	9.3	10.1
Yemen	4.7	–7.0	–4.6	–10.2	–4.4	–3.0	–2.7	–4.0

Source: International Monetary Fund, "Regional economic outlook. Middle East and Central Asia", Washington, D.C., November 2012p, p.34, UAE :United Arab Emirates.

Table 4. MENAP Oil Importers: Selected Economic Indicators

p:projection	Real GDP Growth *(Annual change; percent)*							
	2000–06	**2007**	**2008**	**2009**	**2010**	**2011**	**2012p**	**2013p**
MENAP	4.9	6.8	5.3	4.2	4.0	2.0	2.1	3.3
Afghanistan, Rep. of	…	13.7	3.6	21.0	8.4	5.8	5.2	6.5
Djibouti	2.8	5.1	5.8	5.0	3.5	4.5	4.8	5.0
Egypt	4.4	7.1	7.2	4.7	5.1	1.8	2.0	3.0
Jordan	6.3	8.2	7.2	5.5	2.3	2.6	3.0	3.5
Lebanon	3.0	7.5	9.3	8.5	7.0	1.5	2.0	2.5
Mauritania	4.8	1.0	3.5	–1.2	5.1	4.0	5.3	6.9
Morocco	4.9	2.7	5.6	4.9	3.7	4.9	2.9	5.5
Pakistan	5.1	6.8	3.7	1.7	3.1	3.0	3.7	3.3
Sudan	8.2	12.2	2.3	4.6	2.2	–4.5	–11.2	0.0
Syrian Arab Republic1	4.0	5.7	4.5	5.9	3.4	…	…	…
Tunisia	4.6	6.3	4.5	3.1	3.1	–1.8	2.7	3.3
	Consumer Price Inflation *(Year average; percent)*							
	2000–06	**2007**	**2008**	**2009**	**2010**	**2011**	**2012p**	**2013p**
MENAP	4.5	7.1	13.0	10.2	8.5	9.9	9.7	9.2
Afghanistan, Rep. of	…	8.6	30.5	–8.3	0.9	13.8	9.1	5.0
Djibouti	2.3	5.0	12.0	1.7	4.0	5.1	4.7	2.4
Egypt	5.1	9.5	18.3	11.7	11.4	9.9	9.7	11.4

Jordan	2.7	4.7	13.9	–0.7	5.0	4.4	4.5	3.9
Lebanon	1.3	4.1	10.8	1.2	4.5	5.0	6.5	5.7
Mauritania	6.5	7.3	7.5	2.1	6.3	5.7	5.9	6.1
Morocco	1.7	2.0	3.9	1.0	1.0	0.9	2.2	2.5
Pakistan	5.0	7.8	10.8	17.6	10.1	13.7	11.0	10.4
Sudan	7.6	8.0	14.3	11.3	13.0	18.3	28.6	17.0
Syrian Arab Republic1	3.8	4.7	15.2	2.8	4.4	…	…	…
Tunisia	2.9	3.4	4.9	3.5	4.4	3.5	5.0	4.0
	General Gov. Overall Fiscal Balance ***(Percent of GDP)***							
	2000–06	**2007**	**2008**	**2009**	**2010**	**2011**	**2012p**	**2013p**
MENAP	–4.5	–5.2	–5.6	–5.0	–5.6	–7.0	–7.8	–7.4
Afghanistan, Rep. of	…	–2.0	–4.0	–1.3	0.9	–0.9	–0.8	–0.6
Djibouti	–1.9	–2.6	1.3	–4.6	–0.5	–0.7	0.4	0.8
Egypt	–6.8	–7.5	–8.0	–6.8	–7.8	–9.9	–11.1	–9.8
Jordan2	–3.0	–5.7	–5.5	–8.9	–5.6	–5.7	–6.5	–5.5
Lebanon2	–14.6	–10.8	–9.5	–8.3	–7.7	–6.1	–7.9	–8.3
Mauritania2,3	…	–1.6	–6.5	–5.1	–1.5	–1.5	–2.4	–2.3
Morocco2	–5.0	–0.1	0.7	–1.8	–4.4	–6.9	–6.1	–5.3
Pakistan	–2.8	–5.5	–7.3	–5.0	–5.9	–6.4	–6.4	–7.2
Sudan	–0.9	–2.5	–0.1	–4.2	–0.4	–1.3	–4.0	–3.9

Table 4. (Continued)

Syrian Arab Republic1	–1.9	–3.0	–2.9	–2.9	–4.8	…	…	…
Tunisia	–2.7	–2.8	–0.7	–2.6	–0.9	–3.1	–6.4	–5.3
	Current Account Balance *(Percent of GDP)*							
	2000–06	**2007**	**2008**	**2009**	**2010**	**2011**	**2012p**	**2013p**
MENAP	–0.8	–2.5	–4.1	–4.8	–3.1	–3.5	–5.2	–4.4
Afghanistan, Rep. of	…	5.8	5.1	1.6	3.9	3.3	2.1	0.5
Djibouti	–2.0	–21.4	–24.3	–9.1	–5.8	–12.6	–12.2	–12.5
Egypt	1.6	1.7	0.5	–2.3	–2.0	–2.6	–3.4	–3.3
Jordan	0.2	–17.2	–9.3	–4.9	–7.1	–12.0	–14.1	–9.9
Lebanon	–13.8	–6.8	–9.2	–9.8	–9.6	–14.0	–16.2	–15.6
Mauritania	–16.3	–17.2	–14.8	–10.7	–8.7	–7.5	–23.6	–13.9
Morocco	2.2	–0.1	–5.2	–5.4	–4.3	–8.0	–7.9	–5.4
Pakistan	0.8	–4.8	–8.5	–5.7	–2.2	0.1	–2.0	–1.7
Sudan	–5.7	–5.9	–2.0	–10.0	–2.1	–0.5	–7.8	–6.6
Syrian Arab Republic1	–1.8	–0.2	–1.3	–3.6	–3.3	…	…	…
Tunisia	–2.8	–2.4	–3.8	–2.8	–4.8	–7.3	–7.9	–7.7

Source: International Monetary Fund, "Regional economic outlook. Middle East and Central Asia", Washington, D.C., November 2012p, p.34.

financial institutions and stock markets were among the first institutions to show weakness, the first policy response in many countries was to support their commercial banks by providing credit support and liquidity. Among oil-exporting countries, Kuwait, Saudi Arabia, the UAE, and Libya strengthened their banking systems by offering their commercial banks deposit guarantees. The only oil-importing Arab country to adopt this policy, however, was Jordan. Egypt enhanced its already existing deposit guarantee, and such a policy was also already in place in Morocco (Habibi, 2009:5).

On the demand side, government spending is expected to rise in 2011 as MENA governments have moved quickly towards expanding supportive policy measures and social transfers to help the unemployed and ease the burden of high commodity prices. Partly because of these actions, but also because of rising fuel and food prices, inflation rates are expected to increase in many MENA countries in 2011.The fiscal stance of oil importers in North Africa is expected to worsen in 2011, as revenues decline in response to reduced business activity and expenditures increase reflecting the supportive social policy measures provided by governments. Oil exporters will also see increased expenditures, but these will be offset by higher oil revenues, leading to improvements in their fiscal balances relative to those reached in 2010 and the pre-unrest forecasts. Yemen and Syria however are exceptions (World Bank, 2011:5).

The employment's being high has been a problem in MENA for years, and the prospects for improvements in the near term has been dimmed by the crisis. The impact of the crisis on official unemployment rates has been negligible in most MENA countries however participation rates which were already low compared to other countries prior to the crisis, have declined as discouraged workers dropped out of the labor force and decided not to seek work in the official labor market. Workers in the manufacturing sectors have been especially vulnerable during this crisis. Firms in these sectors scaled down their activities, reduced working hours, and even shed jobs in order to adjust to the drop in external demand. The good news is that the job losses in these sectors were offset in most cases by the job creation in the non-tradable goods and services industries. (World Bank, 2010:5).

Specific policy recommendations to support governments in implementing better policies for job creation are as follows. First, proactive investment policy measures are essential, in particular the harmonization of national investment laws and progress towards a regional investment framework, which would facilitate cross-border investment, namely in services. Second, education and labour policies should address the skills mismatch between market supply and demand and introduce less rigid labour market policies. Third, proactive and innovative policies are required to unleash the female labour force potential. These include enhanced contract flexibility, equal access to social benefits, leveraging new technologies, and the promotion of international business women's networks. Additionally, fostering and strengthening business linkages between local SMEs and MNEs can help small businesses expand and generate more jobs. Finally, targeted policies to encourage investment in high growth and labour intensive sectors such as renewable energies and services can have a direct impact on employment. In conclusion, it should also be noted that the quality of data on FDI flows and employment should be improved to develop more targeted policy recommendations maximising the impact of FDI on employment in the MENA region. (World Economic Forum and the OECD, 2011:11).

Prolonged instability and lack of clarity about the future political transition in the affected countries in the region is the main risk for the forecast. Basicly, up to a reasonable level of political stability returns, investment will be compromised. Sustained tensions would also amplify the negative impact on tourism receipts, which have been a large share of GDP in a number of countries, and could translate into increased cost of capital, further dampening growth prospects (World Bank, 2011:5).

The impacts of higher food prices in the MENA region are also critical. The country's dependence on food and oil imports, and the extent of the passthrough from international to domestic prices dtermine the effects. While the region includes some major oil exporters that are benefiting from the oil price increases, it is also home of a number of countries that rely on imported oil. MENA countries are highly dependent on imported food, particularly cereals, oils, and sugar. In the event of further food price increases, they face the risk of increased import bills, higher domestic inflation, and worsened fiscal balances in cases when governments subsidize food. New estimates of pass-through coefficients for the MENA countries, calculated for this report, indicate that a rise of global food prices has been transmitted to domestic food prices to a significant degree. Transmission from international to domestic food price levels has been notably high for Egypt, Iraq, Djibouti, United Arab Emirates and West Bank and Gaza, while being particularly low in Tunisia and Algeria. Where international food price increases filter into domestic prices, overall inflation tends to be higher(World Bank, 2011:5).

The boost in expected growth in developing MENA in 2012 assumes a move to enhanced political stability. If governments in the countries experiencing unrest are able to gain a reasonable level of legitimacy and begin a credible reform program, growth is likely to quickly return to or surpass pre-revolution levels. Of utmost importance is citizen security and political stability. With security and stability, a few steps toward government reform will reassure investors and the growth rate will improve. There is, of course, a good deal of uncertainty, but the opportunity to move to a path of stronger and more inclusive growth is present. If the MENA countries take the demands of the population for more accountable and transparent governance seriously, and move to a structure that promotes competition and inclusiveness, this will promote robust growth in the region and many more opportunities for the young population (World Bank, 2011:5).

Assuring access to finance without compromising financial stability will be a major challenge in MENA, although issues related to weak regulatory systems, corporate governance and overdependence on the banking system also loom large. The slowdown of credit growth as a result of the crisis has added urgency to the access agenda because the credit tightening expected in the post-crisis period affects disproportionately the underserved segments, typically high risk households and firms. Addressing the stability agenda will be equally challenging. The pre-conditions for effective market discipline are weaker in MENA than in developed countries due to weaker institutions and less sophisticated market players. In addition, the generous support programs in response to the crisis may have further weakened financial institutions. The severity of the financial crisis and the uncertainty about how the financial system will evolve has sparked interest in regional and domestic financial markets. Pursuing financial integration in MENA might be a good strategy given the mix of countries, which include both capital exporters (the GCC countries) and capital importers (oil importing countries), as this would facilitate trade integration (World Bank, 2010:vi)

Enhancing overall competitiveness should be part of the reform agenda to address the challenges and exploit the opportunities present in the Middle East and North Africa (MENA) region. Particularly needed are measures to support a vibrant, competitive, and entrepreneurial private sector. The private sector currently remains stifled by a business environment that is not conducive to the development of enterprises. Corruption, lack of transparency in government decision making, market distortion, and weak global and regional integration hinder competition and reduce efficiency. The development of a dynamic private sector would not only involve the promotion of domestic enterprise but also the opening up of the economy to trade and investment. Although the region has made progress in these areas, the significant increase of foreign direct investment (FDI) registered during the last decade has not been sufficient to reduce the high levels of unemployment. The recent decrease in FDI flows due to the global economic crisis and the impact of the Arab Spring on investors' confidence brings additional challenges (World Economic Forum and the OECD, 2011:6).

In the aftermath of the global financial crisis, several MENA countries experienced significant financial/economic slowdowns. MENA stock markets tumbled, real estate asset prices crashed, loans to the private sector and private capital flows dried up, GDP growth rates turned negative, spreads on sovereign bonds soared, and risk aversion increased dramatically (Neaime, 2012).

CONCLUSION

The MENA countries has faced important changes because of the global economic crisis and the Arab Spring. Economic growth slowed significantly with the global economic and financial crisis of 2008-2009. More recently, a wave of protests driven by longstanding socio-political and economic issues spread across several countries. The global financial crisis of 2008 had important negative impact in MENA through the decline in oil prices and turmoil in international financial markets. MENA was also hit by the secondary effects of the crisis on trade, remittances, and FDI. Countercyclical policies and financial sector support measures are expected to have limited the decline in output in 2009 by encouraging consumption and investment activity.

The impact of the 2008–09 global financial and economic crisis varied substantially among three country groupings in the Middle East and North Africa (MENA): the Gulf Cooperation Council (GCC), developing oil exporters, and oil importers. Among these three groups, the GCC oil exporters were hardest hit because the crisis affected them directly through two different channels: (a) a negative terms-of-trade shock associated with the drop in oil prices; and (b) a financial shock, which destabilized overextended domestic banks and led to the bursting of a real estate bubble. As a result, MENA countries were affected importantly by the global economic crisis by the channels of declining international prices of the oil, decreasing export, deteriorating expectations and financial markets.

REFERENCES

Doaa, S.A., Doaa A. (2010). "The Effect Of The Global Financial Crisis On Migrant Workers Among Mena Countries *International Conference on Economic Modeling* , pp.1-20.

Habibi Nader., (2009). "The Impact of the Global Economic Crisis on Arab Countries: A Year-End Assessment" Middle East Brief, December 2009, No. 40.

International Monetary Fund (2012). "Regional economic outlook. Middle East and Central Asia", Washington, D.C., November.

International Monetary Fund (2012). Coping with High Debt and Sluggish Growth, World Economic And Financial Surveys, World Economic Outlook (WEO), October.

Neaime Simon (2012). "The global financial crisis, financial linkages and correlations in returns and volatilities in emerging MENA stock markets" *Emerging Markets Review* 13, pp. 268–282.

Ritva Reinikka (2010). "The Financial Crisis, Recovery, and ong-Term Growth in the Middle East and North Africa" in "The Day After Tomorrow", Otaviano. Canuto, Marcelo M. Giugale (Edt). World Bank Publications, pp.377-386.

World Bank (2010). "Recovering from the Crisis" Middle East And North Africa Region – A Regional Economic Update, April 2010.

World Bank (2011)."Middle East and North Africa Region Regional Economic Update: MENA Facing Challenges and Opportunities" World Bank May.

World Economic Forum and the OECD (2011). "Arab World Competitiveness Report 2011-2012" World Economic Forum and the OECD pub.

In: Economic and Social Issues …
Editor: Nilgün Çil Yavuz
ISBN: 978-1-62948-152-4

Chapter 6

THE DETERMINANTS OF ECONOMIC FREEDOM IN THE MIDDLE EAST AND NORTH AFRICA

Nurcan Metın[*]
Trakya Universitym, Turkey

ABSTRACT

This paper investigates whether the economic freedom depends on the property rights, the freedom from corruption, the political rights and the civil liberties with the linear balanced pooled least squares models, the country specific fixed and random effects models and the country and period specific fixed and random effects models in the Middle East and North Africa from 1999 to 2012. Furthermore, this paper researches whether the least squares standard errors, the white cross-section standard errors, the white period standard errors, the white diagonal standard errors, the cross-section SUR (panel corrected standard error) standard errors, the cross-section weights (panel corrected standard error) standard errors, the period SUR (panel corrected standard error) and the period weights (panel corrected standard error) standard errors give the similar results for these models. The country and period specific fixed and random effects model results show that the property rights, the freedom from corruption and the political rights from the significant variables have positive effects on the economic freedom, while the civil liberties

[*] nurcanmetin@trakya.edu.tr.

has negative effect on the economic freedom. Also, the model results indicate that the various standard errors give about results for these models. As a result, this empirical research supports the idea that the property rights, the freedom from corruption, the political rights and the civil liberties are the important determinants of economic freedom. In the Middle East and North Africa, we suggest that various government policies should be regulated according to these factors again.

Keywords: Economic freedom; Property rights; Freedom from corruption; Political rights, Civil liberties; MENA

1. Introduction

The economic freedom can be defined as a better quality of life for people. Many authors explore factors affecting economic freedom. From these authors, Burkhart (2000) presents a political economy model of democracy. The main finding is that unbridled capitalism is unnecessary for a democratic polity. Goel and Nelson (2005) examine whether economic freedom or political freedom serves as a deterrent to corrupt activity. Examining different components of economic freedom, they find that not all these components are equally effective in reducing corruption. Doucouliagos (2005) explores the differences between aggregate and disaggregate measures of economic freedom and shows that selection effects are stronger when aggregate measures are used. Gohmann, Hobbs and McCrickard (2008) examine how the entrepreneurial activity and level of employment in U.S. service industries respond to changes in the degree of economic freedom among states. Findings suggest that the relationship between entrepreneurial outcomes and economic freedom varies significantly by industry. Peev and Mueller (2012) examine the interrelationships between democracy, economic freedoms, and economic growth. They find that strong democratic institutions are associated with greater economic freedoms and larger public sectors and public deficits, and that stronger economic freedoms lead to more rapid growth, but large public sectors and public deficits have adverse effects on growth. Apergis, Dincer and Payne (2013) *investigate the causal relationship between income inequality and economic freedom. The results indicate bidirectional causality between income inequality and economic freedom in both the short and the long run.* Alexandrakis and Livanis (2013) perform panel regressions of output per worker, capital intensity, human capital, and total factor productivity in Latin America on measures of economic freedom in five policy areas. Results show that a smaller government raises output per worker in Latin America but not in the OECD.

This paper explores whether the political rights, the civil liberties, the property rights and the freedom from corruption are important determinants of the economic freedom with the linear balanced pooled least squares models, the country specific fixed and random effects models and the country and period specific fixed and random effects models in the Middle East and North Africa from 1999 to 2012. Furthermore, this paper researches whether the various standard errors give the similar results for these models.

2. Data and Description of Variables

In this paper, the data are taken from the http://www.heritage.org and http://www.freedomhouse.org. The economic freedom is taken as the dependent variable. The property rights, the freedom from corruption, the political rights and the civil liberties are taken as the independent variables. While the economic freedom, the property rights, the freedom from corruption are measured on a 0-to-100 scale, with 100 representing the maximum freedom, the political rights and the civil liberties are measured on a 1-to-7 scale, with 1 representing the highest degree of freedom and 7 the lowest (see for more information about description of variables http://www.heritage. org and http://www.freedomhouse.org.The countries, the variables and the descriptive statistics is given in Table 1, 2 and 3. Figure 1 and 2 show the individual cross sections of the variables.

Table 1. MENA Countries

Countries	Year
Algeria	1999-2012
Bahrain	1999-2012
Egypt	1999-2012
Iran	1999-2012
Israel	1999-2012
Jordan	1999-2012
Kuwait	1999-2012
Lebanon	1999-2012
Libya	1999-2012
Morocco	1999-2012

Table 1. (Continued)

Countries	Year
Oman	1999-2012
Qatar	1999-2012
Saudi Arabia	1999-2012
Syria	1999-2012
Tunisia	1999-2012
United Arab Emirates	1999-2012
Yemen	1999-2012

Table 2. Variables

Dependent Variable		Economic Freedom (EF)*
Independent Variables	Rule of Law	Property Rights (PR)*
		Freedom from Corruption (FC)*
	Political Freedom	Political Rights (POR)**
		Civil Liberties (CL)**

*Variables are measured on a 0-to-100 scale, with 100 representing the maximum freedom.

**Variables are measured on a 1-to-7 scale, with one representing the highest degree of freedom and seven the lowest.

Table 3. Descriptive Statistics

	Economic Freedom	*Property Rights*	*Freedom from Corruption*	*Political Rights*	*Civil Liberties*
Mean	58.70000	43.71849	43.25210	5.550420	5.155462
Median	60.40000	50.00000	45.00000	6.000000	5.000000
Maximum	77.70000	90.00000	90.00000	7.000000	7.000000
Minimum	31.50000	10.00000	10.00000	1.000000	2.000000
Std. Dev.	10.46972	18.78528	20.88373	1.418526	1.119915
Skewness	-0.769872	-0.019033	0.113792	-1.875621	-0.561502
Kurtosis	3.035667	2.756794	2.212095	6.693253	3.921260
Jarque-Bera	23.52318	0.600933	6.669835	274.8100	20.92275
Probability	0.000008	0.740473	0.035618	0.000000	0.000029
Sum	13970.60	10405.00	10294.00	1321.000	1227.000
Sum Sq. Dev.	25978.76	83634.14	103362.9	476.8950	297.2479
Observations	238	238	238	238	238

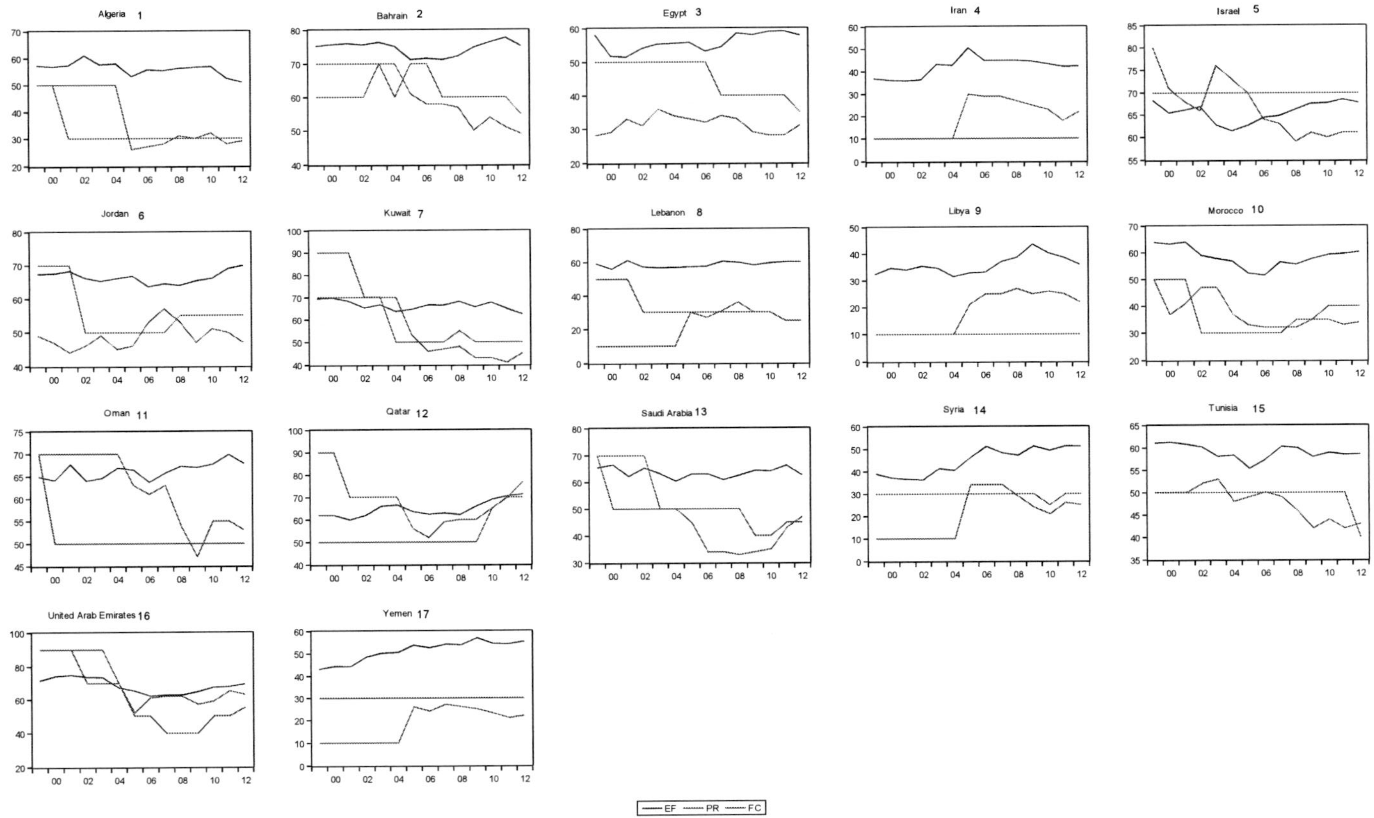

Figure 1. Individual Cross Sections of the Economic Freedom, the Property Rights, the Freedom from Corruption.

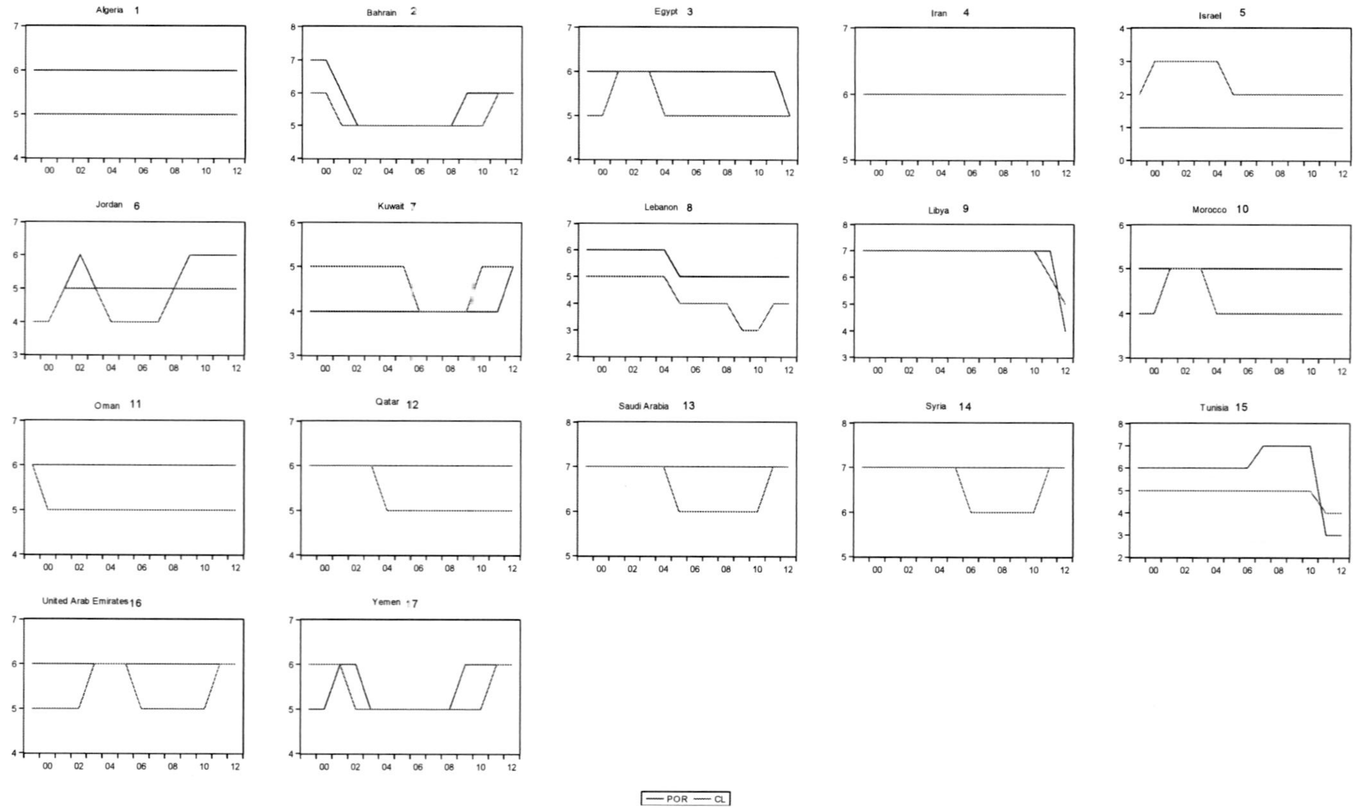

Figure 2. Individual Cross Sections of the Political Rights and the Civil Liberties.

3. Model Specifications and Estimates

In this section, we summarize the model specifications and give the estimates of the linear balanced pooled least squares models, the country specific fixed and random effects models and the country and period specific fixed and random effects models. Furthermore, we give results of the least squares standard errors, the white cross-section standard errors, the white period standard errors, the white diagonal standard errors, the cross-section SUR (Panel Corrected Standard Error: PCSE) standard errors, the cross-section weights (PCSE) standard errors, the period SUR (PCSE) and the period weights (PCSE) standard errors for these models. While the pooled model assumes that there are no effects, the fixed or random effects models allow for either fixed or random effects in either the cross-section or period dimension, or both. While estimates for the pooled model are obtained by the pooled least squares estimator, the estimates for the fixed effects models are obtained by the least squares dummy variable estimator or the fixed effects estimator. The random effects specification assumes that the corresponding effects are realizations of independent random variables with mean zero and finite variance. The random effects specification assumes that the effect is uncorrelated with the idiosyncratic residual. The estimates for the random effects model are obtained by the generalized least squares (GLS) estimator. However, the type of standard errors depends on the choice of coefficient covariance method. The White cross-section method assumes that the errors are contemporaneously (cross-sectionally) correlated (period clustered). The White period method assumes that the errors for a cross-section are heteroskedastic and serially correlated (cross-section clustered). The White (diagonal) method is robust to observation specific heteroskedasticity in the disturbances, but not to correlation between residuals for different observations. While the Cross-section SUR (PCSE) method handles cross-section correlation (period clustering), the Period SUR (PCSE) handles between period correlation (cross-section clustering). The cross-section weights (PCSE) and the period weights (PCSE) use only the diagonal elements and these covariance estimators are robust to heteroskedasticity across cross-sections or periods, respectively, but not to general correlation of residuals. After these brief explanations, we obtain the following outputs in tables. The coefficient estimates have not changed, but the standard errors, t-values, and p-values are some different. The model estimates is evaluated according to these standard errors [Additional details about these topics are provided in Wooldridge (2002, p. 148-153), Arellano (1987), Beck and Katz (1995),

Baltagi (2005), Baltagi and Chang (1994), Hsiao (2003), Hill, Griffiths and Lim (2011) and EViews 8 User's Guide II (2013)].

Pooled Least Squares Estimates

The pooled least squares estimates of the economic freedom are displayed in Table 4 alongside least-squares standard errors, t-values and p- values, and the corresponding White period standard errors, t-values and p-values. Looking at the estimates of the economic freedom in Table 4, we find that the all variables (the property rights, the freedom from corruption, the political rights and the civil liberties) have significantly the effects on the economic freedom.

Table 4. Pooled Least Squares Estimates of Economic Freedom

		Least Squares Std. Errors			White Period Std. Errors		
Variable	Coefficient	Std. Error	t-Statistic	Prob.	Std. Error	t-Statistic	Prob.
Property rights	0.306560	0.028134	10.89628	0.0000	0.058191	5.268159	0.0000
Freedom from corruption	0.169061	0.023844	7.090309	0.0000	0.037787	4.473995	0.0000
Political rights	2.798212	0.389218	7.189315	0.0000	0.886891	3.155079	0.0018
Civil liberties	-4.028913	0.494956	-8.139942	0.0000	1.014414	-3.971665	0.0001
C	43.22508	2.052377	21.06098	0.0000	5.032586	8.589040	0.0000

Country Specific Fixed and Random Effects Estimates

The results from applying the least squares dummy variable estimator to the economic freedom equation for the 17 countries appear in Table 5. Turning to the estimates in Table 5, we find that all of countries are significantly different from zero. In other words, we find that the property rights, the freedom from corruption, the political rights and the civil liberties have significantly the effects on the economic freedom. When we test with Wald test whether there is no individual heterogeneity, we find that the value of the test statistic $F=28.22$ yields a *p-value* of *0.0000* for the economic freedom (Table 6); we reject the null hypothesis that the intercept parameters for all individuals are equal. We conclude that there are differences in individual intercepts, and that the data should not be pooled into a single model with a common intercept parameter. Country specific fixed effects estimates of the economic freedom equation appear in Table 7. We find that the fixed effects estimates are identical to the dummy variable estimates. Also, the fixed effects can be tested with Likelihood Ratio. Two versions of the likelihood ratio test appear in Table 6 and 8, an *F-test* and a X^2 *−test.* The *F-test* is identical to the one we considered earlier and gives the same test result. The random effects estimates are given in Table 9 for the economic freedom. Looking at the estimates of the economic freedom in Table 9, we find that the property rights, the freedom from corruption, the political rights and the civil liberties have significantly the effects on the economic freedom. Also, we find that there is difference between the fixed effects estimates and the random effects estimates for the economic freedom with Hausman test. We conclude that the null hypothesis of no correlation between the explanatory variables and the random effects should be rejected (Table 10). The random effects estimator is inconsistent, and we should use the fixed effects estimator, or should attempt to improve the model specification.

Table 5. Country Specific Dummy Variable Estimates of Economic Freedom

		Least Squares *Std.* Errors			White Period Std. Errors		
Variable	*Coeff.*	*Std. Error*	*t-Statistic*	*Prob.*	*Std. Error*	*t-Statistic*	*Prob.*
Algeria	50.78197	2.733417	18.57820	0.0000	3.540874	14.34165	0.0000
Bahrain	64.80600	2.966168	21.84840	0.0000	4.100306	15.80516	0.0000
Egypt	50.91126	2.782610	18.29623	0.0000	3.698001	13.76724	0.0000
Iran	43.32021	2.836603	15.27186	0.0000	3.643683	11.88913	0.0000
Israel	54.66867	2.045332	26.72851	0.0000	2.949523	18.53475	0.0000
Jordan	57.87179	2.660071	21.75574	0.0000	3.608684	16.03682	0.0000
Kuwait	58.21633	2.557444	22.76348	0.0000	3.609011	16.13083	0.0000
Lebanon	54.68809	2.428539	22.51893	0.0000	3.104493	17.61579	0.0000
Libya	37.79328	3.178163	11.89155	0.0000	4.112356	9.190175	0.0000
Morocco	52.40622	2.385768	21.96619	0.0000	3.114378	16.82719	0.0000
Oman	56.32099	2.957823	19.04137	0.0000	4.031800	13.96919	0.0000
Qatar	54.30713	3.054855	17.77732	0.0000	4.217900	12.87539	0.0000
Saudi Arabia	57.35048	3.346638	17.13675	0.0000	4.504927	12.73061	0.0000
Syria	44.18237	3.206839	13.77754	0.0000	4.245777	10.40619	0.0000
Tunisia	50.97726	2.797372	18.22327	0.0000	3.731616	13.66091	0.0000
United Arab Emirates	56.92566	3.114375	18.27836	0.0000	4.333094	13.13742	0.0000

Table 5. (Continued)

		Least Squares *Std.* Errors			White Period Std. Errors		
Variable	*Coeff.*	*Std. Error*	*t-Statistic*	*Prob.*	*Std. Error*	*t-Statistic*	*Prob.*
Yemen	50.25619	2.597906	19.34489	0.0000	3.459843	14.52557	0.0000
Property rights	0.083504	0.024901	3.353406	0.0009	0.037284	2.239674	0.0261
Freedom from corruption	0.133097	0.021254	6.262186	0.0000	0.044134	3.015744	0.0029
Political rights	1.347451	0.430104	3.132852	0.0020	0.552134	2.440444	0.0155
Civil liberties	- 2.110286	0.455198	- 4.635971	0.0000	0.722714	-2.919946	0.0039

Table 6. ***Testing the Fixed Effects with*** **Wald Test for Economic Freedom**

	Wald Test for Economic Freedom		
Test Statistic	Value	df	Probability
F-statistic	28.22111	(16, 217)	0.0000
Chi-square	451.5378	16	0.0000

Table 7. Country Specific Fixed Effects Estimates of Economic Freedom

		Least Squares Std. Errors			White Period Std. Errors		
Variable	Coefficient	Std. Error	t-Statistic	Prob.	Std. Error	t-Statistic	Prob.
Property rights	0.083504	0.024901	3.353406	0.0009	0.037284	2.239674	0.0261
Freedom from corruption	0.133097	0.021254	6.262186	0.0000	0.044134	3.015744	0.0029
Political rights	1.347451	0.430104	3.132852	0.0020	0.552134	2.440444	0.0155
Civil liberties	-2.110286	0.455198	-4.635971	0.0000	0.722714	-2.919946	0.0039
C	52.69317	2.628088	20.05001	0.0000	3.639614	14.47768	0.0000

Table 8. Likelihood Ratio Test Cross-Section Fixed Effects

	Economic Freedom		
Effects Test	Statistic	d.f.	Prob.
Cross-section F	28.221114	(16,217)	0.0000
Cross-section Chi-square	267.796555	16	0.0000

Table 9. Country Specific Random Effects Estimates of Economic Freedom

		GLS Std. Errors			White Period Std. Errors		
Variable	Coefficient	Std. Error	t-Statistic	Prob.	Std. Error	t-Statistic	Prob.
Property rights	0.125894	0.023572	5.340852	0.0000	0.034084	3.693620	0.0003
Freedom from corruption	0.152858	0.020403	7.491863	0.0000	0.040033	3.818322	0.0002
Political rights	1.333481	0.397582	3.353978	0.0009	0.484455	2.752536	0.0064
Civil liberties	-2.589549	0.434966	-5.953451	0.0000	0.711319	-3.640488	0.0003
C	52.53360	2.522405	20.82679	0.0000	3.416350	15.37712	0.0000

Table 10. Correlated Random Effects - Hausman Test for Economic Freedom

Test cross-section random effects				
Test Summary		Chi-Sq. Statistic	Chi-Sq. d.f.	Prob.
Cross-section random		31.821940	4	0.0000
Cross-section random effects test comparisons:				
Variable	Fixed	Random	Var(Diff.)	Prob.
Property rights	0.083504	0.125894	0.000064	0.0000
Freedom from corruption	0.133097	0.152858	0.000035	0.0009
Political rights	1.347451	1.333481	0.026918	0.9321
Civil liberties	-2.110286	-2.589549	0.018010	0.0004

Country and Period Specific Fixed and Random Effects Estimates

Table 11 gives results from application of the country and period specific fixed effects estimates. We find that the property rights, the freedom from corruption, the political rights and the civil liberties have significantly the effects on the economic freedom. Table 12 shows results from application of the country and period specific random effects estimates. We find that the property rights, the freedom from corruption, the political rights and the civil liberties have significantly the effects on the economic freedom. Furthermore, we reject the null hypothesis according to Likelihood Ratio Test cross-section and period fixed effects for economic freedom (Table 13). We conclude that the data should not be pooled into a single model with a common intercept parameter.

Table 11. Country and Period Specific Fixed Effects Estimates of Economic Freedom

		Least Squares Std. Errors			White Period Std. Errors		
Variable	Coefficient	Std. Error	t-Statistic	Prob.	Std. Error	t-Statistic	Prob.
Property rights	0.134211	0.024573	5.461763	0.0000	0.034643	3.874134	0.0001
Freedom from corruption	0.155704	0.018878	8.247674	0.0000	0.039610	3.930891	0.0001
Political rights	1.150380	0.402807	2.855910	0.0047	0.369200	3.115868	0.0021
Civil liberties	-1.362075	0.475725	-2.863156	0.0046	0.612695	-2.223088	0.0273
C	46.73501	2.611786	17.89389	0.0000	4.449412	10.50364	0.0000
$R^2 = 0.96$	$\bar{R}^2 = 0.95$						

Table 12. Country and Period Specific Random Effects Estimates of Economic Freedom

		GLS Std.Errors			White Period Std. Errors		
Variable	Coefficient	Std. Error	t-Statistic	Prob.	Std. Error	t-Statistic	Prob.
Property rights	0.138397	0.024266	5.703282	0.0000	0.034509	4.010406	0.0001
Freedom from corruption	0.157870	0.020110	7.850148	0.0000	0.039193	4.027975	0.0001
Political rights	1.270084	0.404526	3.139682	0.0019	0.448588	2.831293	0.0050
Civil liberties	-2.221385	0.460185	-4.827158	0.0000	0.673061	-3.300421	0.0011
C	50.22406	2.662508	18.86344	0.0000	3.728235	13.47127	0.0000

Table 13. Likelihood Ratio Test Cross-Section and Period Fixed Effects for Economic Freedom

Effects Test	Statistic	d.f.	Prob.
Cross-section F	32.801411	(16,204)	0.0000
Cross-section Chi-square	303.047856	16	0.0000
Period F	6.254250	(13,204)	0.0000
Period Chi-square	79.834643	13	0.0000
Cross-Section/Period F	23.274964	(29,204)	0.0000
Cross-Section/Period Chi-square	347.631199	29	0.0000

Finally, the country and period specific fixed and random effects models are estimated with the least squares standard errors, the white cross-section standard errors, the white period standard errors, the white diagonal standard errors, the cross-section SUR (Panel Corrected Standard Error) standard errors, the cross-section weights (Panel Corrected Standard Error) standard errors, the period SUR (Panel Corrected Standard Error) and the period weights (Panel Corrected Standard Error) standard errors. We find that the estimation results of the various standard errors give about results for these models (Table 14, 15, 16, 17, 18, 19, 20 and 21).

Table 14 Country and Period Specific Fixed Effects Estimates of Economic Freedom (Least Squares Std. Errors and White Cross-Section Std. Errors)

		Least Squares Std. Errors			White Cross-Section Std. Errors		
Variable	Coefficient	Std. Error	t-Statistic	Prob.	Std. Error	t-Statistic	Prob.
Property rights	0.134211	0.024573	5.461763	0.0000	0.018818	7.131906	0.0000
Freedom from corruption	0.155704	0.018878	8.247674	0.0000	0.013186	11.80805	0.0000
Political rights	1.150380	0.402807	2.855910	0.0047	0.361818	3.179442	0.0017
Civil liberties	-1.362075	0.475725	-2.863156	0.0046	0.627445	-2.170829	0.0311
C	46.73501	2.611786	17.89389	0.0000	2.010622	23.24405	0.0000
$R^2 = 0.96$	$\bar{R}^2 = 0.95$						

Table 15. Country and Period Specific Fixed Effects Estimates of Economic Freedom (White Period Std. Errors and White Diagonal Std. Errors)

		White Period Std. Errors			White Diagonal Std. Errors		
Variable	Coefficient	Std. Error	t-Statistic	Prob.	Std. Error	t-Statistic	Prob.
Property rights	0.134211	0.034643	3.874134	0.0001	0.021851	6.142085	0.0000
Freedom from corruption	0.155704	0.039610	3.930891	0.0001	0.020132	7.734067	0.0000
Political rights	1.150380	0.369200	3.115868	0.0021	0.339763	3.385826	0.0009
Civil liberties	-1.362075	0.612695	-2.223088	0.0273	0.501473	-2.716148	0.0072
C	46.73501	4.449412	10.50364	0.0000	2.428795	19.24206	0.0000
$R^2 = 0.96$	$\bar{R}^2 = 0.95$						

Table 16. Country and Period Specific Fixed Effects Estimates of Economic Freedom (Cross-Section SUR (PCSE) Std. Errors and Cross-Section Weights (PCSE) Std. Errors)

		Cross-Section SUR (PCSE) Std. Errors			Cross-Section Weights (PCSE) Std. Errors		
Variable	Coefficient	Std. Error	t-Statistic	Prob.	Std. Error	t-Statistic	Prob.
Property rights	0.134211	0.019937	6.731935	0.0000	0.022523	5.958810	0.0000
Freedom from corruption	0.155704	0.016765	9.287194	0.0000	0.018920	8.229642	0.0000
Political rights	1.150380	0.364535	3.155745	0.0018	0.385354	2.985255	0.0032

Table 16. (Continued)

		Cross-Section SUR (PCSE) Std. Errors			Cross-Section Weights (PCSE) Std. Errors		
Variable	Coefficient	Std. Error	t-Statistic	Prob.	Std. Error	t-Statistic	Prob.
Civil liberties	-1.362075	0.473833	-2.874588	0.0045	0.458049	-2.973644	0.0033
C	46.73501	2.598913	17.98252	0.0000	2.531135	18.46406	0.0000
$R^2 = 0.96$	$\bar{R}^2 = 0.95$						

Table 17. Country and Period Specific Fixed Effects Estimates of Economic Freedom (Period SUR (PCSE) Std. Errors and Period Weights (PCSE) Std. Errors)

		Period SUR (PCSE) Std. Errors			Period Weights (PCSE) Std. Errors		
Variable	Coefficient	Std. Error	t-Statistic	Prob.	Std. Error	t-Statistic	Prob.
Property rights	0.134211	0.046508	2.885775	0.0043	0.026133	5.135698	0.0000
Freedom from corruption	0.155704	0.038296	4.065820	0.0001	0.019359	8.043090	0.0000
Political rights	1.150380	0.535380	2.148715	0.0328	0.400601	2.871636	0.0045
Civil liberties	-1.362075	0.707193	-1.926032	0.0555	0.481735	-2.827439	0.0052
C	46.73501	4.179981	11.18067	0.0000	2.587082	18.06476	0.0000
$R^2 = 0.96$	$\bar{R}^2 = 0.95$						

Table 18. Country and Period Specific Random Effects Estimates of Economic Freedom (Least Squares Std. Errors and White Cross-Section Std. Errors)

		Least Squares Std. Errors			White Cross-Section Std. Errors		
Variable	Coefficient	Std. Error	t-Statistic	Prob.	Std. Error	t-Statistic	Prob.
Property rights	0.138397	0.024266	5.703282	0.0000	0.015062	9.188757	0.0000
Freedom from corruption	0.157870	0.020110	7.850148	0.0000	0.019691	8.017584	0.0000
Political rights	1.270084	0.404526	3.139682	0.0019	0.285179	4.453637	0.0000
Civil liberties	-2.221385	0.460185	-4.827158	0.0000	0.671217	-3.309490	0.0011
C	50.22406	2.662508	18.86344	0.0000	1.760191	28.53330	0.0000

Table 19. Country and Period Specific Random Effects Estimates of Economic Freedom (White Period Std. Errors and White Diagonal Std. Errors)

		White Period Std. Errors			White Diagonal Std. Errors		
Variable	Coefficient	Std. Error	t-Statistic	Prob.	Std. Error	t-Statistic	Prob.
Property rights	0.138397	0.034509	4.010406	0.0001	0.020768	6.664037	0.0000
Freedom from corruption	0.157870	0.039193	4.027975	0.0001	0.021274	7.420941	0.0000
Political rights	1.270084	0.448588	2.831293	0.0050	0.365884	3.471271	0.0006
Civil liberties	-2.221385	0.673061	-3.300421	0.0011	0.507570	-4.376507	0.0000
C	50.22406	3.728235	13.47127	0.0000	2.466043	20.36625	0.0000

Table 20. Country and Period Specific Random Effects Estimates of Economic Freedom (Cross-Section SUR (PCSE) Std. Errors and Cross-Section Weights (PCSE) Std. Errors)

		Cross-Section SUR (PCSE) Std. Errors			Cross-Section Weights (PCSE) Std. Errors		
Variable	Coefficient	Std. Error	t-Statistic	Prob.	Std. Error	t-Statistic	Prob.
Property rights	0.138397	0.020764	6.665288	0.0000	0.022930	6.035671	0.0000
Freedom from corruption	0.157870	0.019956	7.911034	0.0000	0.020110	7.850300	0.0000
Political rights	1.270084	0.368702	3.444745	0.0007	0.373099	3.404146	0.0008
Civil liberties	-2.221385	0.564341	-3.936248	0.0001	0.456295	-4.868314	0.0000
C	50.22406	2.917490	17.21482	0.0000	2.503238	20.06364	0.0000

Table 21. Country and Period Specific Random Effects Estimates of Economic Freedom (Period SUR (PCSE) Std. Errors and Period Weights (PCSE) Std. Errors)

		Period SUR (PCSE) Std. Errors			Period Weights (PCSE) Std. Errors		
Variable	Coefficient	Std. Error	t-Statistic	Prob.	Std. Error	t-Statistic	Prob.
Property rights	0.138397	0.041933	3.300442	0.0011	0.025949	5.333478	0.0000
Freedom from corruption	0.157870	0.037151	4.249405	0.0000	0.020619	7.656375	0.0000
Political rights	1.270084	0.537605	2.362485	0.0190	0.433700	2.928485	0.0037
Civil liberties	-2.221385	0.668481	-3.323033	0.0010	0.470011	-4.726238	0.0000
C	50.22406	4.024105	12.48080	0.0000	2.755916	18.22409	0.0000

CONCLUSION

The first goal in this paper is to explore whether the economic freedom depends on the property rights, the freedom from corruption, the political rights and the civil liberties with panel data models in the Middle East and North Africa from 1999 to 2012. Another goal is to find whether the least squares standard errors, the white cross-section standard errors, the white period standard errors, the white diagonal standard errors, the cross-section SUR (panel corrected standard error) standard errors, the cross-section weights (panel corrected standard error) standard errors, the period SUR (panel corrected standard error) and the period weights (panel corrected standard error) standard errors give the similar results for these models. The first finding is that the property rights, the freedom from corruption and the political rights from the significant variables have positive effects on the economic freedom, while the civil liberties has negative effect on the economic freedom according to the estimates of the economic freedom in the country and period specific fixed and random effects models. The second finding is that the various standard errors give about results for these models. Consequently, this empirical research supports the idea that the property rights, the freedom from corruption, the political rights and the civil liberties are the important determinants of economic freedom. In the Middle East and North Africa, we suggest that various government policies should be regulated according to these factors again.

REFERENCES

Alexandrakis, C. and Livanis, G. (2013). Economic freedom and economic performance in latin america: a panel data analysis, *Review of Development Economics*, 17(1), 34–48.

Apergis, N., Dincer, O. And Payne, J. (2013). Economic freedom and income inequality revisited: evidence from a panel error correction model, *Contemporary Economic Policy,* DOI: 10.1111/j.1465-7287.2012. 00343.x.

Arellano, M. (1987). Computing robust standard errors for within-groups estimators, *Oxford Bulletin of Economics and Statistics*, 49, 431-434.

Baltagi, B. (2005). *Econometric analysis of panel data,* (Third Edition). West Sussex, England: John Wiley & Sons.

Baltagi, B. and Chang, Y. (1994). Incomplete panels: A comparative study of alternative estimators for the unbalanced one-way error component regression model," *Journal of Econometrics*, 62, 67-89.

Beck, N. and Katz, J. (1995). What to do (and not to do) with time-series cross-section data, *American Political Science Review*, 89(3), 634-647.

Burkhart, R. (2000). Economic freedom and democracy: post–cold war tests, *European Journal of Political Research*, 37(2), 237–253.

Doucouliagos, C. (2005). Publication bias in the economic freedom and economic growth literature, *Journal of Economic Surveys*, 19(3), 367–387.

EViews 8 User's Guide II (2013). ISBN: 978-1-880411-13-1.

Goel, R. and Nelson, M. (2005). Economic freedom versus political freedom: cross-country influences on corruption, *Australian Economic Papers*, 44(2), 121–133.

Gohmann, S., Hobbs, B. and McCrickard, M. (2008). Economic freedom and service industry growth in the United States, *Entrepreneurship Theory and Practice*, 32(5), 855–874.

Hill, R.C., Griffiths, W. E. and Lim, G. C. (2011). *Principles of econometrics* (4th Edition). Wiley, USA.

Hsiao, C. (1986, 2003). *Analysis of panel data* (1st and 2nd Editions). Cambridge, UK: Cambridge University Press.

Peev, E. and Mueller, D. (2012). Democracy, Economic Freedom and Growth in Transition Economies, *Kyklos*, 65(3), 371–407.

Wooldridge, J. M. (2002). *Econometric analysis of cross section and panel data*, Cambridge, MA: The MIT Press.

In: Economic and Social Issues …
Editor: Nilgün Çil Yavuz
ISBN: 978-1-62948-152-4

Chapter 7

HUMAN CAPITAL CONVERGENCE IN TURKEY: SPATIAL DYNAMIC PANEL DATA ANALYSIS

***Fatma Zeren*[1*] *and Sevinç Yaraşır Tülümce*[2†]**
[1]Department of Econometrics, Inonu University, Turkey
[2]Department of Public Finance Pamukkale University, Turkey

ABSTRACT

Recently, growth and convergence models have become an important method of explaining human capital. The incorporation of human capital into growth models, human capital's contribution to capital growth, and modern growth theories are the subjects of several studies. Human capital can be explained as the value invested in humans and the improvement of their skills. Convergence is based on the concept that regions that were initially the leaders grow slower than underdeveloped regions. Convergence analyses generally focus on income, but convergence of education and another socioeconomic indicator is disregarded. This study analyzes regional convergence of human capital in Turkey from 2002 to 2009 with spatial dynamic panel data and reviews convergence of education. In empirical analysis, the number of associate degree and bachelor's degree students registered in NUTS-I regions is used as the human capital variable.

* fatma.zeren@inonu.edu.tr.
† syarasir@pau.edu.tr.

Keywords: Human Capital, Convergence, High Education, Spatial Dynamic Panel
JEL: E24, I24, O47, C31

1. Introduction

Human capital's influence on growth has been studied for years. Conventional growth theories explain growth differences between countries with capital stock owned. Factors such as physical capital and effort are taken into consideration in conventional growth theories. However, it is known that neoclassic theories do not provide efficient growth explanations. Today, conventional growth theories have been expanded, and models of economic growth incorporate several factors such as the importance of geographical location, foreign trade limits, the impact of institutions, and human capital. Because human capital is reviewed within the scope of growth theories, the relationship between human capital and growth is a part of the majority of these empirical studies. Empirical studies in different countries reveal the importance of human capital's influence on growth.

On the other hand, there might be income differences between countries or between regions or cities within a country. There are many significant factors when comparing growth rates between countries or regions and for closing the different. Technological expansion, the role of globalization, and the impact of human capital are some examples of these factors. The convergence hypothesis, based on neoclassical growth models, explains that countries that were initially the leaders countries have a slower growth rates than underdeveloped countries. Because of the fast growth rates of underdeveloped countries or regions, the gap between the two groups is reduced. In the literature, there are several income convergence studies conducted on the basis of countries and regions. Convergence analyses focus on income dynamics. However, the fact that socio-economic differences experienced by low-income regions are important in terms of the imbalance between regions is disregarded. Thus, the impact of indicators, such as education and life expectancy, should be examined along with income differences. Low-income regions commonly have similar economic performances, but differences in education indicators such as human capital create imbalances. Accordingly, studying convergence of human capital is a vary important. Very few studies discuss convergence of human capital. The studies related to convergence of human capital were conducted for countries such as Greece, Peru, and Canada.

This study explains the human capital theory and convergence theory within the scope of theories related to the convergence of human capital. Convergence of human capital is then discussed and the literature reviewed. The last section of the study tests convergence of human capital between 2002 and 2009 in NUTS-I regions of Turkey with spatial dynamic panel data analyses. As is known, regions in Turkey have vast social, economic, and cultural differences. Fiscal policy particularly aims at ensuring economic growth and eliminating regional imbalances. Thus, the government should eliminate regional imbalances by valuing human capital investments and embracing incentive policies. Accordingly, the goal of this study is to analyze differences between regional education performances and reveal the regional convergence of education.

2. Theories Related to Convergence of Human Capital

Conventional growth theories fail to fully explain economic growth with capital stock and manpower. The variables of conventional growth models and other variables should be taken into consideration per the new theory concept. Human capital is one of the most important variables used for explaining economic growth. Several empirical studies explain and establish education's contribution to growth within the human capital theory. Accordingly, the importance of human capital should first be explained within growth theories using the human capital theory. Then the convergence hypothesis within growth theories will be discussed, because the goal is to review convergence of human capital.

2.1. Human Capital Theory

Human capital is described as "skills attributed to the individual and other qualities gained" (Tekir, 1987: 4). The human capital theory is considered to be the theory examining expenses made for issues such as education, domestic migration and emigration, health care, in-service training, and human capital theory offers significant advantages to an economy (Schultz, 1971: 8). The human capital concept covers information, skills, and all other qualities gained as a result of manpower activities, which are one of the production factors. In other words, human capital covers all investments that include positive values enhancing productivity and efficiency in terms of education, health care, professional skills, and other personal qualities. Activities enhancing these positive values are also considered investments. The aspect most fit for measurement among human capital investments is the quality of education services. At the micro level, education is discussed in terms of people and members of the community, whereas at the macro level, education's contribution to the country as a human capital element is discussed. The advantage brought by education at the micro level includes increased personal income; the advantage at the macro level reveals education's contribution to growth by corrected income distribution, reduced regional imbalances, and technological development. In fact, personal and social advantages introduced by education necessitate considering education a human capital investment. Per the human capital theory, the most influential factor on a country's development is increasing the number of educated people and their level of education.

Acclaimed economists such as Smith, Malthus, Ricardo, Mc.Culloch, Marx, and Fisher argue that capital invested in people is the most valuable investment. However, other philosophers, such as Mill, believe that considering people as properties (like a factor of physical capital) would be wrong (as quoted in Becker, 1964: 55). Although Marshall's view that people cannot be addressed as capital under market conditions and practice was a great inspiration for the following generations of economist, his work titled "*Principles of Economics*" described education as a form of national investment (as quoted in Marshall, 1963: 83). Marshall explained that public and private expenses paid for education should not be evaluated only in terms of direct products; education is an important tool for revealing the skills a person has (Schultz, 1971: 27). Accordingly, human capital is the basis for ensuring effective continuance of physical capital.

The strongest aspect of evidence that education is an investment is the positive relationship between educational expenses paid by an individual and that individual's income. For example, continuing each level of education creates a wage difference in comparison to the previous one and thus increases a person's "lifelong net income." Age-income profiles are used for examining human capital investments on earnings. These profiles illustrate average annual incomes of people having the same educational background but at different ages. Thus, human capital investments have a full positive effect on earnings (Havermesh and Rees, 1988: 66). The most important evidence of earning profiles increasing throughout a person's life are the indicators in labor market. The best explanation provided in this matter is the human capital model, in which increases in lifelong earnings of people directly responding to increase in productivity is evident (Hellerstein and Neumark, 2001: 90). To realize economic growth and sustainable economic development, we need physical capital and an educated workforce. This activity area, which is crucial for economic and social development, can be evaluated as consumption and investment in macro terms. If knowledge obtained through education is used for purposes other than one's profession and evaluated in terms of prestige, then it is considered consumption. If the knowledge and skills are used to enhance productivity, then education is considered an investment.

2.1.1. Education in Human Capital Theory; "Higher Education"

In the past, formation of human capital and its impact on economies was disregarded. However, Schultz, believing that insufficient educational investment is the reason some countries fail to develop, founded education economy. Later, several economists focused on investments made in human capital and started to examine the advantages of educational investments, because it was noted that education not only contributes to development but is also a vital element of regional growth.

Higher education has a unique position within human capital theory because higher education plays a crucial role in training executives of a country, motivating scientific and technological advancements, and, at the macro level, contributing to the economy and country through technological developments. Additionally, the quality of education received by the individuals making up the community is used as criteria to determine the development level of countries. Universities, offering the highest level of education, are outstanding institutions thanks to their contributions to the technological, and scientific fields and the cultural, economic, and social advantages they offer to their regions and locations. Thus, higher education institutions have crucial functions such as scientific research and offering qualified manpower to the community.

At the micro level, the direct advantages of a higher education are increased income, prestige, and respectability, whereas the external advantages offered to the community are described as "social advantages." Schultz listed the benefits of education. This list includes economic advantages the discovery of new talents, enhancement of skills to adapt to different jobs, and the provision of manpower for sustaining economic growth. Also, becoming better citizens, improving the level of culture in the community, offering better education opportunities to the next generations, and such other elements are examples of the social advantages offered by education (Cohn, 1972: 125). Education not only enhances the productivity of a person but also contributes to the process of enhancing productivity of other people (Barr, 1991: 159). Education in general, but particularly higher education, is considered to be an important tool for issues such as health care, overpopulation, poverty, and economic and political instability.

2.1.2. Human Capital in Growth Models

Human capital is both the result and cause of economic growth processes. The relationship between human capital and economic growth plays a crucial role in sustaining economic development (Mincer, 1996: 29). Countries having significant human capital easily and rapidly develop new ideas and products or adapt to ideas and products developed externally. Thus, a follower country having a significant level of human capital might develop faster than the leading country it follows (Mincer, 1996: 29). There is an important positive relationship between growth rate and human capital. If developing countries manage to make higher human capital investments per capita, these countries enhance their opportunities to catch up with developed countries. Although poorer countries need educated manpower more than wealthy countries, education investments in such countries are restricted because there is a lack of resources that can be allocated for education (Meler, 1976: 526).

The empirical studies in the literature reveal that increases in national income are more effective than increases in production factors. According to Schultz (1971), this difference can be measured with investments made in human capital. The advantages offered by investing in education cannot be offered by any other investment. Education investments are reflected in the quality of the workforce in the long run. A study of education vs. productivity done in 1995 and covering over 3,100 offices in the United States concludes that a 10 percent increase in the workforce's education level offers a 5.8 percent increase in factor productivity, whereas a 10 percent increase in capital stock, in other words, level of hardware, increases productivity by only 3.4 percent. Thus, the marginal value of investing in human capital is approximately three times more than investing in machines (Eicher, 2000: 381).

Another study examining education's impact on economic growth in the United States from 1960 to 1980 determines that the total real national income growth rate was 3.33%, and 0.64% of this rate was education's contribution. Education's contribution in total real national income growth rate was 19% (Cohn, 1972: 56).

A study by Barro (2001) examines 98 countries and their circumstances from 1960 to 1985. The study concludes that countries having higher human capital in the beginning achieve higher economic growth in the following years. In a later study, Barro (2001) looks at 100 countries from 1965 to 1995 and concludes that growth has a positive relationship with high school graduation rates. The study alsı found that the percentage of people with a higher education plays a crucial role in the country's ability to embrace new Technologies.

In their study, Azzoni and Servo (2002) determine that education is an important indicator for explaining regional differences within Brazil. They argue that the more we invest in education, the more we will grow.

Benhabib and Spiegel's (1994) study covering the years 1965–1985 concludes that human capital has indirect influence on economic growth via the growth of total factor productivity. Accordingly, the creation of technology is directly influenced by human capital, and adaptation to external technologies is faster. The study also indicates that if knowledge gained as a result of human capital cannot be used in a positive way, education's positive influence on growth is jeopardized.

Mankiw et al. (1992) focuses on the relationship between capital stock, population, trained manpower, physical capital, and growth and concludes that human capital has an outstanding impact on growth when considering the number of people enrolled in high school as human capital. They review the flexibility of the variables of growth and conclude that the flexibility of the educated workforce for the three categories of countries was between 0.66 and 0.76 whereas physical capital flexibility coefficient was between 0.69 and 0.28. The analysis focuses on the period from 1960 to 1985. The study also examined the convergence of country categories. The study also concluded that there is a relationship between human capital and savings held by the population.

In their study, Baldacci et al. (2004) conclude that human capital has positive effects on growth and that advancements in human capital will result in higher incomes. Increasing education expenses by one percent of GDP will create a 1.4 percent increase in growth within a period of fifteen years. The findings further suggest that the effect of educational expenses can be observed within the first year.

Wang and Yao's (2001) study focusing on China in the years 1952–1999 argue that human capital makes significant contributions to wealth, causing growth to develop rapidly. Total factor productivity was significant and positive from 1978 to 1999. However, the study concludes that growth in human capital dramatically decreased during the reformation period of 1978–1999.

McDonald and Roberts (2002) conclude that health and education make positive contributions to economic growth as human capital.

As seen in these studies, human capital's contributions to growth are undeniable. Physical capital and specialized training further enhance the marginal productivity of human capital. Physical capital does not grow depending on external factors. In reality, demand for both human and physical capital is increasing with the need to adapt to recent advancements in technology and reduce costs (Mincer, 1996: 37). Thus, without a doubt, education in general, and particularly higher education, contributes to economic development. Increased efforts, manpower, and productivity are the results of education. As for increasing social productivity, education's role as an income equalizer is important for determining policies governing educational productivity.

2.2. Convergence Theory

Convergence can be defined as certain poor countries, regions, or cities growing faster than wealthy countries, regions, or cities, reducing the gap between them in time. Abramowitz and David (1996) define convergence as follows: "Regions or economies, which are behind the leading region or economy under certain conditions, have the skills and ability to grow faster in comparison to the region or economies which were the leaders in the beginning". In this scope, the convergence hypothesis has three basic macro resources and theoretical bases. These are technological progress, the neoclassical growth model, and the role of globalization (Rassekh, 1998: 86).

a) Technological progress: Economists believe that implementing and achieving a new form of technology will create a spill-over effect and contribute to the growth of underdeveloped economies or regions. It is indicated that technology is a public property and technological progress is the basis of catching up and convergence. Although multinational companies are effective tools for transferring new technologies, the remaining segments of technology fail to receive technology in the same manner. Thus, economies keeping up with technology transfers and technological progress will be closer to wealthy economies and catch a huge opportunity. In this mode, increasing the quality of human capital facilitates the following countries' ability to keep up with technology transfers and innovations.

b) Neoclassical growth model: The growth model developed by Solow et al. assumes that each economy will converge to its steady-state income level.. The model accepts that convergence takes place in steady-state. If an economy has a lower capital-labor rate in the initial steady-state, then it will grow faster than others because a lower capital-labor rate means capital has higher marginal productivity. If a group of economies converge to the same equilibrium income, an economy having a lower starting income would grow faster in comparison to the leading economy.

c) Role of globalization: Although Smith agrees that trade relationships between poor and wealthy countries are beneficial to both countries, he also mentions that this will cause income divergence because Smith believes that productivity in the manufacturing sector improves faster than productivity in the agriculture sector. On the other hand, a study by Sachs and Warner (1995) examines the relationship between trade liberalization and economic convergence and concludes that trading barriers should be eliminated or reduced so that poor countries can catch up with wealthy countries. The study focused on protection of property rights and international trading in 117 economies between the years 1979 and 1985. The studies by Williamson and Ben-David conclude that there is a link between international trading and convergence. Despite the findings of this study, it is not possible to draw a clear conclusion about international trading and globalization's impact on convergence.

In brief, the convergence hypothesis assumes that economies having income much lower than their own steady-state income grow faster; and economies closer to or above their own steady-state grow slower. The theoretical principles of the convergence hypothesis are based on Solow's neoclassical growth model. The neoclassical growth model also suggests that relatively poor regions or economies will grow faster. Thus, per the convergence hypothesis, incomes of the mentioned country or regions will converge on each other.

In the literature, there are two basic criteria for the convergence hypothesis. These are β and σ convergences. The criterion for examining the capital income progress of an economy over time is known as σ convergence. β convergence is categorized as an absolute and conditional convergence and focuses on establishing the relationship between per-capita income growth rates and initial per-capita income levels (Yamanoğlu, 2009: 8). Absolute convergence does not take into consideration unique qualities of economies or regions, whereas conditional convergence takes into consideration the characteristics of different economies or regions. Conditional convergence is based on economies or regions converging to their own income equilibrium points. Absolute convergence focuses on economies or regions converging to a common steady-state income level. β convergence, introduced to the literature by Baumol's study (1986), argues that there is a negative relationship between the per-capita income of an economy at the beginning and the growth rate of per-capita income in the following periods. However, σ convergence argues that the standard deviation of per-capita income gradually decreases over time. β convergence is a necessary but not sufficient condition of σ convergence's existence (Paas et al., 2007). In other words, the existence of β convergence does not require the existence of σ convergence because there might be economic shocks causing divergence of economies over time (Jones, 2002: 28). The β value calculated expresses a coefficient indicating the convergence rate. A positive coefficient value requires accepting the existence of convergence, whereas a negative value requires accepting the existence of divergence.

The convergence hypothesis is supported by several empirical studies focusing on countries and regions/cities within countries. Just as in many other countries, Turkey is tested in terms of income convergence related to β and σ convergences. Filiztekin's study (1998) suggests that there was conditional σ convergence between cities in Turkey from 1975 to 1995 but there was no absolute β convergence. Kılıçaslan and Özatağan (2007) conclude that there was convergence between Turkish cities from 1987 until 2000. Karaalp and Erdal (2009) conclude that there was convergence between cities within all regions studied except the Aegean region, but there was no convergence between the regions. Berber et al. (2000) tests seven geographical regions of Turkey by focusing on the period from 1975 to 1997 and concludes that there was divergence rather than convergence. Likewise, studies by Erk et al. (2000), Gezici and Hewing (2001), Karaca (2004), Altınbaş et al. (2002), and Doğruel (2003) concluded that there was no convergence in terms of cities and regions of Turkey.

3. Human Capital Convergence

In developing countries, education is an important socio-economic criterion because the level of education has a positive correlation with the economic performances of regions (Elias and Rey, 2011: 108). Empirical studies in the literature provide evidence that there is a positive relationship between education as human capital and growth. Neoclassical growth models provide evidence related to β convergence among regions and countries. However, if we bear in mind the human capital stock, explaining growth with neoclassical model becomes harder, especially in an open economy. Human capital should be used to explain a section of the per-capita income, but the neoclassical growth model is not enough to explain this. In the neoclassical growth model, the law of diminishing returns applies to input, and, depending on the criterion, output is considered to be fixed; also, technology is included in the manufacturing function as an external factor. In this concept, it is considered that the per-capita manufacturing increase rate will be zero in developed and developing economies in the long-run and the economies will be steady. These circumstances cause convergence, whereas the gap between technologies and growth-rate differences between countries cause divergence. In recent years, conditional convergence and modern growth theories emerged beside the salt convergence hypothesis. It is argued that the neoclassical growth model disregards human capital's influence on population and savings. Barro and Mankim et al. (1992) argued that human capital should be included in growth models. The studies provide evidence of a correlation between human capital and a country's savings and population-increase rates. The new extended model explains approximately 80 percent of the growth in countries (Mankiw et al., 1992: 408-409). Thus, modern growth theories incorporate human capital and technology and focus on analyzing factors having an impact on growth.

Although physical capital has perfect mobility in an open economy, if human capital per laborer falls below the steady-state income equilibrium level, then convergence of per-capita income at the steady-state level will slow. In classical theories considering labor and physical capital as input, the marginal productivity of labor in poor countries or regions, having lower capital per laborer in the initial state, will be higher than the marginal productivity of labor in wealthy regions. In this case, flow of capital should be readjusted from wealthy to poor countries. Barro, Mankim, and Sala-i Martin (1995) suggest that lack of human capital in poor regions will result in a drastic decrease in the marginal productivity of physical capital. Contrary to the classical model, the marginal productivity of capital will be the same in poor and rich regions during the transition to the steady-state balance of each economy (Liaskos and Papadas, 2009: 4). Mankiw, Romer, and Weil (1992) argue that the quality and nature of human capital should be taken into consideration for regional convergence. Developments and advancements in growth models reveal that human capital offers important insights about regional convergence. Quantitative analyses of human capital convergence had a tendency towards analyses of the purpose of establishing human capital's contribution to economic growth and convergence. Just like the studies of Barro, Mankiw, and Sala-i Martin (1995), human capital is included in the Cobb Douglas manufacturing function. The studies of economists such as Barro, Levine, Renelt, and Mankiw conclude that the countries' conditional convergence per year is 2 percent after controlling for differences in investment rates, initial human capital stock, and some other variables. Thus, classical growth models fail to fully explain the impact of variables related to convergence (Barro et al., 1995: 103-104).

These latest versions of neoclassical growth models discuss convergence and growth processes in terms of human capital and take into consideration several variables related to the quality and nature of human capital. Human capital is approximated by educational achievement measured in different ways. Human capital stock covers education, on-the-job training, and experience. It is difficult to measure job training and experience. Thus, the studies include educational indicators in the models. Some economists also mention that the quality and nature of education might vary from one region to another and point to difficulties related to including human capital in models. However, these difficulties can be eliminated by assuming that the quality of education is the same in all regions of a country.

In the literature, there are several studies on the factors having an impact on convergence and growth. Most of the studies focusing on regional convergence are about dynamics of income. However, analysis of spatial convergence should take into consideration socio-economic factors because regional differences are caused by the social, economic, and cultural values of regions. Especially in developing countries, variable social indicators among regions, such as educational performance and life expectancy, are the basis of regional differences. Thus, analysis of convergence of human capital has become the subject of research in recent years. However, there are very few studies focusing on regional convergence of human capital. The study by Liaskon and Panadas (2009) analyzes the convergence of human capital by examining the percentage of the population that was educated in NUTS-III regions of Greece from 1971 until 2001. The study concludes that both time and space have an impact, and they obtained conditional β convergence. However, other findings suggest that there is no actual convergence for the period analyzed.

The study by Sub-Smith (2001) calculates convergence rates for 100 countries for the period of 1970–1996. The study concludes that there is significant β convergence and that there is a close connection between education and health-care investments. Other findings conclude that there is conditional and unconditional convergence in terms of various indicators.

The study by Coulombe-Tremblay (1998) focuses on explaining the majority of the per-capita income growth profile in Canada from 1951 to 1996 by using human capital indicators. The empirical section of the study includes new neoclassical growth models. The study offers evidence that the dynamics of human capital stock accelerate growth. In the convergence process, physical capital stock is explained by human capital stock and per-capita income disparities between economies or regions are explained by disparities in human capital stock. Other findings suggest that different levels of education and different groups achieved different rates related to the convergence of human capital in Canadian cities.

Elias and Rey (2011) analyzes the convergence of education among regions in Peru for the years 1993–2005. The study conclude that there is regional educational convergence in various regions of Peru. The findings of the study show that a region's educational growth also displayed strong spatial autocorrelation, indicating that a region's movement towards convergence tends to be similar to its neighbors.

4. Econometric Methodology

4.1. β Convergence Models

Since the publication of the articles of Barro and Sala-i-Martin (1991, 1995), numerous studies have examined β convergence between different countries and regions. Absolute convergence is usually tested following a cross-sectional model:

$$\frac{1}{T}\ln\left(\frac{Y_{n,t}}{Y_{n,0}}\right) = \alpha + \beta \ln Y_{n,0} + V_n$$

where T is the number of periods (years) under study; $Y_{n,t}$ is human capital at the year t, $Y_{n,0}$ is the human capital of a province at the initial year, and V_n is the stochastic error term. There is absolute β convergence when the estimate of β is significantly negative.

The panel specification for the absolute convergence model takes the following form:

$$\ln\left(\frac{y_{n,t+k}}{y_{n,t}}\right) = c_n + \alpha_t + \beta \ln y_{n,t} + v_{n,t}$$

where c_n is a time invariant and captures any individual-specific effect and α_t is an individual invariant and captures any time-specific effect.

4.2. Spatial Dynamic Panel Data Analysis

Spatial econometrics is a subfield of econometrics that deals with the treatment of spatial autocorrelation and spatial heterogeneity in regression models for cross-sectional and panel data (Anselin 1988; Elhorst 2003).

Spatial autocorrelation may be generally defined as the coincidence of value similarity with locational similarity. In case of positive autocorrelation high or low values for a random variable tend to cluster in space whereas in case of negative spatial autocorrelation locations tend to be surrounded by neighbors with very dissimilar values (Anselin Bera, 1998:241).

The common method of handling spatial autocorrelation is the weight matrix approach. This weight matrix W is nonstochastic; that is, the researcher takes W as known *a priori*. W is an $(n \times n)$ matrix with zeros on its main diagonal. The off-diagonal elements, w_{ij}, represent a spatial relationship between location i and j. There are two principal ways to form W: a contiguity approach and a distance approach. When two locations share a common boundary or are within a given distance of each other, w_{ij} are non-zero and zero in all other conditions. For ease of interpretation, the elements of the spatial weights matrix are generally row-standardized, such that for each *i*, $\sum_j w_{ij} = 1$.

Lee and Yu (2010) developed a spatial dynamic panel data model with both time and individual fixed effects. This model is as follows.

$$Y_{nt} = \lambda_0 W_n Y_{nt} + \gamma_0 Y_{n,t-1} + \rho_0 W_n Y_{n,t-1} + X_{nt}\beta_0 + c_{n0} + \alpha_{t0} l_n + V_{nt},$$
$$t = 1,2,\ldots,T \qquad (1)$$

where $Y_{nt} = (y_{1t}, y_{2t}, \ldots, y_{nt})'$ and $V_{nt} = (v_{1t}, v_{2t}, \ldots, v_{nt})'$ are $(n \times 1)$ column vectors. X_{nt} is an $(n \times k_x)$ matrix of nonstochastic regressors, c_{n0} is an $(n \times 1)$ column vector of individual fixed effects, α_{t0} is a scalar of time effect, l_n is an $(n \times 1)$ column vector of ones, v_{it} is i.i.d. across *i* and *t* with zero mean and variance σ_0^2, and W_n, is an $(n \times n)$ spatial weight matrix. In (1), Lee and Yu (2010) used a data transformation approach to estimate all the parameters of achieved effective estimates asymptotically.

They introduce a data transformation approach to eliminate the time effects. Because they assumed that the estimates of the transformed approach have faster rates of convergence than the rates of convergence of the direct estimates and when *n* is a fixed finite number, the estimates of the direct approach is inconsistent whereas the estimates of the transformation approach can stil be consistent and asymptotically normal. Let $J_n = I_n - \frac{1}{n} l_n l_n'$ be the deviation from the group mean transformation. Let $\left(F_{n,n-1}, l_n/\sqrt{n}\right)$ be the orthonormal matrix of eigenvectors of J_n. $F_{n,n-1}$ corresponds to the eigenvalues of one, and $l_n/\sqrt{n}$ corresponds the eigenvalue of zero.

The transformed formulation of (1) (Lee and Yu, 2010: 567) is as follows:

$$Y_{nt}^* = \lambda_0 W_n^* Y_{nt}^* + \gamma_0 Y_{n,t-1}^* + \rho_0 W_n^* Y_{n,t-1}^* + X_{nt}^* \beta_0 + c_{n0}^* + V_{nt}^* \qquad (2)$$

where $W_n^* = F_{n,n-1}' W_n F_{n,n-1}$, $Y_{nt}^* = F_{n,n-1}' J_n Y_{nt}$, $X_{nt}^* = F_{n,n-1}' J_n X_{nt}$, $c_{n0}^* = F_{n,n-1}' J_n c_{n0}$, $V_{nt}^* = F_{n,n-1}' J_n V_{nt}$, and V_{nt}^* are an $(n-1)$ dimensional disturbance vector with zero mean and variance matrix $\sigma_0^2 I_{n-1}$.

V_{nt}^{*} will be $N\left(0,\sigma_0^2 I_{n-1}\right)$ and (2) is estimated by maximum likelihood. The log likelihood function of (2) is as follows:

$$\ln L_{n,T}\left(\theta, c_n^{*}\right) = -\frac{(n-1)T}{2}\ln 2\pi - \frac{(n-1)T}{2}\ln\sigma^2 + T\ln\left|I_{n-1} - \lambda W_n^{*}\right| - \frac{1}{2\sigma^2}\sum_{t=1}^{T} V_{nt}^{*\prime}(\theta) V_{nt}^{*}(\theta) \tag{3}$$

where $V_{nt}^{*}(\theta) = \left(I_{n-1} - \lambda W_n^{*}\right)Y_{nt}^{*} - Z_{nt}^{*}\delta - c_n^{*}$, $Z_{nt} = \left(Y_{n,t-1}, W_n Y_{n,t-1}, X_{nt}\right)$, and $\delta = \left(\gamma,\rho,\beta'\right)'$. They established that the log likelihood function (3) Y_{nt}^{*} can be expressed in terms of Y_{nt} as

$$\ln L_{n,T}(\theta,c_n) = -\frac{(n-1)T}{2}\ln 2\pi - \frac{(n-1)T}{2}\ln\sigma^2 - T\ln(1-\lambda) + T\ln\left|I_n - \lambda W_n\right| - \frac{1}{2\sigma^2}\sum_{t=1}^{T} V_{nt}'(\theta) J_n V_{nt}(\theta) \tag{4}$$

where $V_{nt}(\theta) = \left(I_n - \lambda W_n\right)Y_{nt} - Z_{nt}\delta - c_n$ and J_n may be see as the generalized inverse of $\sigma_0^{-2}Var\left(J_n V_{nt}\right)$.

Using first-order conditions, they concentrate out c_n in (4) and acquired concentrated likelihood function. For the concentrated likelihood function, the first-order derivatives provide a parameter estimations. They established that this estimations are consistent.

5. Data and Empirical Results

This study tests convergence of human capital for 12 NUTS-I regions of Turkey for the period of 2002–2009 by using a human capital indicator and spatial dynamic panel data analysis. The number of associate-degree and bachelor's-degree students enrolled in higher education is considered the human capital indicator. Human capital data was provided by the Turkish Statistical Institution. Because data on the basis of cities is restricted in Turkey, only absolute convergence is examined in this analysis. The β convergence model achieved as a result of analyzing human capital convergence with dynamic spatial data is as follows:

$$\ln\left(\frac{Y_{n,t}}{Y_{n,t-1}}\right) = \lambda_0 W_n \ln\left(\frac{Y_{n,t}}{Y_{n,t-1}}\right) + \gamma_0 \ln\left(\frac{Y_{n,t}}{Y_{n,t-1}}\right)_{n,t-1} + \rho_0 W_n \ln\left(\frac{Y_{nt}}{Y_{n,t-1}}\right)_{n,t-1} + \beta_0 \ln Y_{n,t-1} + c_{n0} + \alpha_{t0} l_n + V_{nt}$$

Weight matrix (W) has been formed according to critical cut-off neighborhoods. Components of the W matrix are determined as follows:

$$w_{ij} = \begin{cases} 1, & 0 \leq d_{ij} \langle d^* \\ 0, & otherwise \end{cases}$$

where d_{ij} is the physical distance between two regions i and j and d^* is a certain critical threshold value. For the present study, the threshold value d^* is set to the minimum distance required to ensure that each location has at least one neighbor. Figure 1 shows the distribution of human capital growth across region for the 2002 and Figure 2 shows the distribution of human capital growth across region for the 2009.

This figures is evident that spatial spillover is present. The results of estimation are given in Table 1.

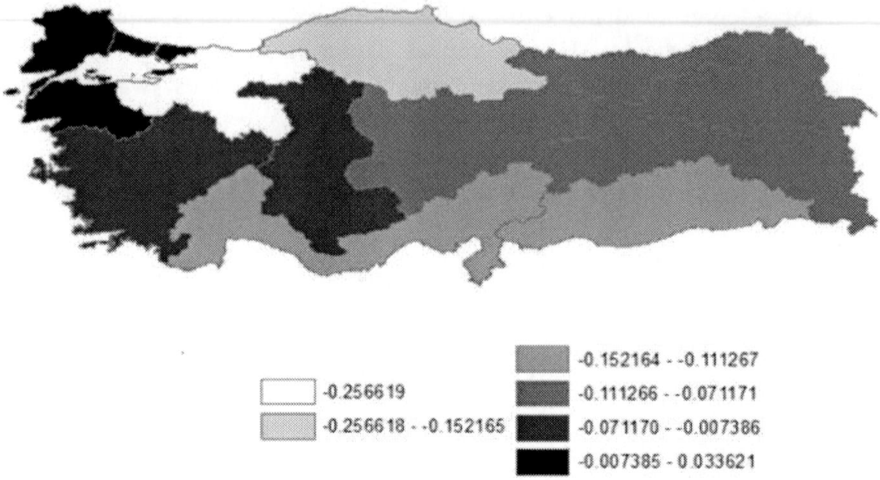

Figure 1. The Distribution of Human Capital Growth for 2002.

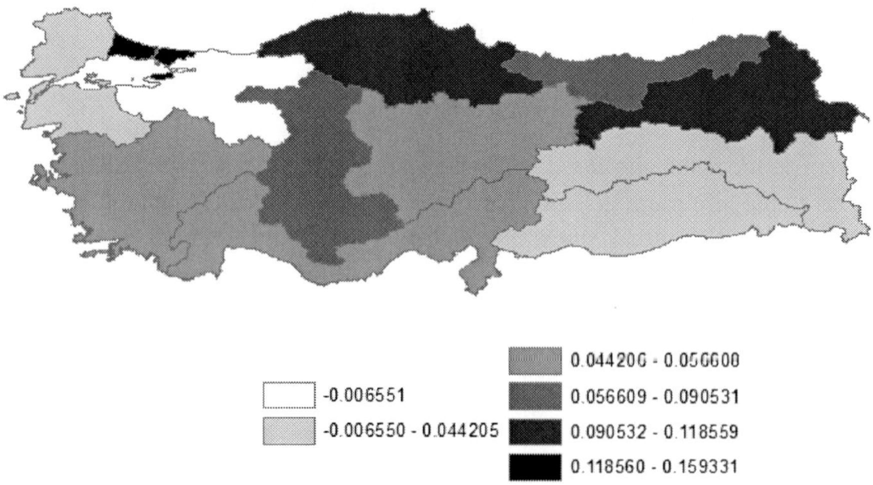

Figure 2. The Distribution of Human Capital Growth for 2009.

Table 1. The Estimation of Spatial Dynamic Panel

Coefficients	Coefficient Estimates
$\tilde{\lambda}_0$	0.3875* (2.871)
$\tilde{\gamma}_0$	0.3029* (2.097)
$\tilde{\rho}_0$	-0.2688* (-2.921)
$\tilde{\beta}_0$	0.2068* (2.206)
Constant	0.0038** (6.945)

Note: Values in parentheses are t-statistics. Significance indicated by *(1%), **(5%).

Per the estimation results of Table 1, signs of all coefficients are as expected, excluding the estimate of $\tilde{\rho}$, lagged neighborhood coefficient. The estimation of $\tilde{\lambda}_0$ coefficient measuring the effect of neighboring regions and the estimation of $\tilde{\gamma}_0$ coefficient measuring impact of lagged dependent variable are significant. As expected, the sign of the estimated coefficients is positive. Also as expected, $\tilde{\beta}_0$, the human capital convergence coefficient estimation, is positive. It is clear that there isn't convergence between NUTS-I level regions of Turkey.

CONCLUSION

All kinds of values related to enhancing people's talents, skills, and capabilities are known as human capital. Education and health-care expenses, for example, are important items of human capital. Universities have unique importance among educational services and expenses. Universities contribute technology and science while offering several social, cultural, and economic advantages to their regions. Universities provide educated manpower, also know as human capital. There is a positive correlation between increased workforce productivity and educated people. Besides, regions or economies having high levels of human capital easily apply and adapt to new technologies. Accordingly, investing in human capital is a factor that accelerates the economic growth of regions. In other words, increased quality of manpower is a factor triggering growth.

Several empirical studies in the literature demonstrate that human capital enhances the productivity of labor and contributes to growth. Thus, human capital has undeniable influence on growth. However, the convergence hypothesis focuses on growth by studying the convergence of income. As a matter of fact, income levels of low-income regions or cities in developing countries resemble each other, but educational differences are the basis of regional differences. Accordingly, recent studies in the literature offer empirical findings related to convergence of human capital. In convergence of human capital, it is assumed that regions initially having lower human capital will achieve a growth rate higher than the leading regions in the following years. Accordingly, there is a convergence of human capital between underdeveloped regions and leading regions. Spatial dynamic panel data analysis was used to test the existence of human capital convergence in Turkey in the period of 2002–2009 by analyzing 12 regions at NUTS-I level. Per the findings, convergence of human capital was not achieved in the regions. Regions initially having low human capital did not achieve faster growth rates than wealthy regions. This result conforms to the expectations because the study does not take into consideration the unique aspects of those regions. Disparities between regions of Turkey cause this result.

As for the number of students registered for higher education, students prefer universities located in the western regions and developed locations of the country. Thus, these regions experienced increased human capital but did not experience a decrease in marginal productivity of labor. On the contrary, underdeveloped regions having lower human capital did not demonstrate marginal productivity of labor higher than wealthy regions. In regions where there is a lack of human capital, marginal productivity of capital and labor is low. Thus, achieving convergence of human capital between regions of Turkey will be be difficult. The government should increase investments in human capital and implement policies for eliminating differences between the regions. In short, convergence of human capital is not determined for the period examined.

REFERENCES

Abramowitz, M., P. David, "Convergence and Deferred Cartch Up", in Ralph Landau, Timothy Taylor and Gavin Wrigth, eds., The Mosaic of Economic Growth, Standford: *Stanford University Press,* 1996, s. 21.

Altinbas, S., F: Doğruel, M. Guneş, "Türkiye'de Bölgesel Yakınsama: Kalkınmada Öncelikli İller Politikası Başarılı mı?", VI. ODTU Uluslararası Ekonomi Kongresi, 11-14 Eylül, Ankara, 2002.

Anselin, L. Spatial Econometrics: Methods and Models, Kluwer Academic Publishers, Dordrecht, The Netherlands, 1988

Anselin, L. And Bera, A. 1998, Spatial Dependence in Linear Regression Models with an Introduction to Spatial Econometrics. In: Ullah A and Giles D (eds), *Handbook of Applied Economic Statistics,* Marcel Dekker, New York, 237 - 289

Azzoni, C.R., L. M. Servo, "Education, Cost of Living and Regional Wage Inequality in Brazil", *Papers in Regional Science,* 81 (2), 2002, 157-175.

Baldacci, A., B. Clements, S. Gupta, O. Cui, "Social Spending, Human Capital, Growth in Developing Countries: Implications for Achieving the MDGs", *IMF Working Paper,* WP/04/217, November 2004.

Barr, N., "Income-Contingent Student Loans: An Idea Whose Time Has Come", Economics, Culture and Education: *Essay In Honour of Mark Blaug,* 1991.

Barro, R. J., "Economic Growth In A Cross Section of Countries", *The Quarterly Journal of Economics,* 106 (2), May 1991, 407-444.

Barro, R.J., X. Sala-I Martin, "Convergence Across States and Regions", *Brookings Papers on Economic Activity,* 1991, 107-182.

Barro, R.J., X. Sala-I Martin, "Convergence", *Journal of Political Economy,* 100, 1992, 223-251.

Barro, R., G. Mankiw, X. Sala-I Martin, "Capital Mobility in Neocalassical Models of Growth", *The American Economic Review,* March 1995, 103-115.

Barro, R. J., "Human Capital and Growth", *The American Economic Review,* Vol 91, No: 2, May 2001.

Becker, G. S., Human Capital, National Bureau of Economic Research, New York, 1964,

Benhabib, J., M. M. Spiegel, "The Role of Human Capital In Economic Development: Evidence From Aggregate Cross-Country Data*", Journal of Monetary Economics,* 34(2), 1994.

Berber, M., R. Yamak, S. Artan, "Türkiye'de Yakınlaşma Hipotezinin Bölgeler Bazında Geçerliliği Üzerine Ampirik Bir Çalışma: 1975-1997", *Ulusal Bölge Bilimi ve Bölge Planlama Kongresi Bildiriler Kitabı,* 2000, 51-59.

Cohn, E. , The Economics of Education, Lexington Books, D. C. *Health and Company,* London, 1972

Coulombe, S., J. F. Tremblay, "Human Capital and Regional Convergence İn Canada", *CSLS Conference on the State of Living Standarts and The Quality of Life in Canada,* October 30-21, 1998, Ontario.

Doğruel, F., A. S. Doğruel, "Türkiye'de Bölgesel Gelir Farklılıkları ve Büyüme", A. H. Köse, F. Şenses, E. Yeldan, İktisat Üzerine Yazılar I: Küresel Düzen, Birikim, Devlet ve Sınıflar-Korkut Boratav'a Armağan İçinde", İstanbul, İletişim Yayınları, 2003, 287-318.

Eicher, J. C., "Avrupa'da Yükseköğretimin Maliyeti ve Finansmanı", Çev. Harun CANSIZ, Marmara Üniversitesi Yayın No : 600, İstanbul, 2000.

Elhorst, P.J. "Specification and Estimation of Spatial Panel Data Models",*International Regional Science Review,* 26(3), 244-268, 2003

Elias, M., S. J. Rey, "Educational Performance and Spatial Convergence in Peru", Region et Developpement n, 22, 2011, 107-135.

Erk,N., S. Ateş, T. Direkci, "Convergence and Growth Within GAP Region and Overall Turkey's Region", IV. ODTU Uluslararası Ekonomi Kongresi, 13-16 Eylül, Ankara, 2000.

Filiztekin, A., "Convergence Across Industries and Provinces in Turkey", Koç University Working Paper, No. 1998/8.

Gezici, F., G.J.D. Hewings, "Regional Convergence and The Economic Perfprmance pf Peripheral Areas in Turkey", REAL *Discussion Paper,* No. 01-T-13, 2001.

Havermesh, D. S., A. Rees, *The Economics of Work and Pay,* Fourth Edition, New York, 1988.

Hellerstein, J. K., D. Neumark, "Are Earnings Profiles Steeper Than Productivity Profiles?", *The Journal of Human Resources,* Vol: XXX, Issue: 1, 2001.

Jones, B., "Economic integration and convergence of per-capita income in West Africa", *African Development Review,* 14(1), 2002, 18–47

Karaalp, H. S., F. Erdal, "Türkiye'de İller ve Bölgeler Arsaında Gelir Farklılıkları: Bir Sigma Yakınsama Analizi", I. *Uluslararası Davraz Kongresi, Bildiriler Kitabı,* 2009, 27-39.

Karaca, O., "Türkiye'de Bölgeler Arası Gelir Farklılıkları: Yakınsama Var mı?", *Türkiye Ekonomi Kurumu Tartışma Metni,* No: 2004/7.

Kilicaslan, Y., G. Özatağan, "Impact of Relative Population Change on Regional Income Convergence: Evidence From Turkey", *Review of Urban Regional Development Studies,* 19 (3), 2007, 210-223.

LEE, L.F. And J. YU, A spatial dynamic panel data model with both time and individual fixed effects. *Econometric Theory* 26, 2010, 564-597.

Liaslos, G., C. Papadas, "Human Capital Convergence in Greece: A Panel Data Analysis", *Working Paper,* 2009 (10).

Mankiw, G., D. Romer, D. Weil, "A Contribution to the Empirics of Economic Growth", *Quarterly Journal of Economics,* 107(2), 1992.

Marshall, A., "Education and Invention", Ed. Charles S. Benson, *Perspectives On The Economics of Education,* 1963.

Mcdonals, C. S, J. Roberts, "Growth and Multiple Forms of Human Capital in An Augmented Solow Model: A Panel Data Investigation", *Economic Letters,* 74, 2002.

Meler, G. M., Leading Issues In Economic Development, Third Edition, New York, *Oxford University Press,* 1976.

Mincer, J., "Economic Development, Growth of Human Capital and The Dynamics of The Wage Structure", *Journal of Economic Growth,* March 1996.

Paas, T., A. Kuusk, F. Schlitte, A. Vörk, "Econometric Analysis of Income Convergence in Selected EU Countries and Their Nuts III Level Regions", The University of Tartu Faculty of Economics and Business *Administration Working Paper ,* No. 60, 2007.

Rassekh, F., "The Convergence Hypothesis: History, Theory, and Evidence", *Open Economics Review,* 9, 1998, 85-105.

Schultz, T. W., Investment In Capital, The Role of Education and of Research, *The Free Pres A Division of The Macmillan Company*, 1971.

Sub, R., S. Smith, "Human Capital Convergence: International Evidence", March 2001, *IMF Working Paper.*

Tekir, S., "Bir Kamusal Hizmet Olarak Eğitim Beşeri Sermaye Yatırımlarının Önemi", *Dokuz Eylül Üniversitesi, İ.İ.B.F. Dergisi, Cilt : 2, Sayı : 1,* 1987.

Yamanoğlu, K.B., "Türkiye'de İller Arası Mali Yakınsama", Paper presented at EconAnadolu 2009: Anadolu International Conference in Economics June 17-19 2009, *Eskişehir,* Turkey.

Wang, Y., Y. Yao, "Sources of China's Economic Growth, 1952-1999: İncorporating Human Capital Accumulation", The World Bank, July 2001.

In: Economic and Social Issues …
Editor: Nilgün Çil Yavuz
ISBN: 978-1-62948-152-4

Chapter 8

THE FACTORS AFFECTING THE RULE OF LAW IN THE MIDDLE EAST AND NORTH AFRICA

Nurcan Metın [*]
Trakya University, Turkey

ABSTRACT

This paper examines the effects of the fiscal freedom, the government spending, the business freedom, the monetary freedom, the trade freedom, the investment freedom and the financial freedom on the rule of law (the property rights and the freedom from corruption) with the linear balanced pooled least squares models, the country specific fixed and random effects models and the country and period specific fixed and random effects models in the Middle East and North Africa from 1999 to 2012. From these models, the country and period specific fixed effects model results indicate that the business freedom, the monetary freedom and the financial freedom have significantly the effects on the property rights, while the fiscal freedom and the government spending have significantly the effects on the freedom from corruption. The country and period specific random effects model results indicate that the business freedom, the monetary freedom and the financial freedom have significantly the effects on the property rights, while the fiscal freedom, the government spending, the business freedom and the monetary

[*] E-mail: nurcanmetin@trakya.edu.tr

freedom have significantly the effects on the freedom from corruption. *Furthermore*, the results indicate that *the other variables have a positive impact* on the property rights and on the freedom from corruption, while the government spending *has a negative effect* on the freedom from corruption.

As a result, this empirical research supports the idea that the business freedom, the monetary freedom, the financial freedom, the fiscal freedom and the government spending are the important determinants of rule of law. In the Middle East and North Africa, we suggest that various government policies should be regulated according to these factors again.

Keywords: Property rights; Freedom from corruption; Rule of law; MENA

1. Introduction

The rule of law can be defined as the power and influence of law in society. Why the rule of law matters. Robinson (2008) says that "Without the rule of law, government officials are not bound by agreed standards of conduct. Without the rule of law, the dignity and equality of all people is not affirmed, and their ability to seek redress for grievances and fulfilment of societal commitments is limited. Without the rule of law, we have no way to ensure meaningful participation by people in formulating and enacting the norms and standards which organize society".

Looking at the literature, it is possible to see many studies about this topic. Some of these are summarized as follows. Graeff and Mehlko (2003) investigate the impact of various components of economic freedom on corruption. They find that there is a strong relation between economic freedom and corruption, and that this relation depends on a country's level of development. Licht, Goldschmidt and Schwartz (2007) examine the rule of law, corruption, and democratic accountability. They find that these norms correlate systematically and strongly with national scores on cultural dimensions and also differ across cultural regions of the world. Aidt, Dutta and Sena (2008) study the role of political accountability as a determinant of corruption and economic growth. Haggard and Tiede (2011) analyze the rule of law and economic growth.

They find that the correlation among different components of the rule of law concept are not tight among developing countries and that some inferences about the effects of property rights protection may not be warranted. Olsson and Hansson (2011) demonstrate that there is a robust negative relationship between the size of country territory and a measure of the rule of law for a large cross-section of countries. They show some evidence that whether the capital is centrally or peripherally located within the country matters for the average level of rule of law. Apergis, Dincer and Payne (2012) investigate the relationship between economic freedom and corruption using data from U.S. states covering almost a quarter of a century. They show that in the long-run economic freedom, per capita income, and education have a negative and statistically significant impact on corruption whereas income inequality has a positive and statistically significant impact.

Dawson (2013) examines the social determinants of the rule of law by comparing Jamaica and Barbados. He finds that the rule of law not only depends on characteristics of the state, but also on characteristics of society. Pieroni and d'Agostino (2013) show that the extent of the macro-effects on the measures of (micro) economic freedom for corruption can explain why a lack of competition policies and government regulations may yield more corruption.

Our aim in this paper is to examine the effects of the fiscal freedom, government spending, the business freedom, the monetary freedom, the trade freedom, the investment freedom and the financial freedom on the rule of law (the property rights and the freedom from corruption) with the linear balanced pooled least squares models, the country specific fixed and random effects models and the country and period specific fixed and random effects models in the Middle East & North Africa from 1999 to 2012.

2. Data and Description of Variables

In this paper, the data are taken from the http://www.heritage.org. The property rights and the freedom from corruption to explain the rule of law are taken as the dependent variables. The fiscal freedom, the government spending, the business freedom, the monetary freedom, the trade freedom, the investment freedom and the financial freedom are taken as the independent variables.

All of the variables are measured on a 0-to-100 scale. 100 represents the maximum freedom (see for more information about the description of variables http://www.heritage.org). The countries, the variables and the descriptive statistics is given in Table 1, 2 and 3. Figure 1 shows the individual cross sections of the variables.

Table 1. MENA Countries

Countries	Year
Algeria	1999-2012
Bahrain	1999-2012
Egypt	1999-2012
Iran	1999-2012
Israel	1999-2012
Jordan	1999-2012
Kuwait	1999-2012
Lebanon	1999-2012
Libya	1999-2012
Morocco	1999-2012
Oman	1999-2012
Qatar	1999-2012
Saudi Arabia	1999-2012
Syria	1999-2012
Tunisia	1999-2012
United Arab Emirates	1999-2012
Yemen	1999-2012

Table 2. Variables

Dependent Variables	Rule of Law	Property Rights (PR)*
		Freedom from Corruption (FC)*
Independent Variables	Limited Government	Fiscal Freedom (FF)*
		Government Spending (GS)*
	Regulatory Efficiency	Business Freedom (BF)*
		Monetary Freedom (MF)*
	Open Markets	Trade Freedom (TF)*
		Investment Freedom (IF)*
		Financial Freedom (FNF)*

* Variables are measured on a 0-to-100 scale. 100 represents the maximum freedom.

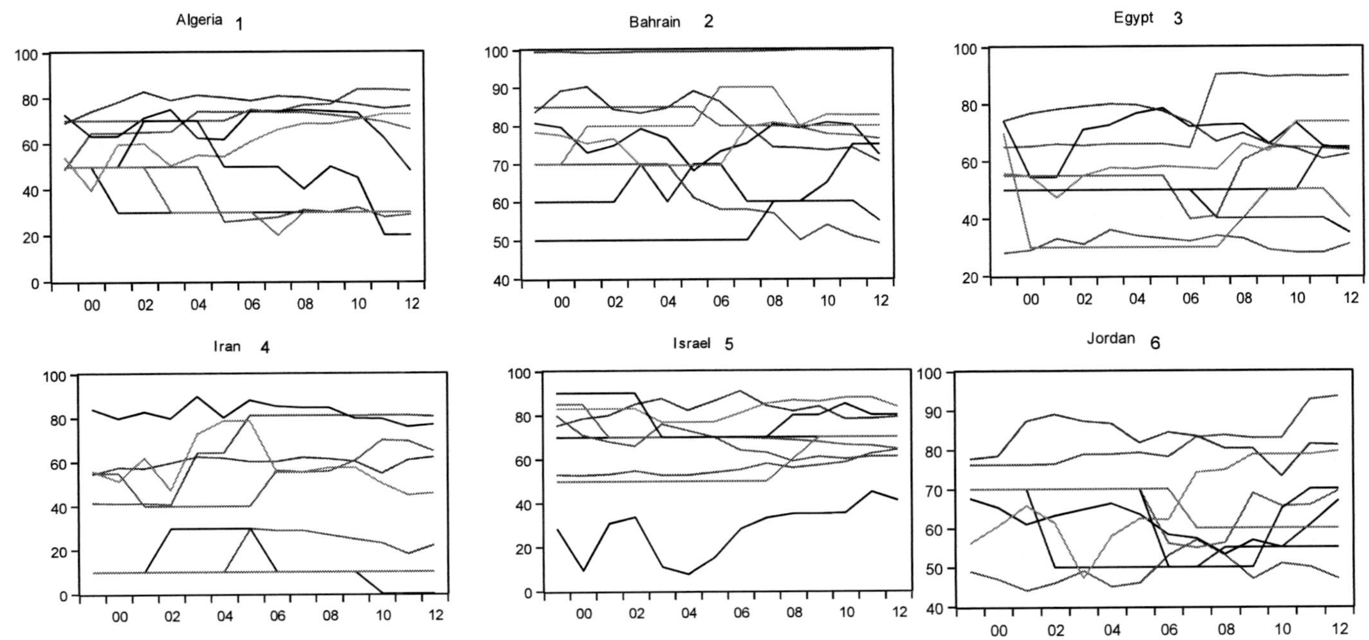

Figure 1. (Continued)

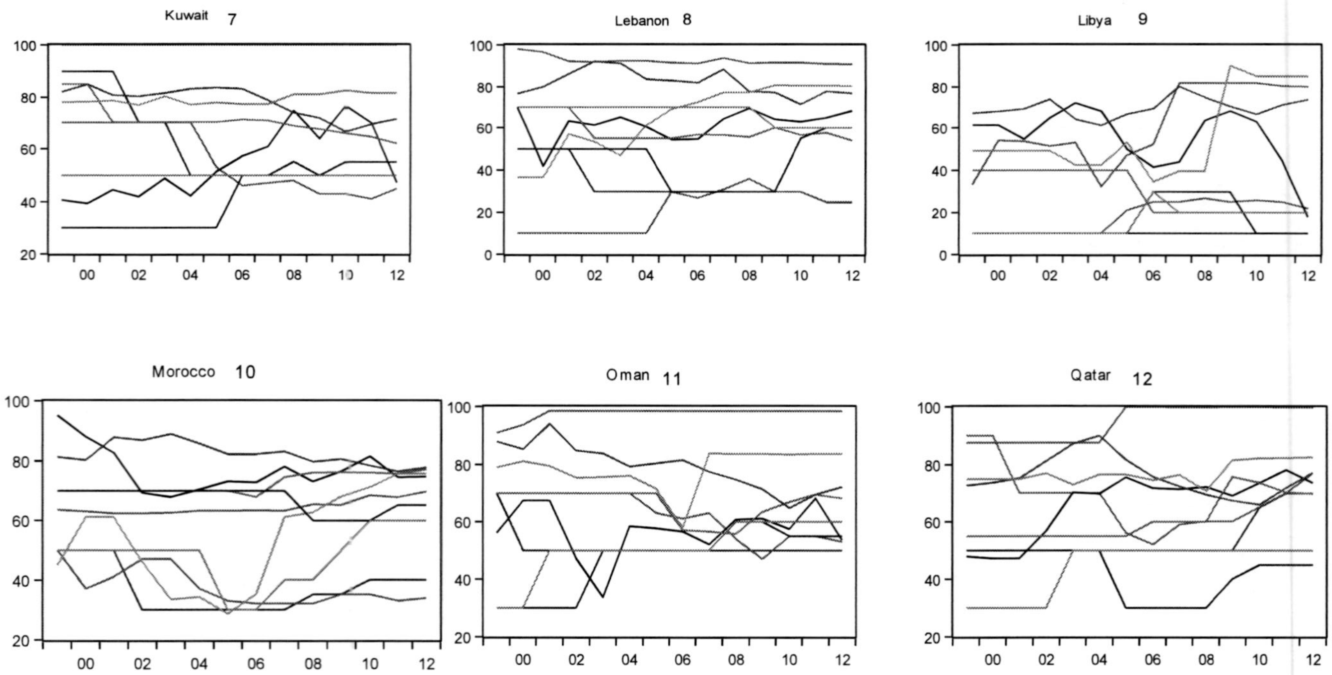
Kuwait 7
Lebanon 8
Libya 9
Morocco 10
Oman 11
Qatar 12
100
80
60
40
20
0
00
02
04
06
08
10
12

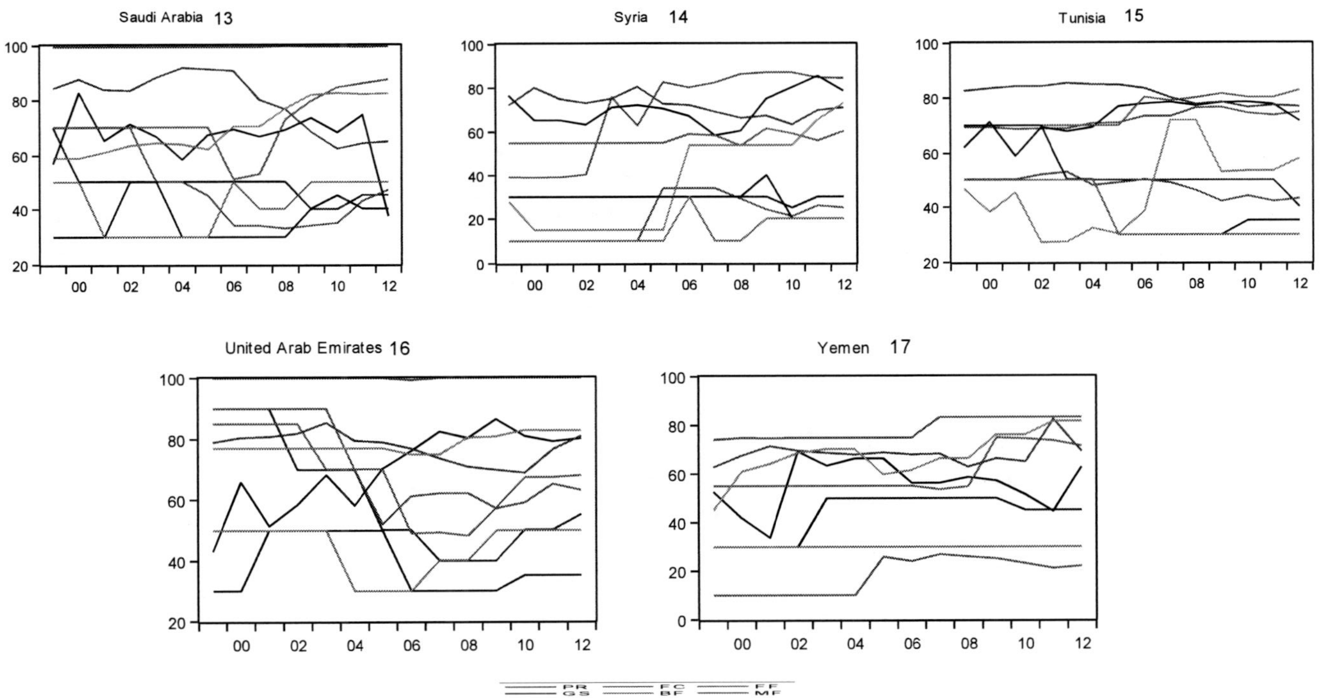

Figure 1. Individual Cross Sections of Variables.

Table 3. Descriptive Statistics

	Property Rights	Freedom from Corruption	Fiscal Freedom	Government Spending
Mean	43.71849	43.25210	81.31008	64.19832
Median	50.00000	45.00000	83.20000	67.30000
Maximum	90.00000	90.00000	99.90000	95.10000
Minimum	10.00000	10.00000	32.30000	7.600000
Std. Dev.	18.78528	20.88373	17.44617	15.12830
Skewness	-0.019033	0.113792	-0.692691	-1.163053
Kurtosis	2.756794	2.212095	2.616093	4.696627
Jarque-Bera	0.600933	6.669835	20.49448	82.20236
Probability	0.740473	0.035618	0.000035	0.000000
Sum	10405.00	10294.00	19351.80	15279.20
Sum Sq. Dev.	83634.14	103362.9	72135.46	54241.12
Observations	238	238	238	238

	Business Freedom	Monetary Freedom	Trade Freedom	Investment Freedom	Financial Freedom
Mean	64.14370	76.51933	65.71765	44.91597	42.98319
Median	69.40000	78.05000	70.75000	50.00000	50.00000
Maximum	87.50000	94.00000	90.00000	90.00000	90.00000
Minimum	20.00000	54.60000	15.00000	0.000000	10.00000
Std. Dev.	13.53387	8.298429	16.78378	19.10424	19.97698
Skewness	-1.009001	-0.389543	-1.046743	-0.033016	0.024510
Kurtosis	4.628055	2.520629	3.611916	2.631566	2.310613
Jarque-Bera	66.66869	8.297980	47.17481	1.389360	4.736774
Probability	0.000000	0.015780	0.000000	0.499234	0.093632
Sum	15266.20	18211.60	15640.80	10690.00	10230.00
Sum Sq. Dev.	43410.29	16320.75	66761.79	86498.32	94581.93
Observations	238	238	238	238	238

3. Model Specifications and Estimates

This section summarizes the model specifications and gives the estimates of the linear balanced pooled least squares models, the country specific fixed and random effects models and the country and period specific fixed and random effects models. While the pooled model assumes that there are no effects, the fixed or random effects models allow for either fixed or random effects in either the cross-section or period dimension, or both. While the estimates for the pooled model are obtained by the pooled least squares estimator, the estimates for the fixed effects models are obtained by the least squares dummy variable estimator or the fixed effects estimator. The random effects specification assumes that the corresponding effects are realizations of independent random variables with mean zero and finite variance. The random effects specification assumes that the effect is uncorrelated with the idiosyncratic residual.

The estimates for the random effects model are obtained by the generalized least squares (GLS) estimator. However, the type of standard errors depends on the choice of coefficient covariance method. For the standard error estimates in these models, we prefer to use the White period method (cluster-robust standard errors) because the *White period* method assumes that the errors for a cross-section are heteroskedastic and serially correlated (cross-section clustered). The coefficient covariances are calculated using a White cross-section clustered estimator. We obtain the following outputs in the last three columns of tables. The coefficient estimates have not changed, but the standard errors, t-values, and p-values are different. The model estimates is evaluated according to White period standard errors in the last three columns of tables [Additional details on models are provided in Baltagi (2005), Baltagi and Chang (1994), Hsiao (2003), and Hill, Griffiths and Lim (2011)].

Pooled Least Squares Estimates

The pooled least squares estimates of the rule of law are displayed in Table 4 and 5 alongside least-squares standard errors, t-values and p- values, and the corresponding White period standard errors, t-values and p-values. Looking at the estimates of the property rights and the freedom from corruption in Table 4 and 5, we find that the government spending, the business freedom and the monetary freedom have significantly the effects on the property rights, and that the business freedom, the monetary freedom and the trade freedom have significantly the effects on the freedom from corruption.

Table 4. Pooled Least Squares Estimates of Property Rights

		Least Squares Std. Errors			White Period Std. Errors		
Variable	Coefficient	Std. Error	t-Statistic	Prob.	Std. Error	t-Statistic	Prob.
Fiscal freedom	0.128550	0.058511	2.197009	0.0290	0.076004	1.691354	0.0921
Government spending	-0.257457	0.053911	-4.775597	0.0000	0.085985	-2.994219	0.0031
Business freedom	0.534168	0.064826	8.240020	0.0000	0.158976	3.360058	0.0009
Monetary freedom	0.501762	0.110028	4.560321	0.0000	0.166436	3.014747	0.0029
Trade freedom	0.139848	0.057458	2.433926	0.0157	0.078592	1.779424	0.0765
Investment freedom	0.106438	0.056037	1.899409	0.0588	0.093138	1.142800	0.2543
Financial freedom	0.130695	0.059972	2.179252	0.0303	0.148590	0.879567	0.3800
C	-42.45256	10.23942	-4.145993	0.0000	15.59262	-2.722606	0.0070

Table 5. Pooled Least Squares Estimates of Freedom from Corruption

		Least Squares Std. Errors			White Period Std. Errors		
Variable	Coefficient	Std. Error	t-Statistic	Prob.	Std. Error	t-Statistic	Prob.
Fiscal freedom	0.241769	0.075962	3.182755	0.0017	0.124071	1.948643	0.0526
Government spending	-0.168602	0.069990	-2.408954	0.0168	0.107316	-1.571077	0.1175
Business freedom	0.437623	0.084160	5.199887	0.0000	0.155990	2.805456	0.0055
Monetary freedom	0.836511	0.142843	5.856152	0.0000	0.185799	4.502244	0.0000
Trade freedom	0.391091	0.074595	5.242894	0.0000	0.161719	2.418342	0.0164
Investment freedom	0.112367	0.072750	1.544566	0.1238	0.095956	1.171034	0.2428
Financial freedom	-0.131252	0.077859	-1.685765	0.0932	0.222370	-0.590241	0.5556
C	-82.76932	13.29328	-6.226402	0.0000	23.47504	-3.525844	0.0005

Table 6. Country Specific Dummy Variable Estimates of Property Rights

		Least Squares Std. Errors			White Period Std. Errors		
Variable	Coefficient	Std. Error	t-Statistic	Prob.	Std. Error	t-Statistic	Prob.
Algeria	-11.44057	12.46582	-0.917755	0.3598	18.19960	-0.628617	0.5303
Bahrain	6.868678	14.52568	0.472865	0.6368	21.55355	0.318680	0.7503
Egypt	8.766865	11.73270	0.747217	0.4558	16.31289	0.537420	0.5915
Iran	-15.65046	10.21154	-1.532625	0.1268	12.56890	-1.245173	0.2144
Israel	14.61673	13.22439	1.105287	0.2703	22.77757	0.641716	0.5217
Jordan	6.426148	13.33821	0.481785	0.6305	19.95385	0.322051	0.7477
Kuwait	15.18477	12.84974	1.181718	0.2386	19.93900	0.761561	0.4472
Lebanon	-12.98843	12.93104	-1.004438	0.3163	18.77430	-0.691820	0.4898
Libya	-15.25317	9.591234	-1.590324	0.1132	12.85591	-1.186471	0.2368
Morocco	-10.83674	13.30331	-0.814590	0.4162	18.94170	-0.572110	0.5678
Oman	6.355506	12.88954	0.493075	0.6225	19.59157	0.324400	0.7460
Qatar	14.06055	12.47144	1.127420	0.2608	18.00710	0.780834	0.4358
Saudi Arabia	4.537670	12.94655	0.350493	0.7263	19.09387	0.237651	0.8124
Syria	-3.738540	10.85776	-0.344320	0.7309	14.33265	-0.260841	0.7945
Tunisia	1.593761	12.74909	0.125010	0.9006	18.34290	0.086887	0.9308
United Arab Emirates	18.68122	12.92150	1.445747	0.1497	18.73354	0.997207	0.3198
Yemen	-6.993446	11.23258	-0.622604	0.5342	16.66807	-0.419571	0.6752
Fiscal freedom	-0.085375	0.057213	-1.492226	0.1371	0.074462	-1.146550	0.2528
Government spending	-0.129761	0.051920	-2.499253	0.0132	0.100363	-1.292915	0.1974
Business freedom	0.389598	0.064400	6.049651	0.0000	0.166298	2.342767	0.0201
Monetary freedom	0.347493	0.091436	3.800378	0.0002	0.153055	2.270376	0.0242
Trade freedom	-0.015064	0.047644	-0.316190	0.7522	0.070796	-0.212786	0.8317
Investment freedom	-0.030514	0.048331	-0.631351	0.5285	0.063548	-0.480176	0.6316
Financial freedom	0.199694	0.062905	3.174513	0.0017	0.065097	3.067638	0.0024

Table 7. Country Specific Dummy Variable Estimates of Freedom from Corruption

		Least Squares Std. Errors			White Period Std. Errors		
Variable	Coefficient	Std. Error	t-Statistic	Prob.	Std. Error	t-Statistic	Prob.
Algeria	-16.96788	14.99040	-1.131917	0.2589	19.98716	-0.848939	0.3969
Bahrain	-1.598920	17.46742	-0.091537	0.9272	25.24056	-0.063347	0.9495
Egypt	-18.34136	14.10880	-1.299994	0.1950	18.73790	-0.978838	0.3288
Iran	-16.60722	12.27958	-1.352425	0.1777	16.69958	-0.994469	0.3211
Israel	-1.368137	15.90258	-0.086032	0.9315	19.14502	-0.071462	0.9431
Jordan	-12.14183	16.03946	-0.756997	0.4499	22.03497	-0.551025	0.5822
Kuwait	-7.655275	15.45207	-0.495421	0.6208	21.53627	-0.355460	0.7226
Lebanon	-38.88486	15.54983	-2.500662	0.0131	22.34773	-1.739992	0.0833
Libya	-23.82770	11.53365	-2.065929	0.0400	14.84193	-1.605431	0.1099
Morocco	-17.08248	15.99750	-1.067822	0.2868	21.53371	-0.793290	0.4285
Oman	-0.540844	15.49993	-0.034893	0.9722	21.24327	-0.025460	0.9797
Qatar	11.54548	14.99715	0.769845	0.4422	20.35484	0.567210	0.5712
Saudi Arabia	-11.94944	15.56848	-0.767540	0.4436	22.20982	-0.538025	0.5911
Syria	-24.55461	13.05668	-1.880617	0.0614	18.70342	-1.312840	0.1906
Tunisia	-7.458139	15.33103	-0.486473	0.6271	21.82063	-0.341793	0.7328
United Arab Emirates	12.67892	15.53836	0.815975	0.4154	21.57748	0.587599	0.5574
Yemen	-34.16226	13.50740	-2.529151	0.0122	17.72948	-1.926861	0.0553
Fiscal freedom	0.162678	0.068800	2.364510	0.0189	0.128817	1.262857	0.2080
Government spending	-0.250487	0.062435	-4.011980	0.0001	0.096055	-2.607742	0.0098
Business freedom	0.187233	0.077442	2.417713	0.0165	0.101554	1.843691	0.0666
Monetary freedom	0.507235	0.109954	4.613155	0.0000	0.137486	3.689348	0.0003
Trade freedom	0.068928	0.057292	1.203100	0.2303	0.107098	0.643602	0.5205
Investment freedom	0.057739	0.058120	0.993452	0.3216	0.094040	0.613985	0.5399
Financial freedom	0.010433	0.075645	0.137926	0.8904	0.148160	0.070420	0.9439

The results from applying the least squares dummy variable estimator to the property rights equation and the freedom from corruption equation for the 17 countries appear in Table 6 and 7. Turning to the estimates in Table 6, we find that none of countries are significantly different from zero. However, we find that the business freedom, the monetary freedom and the financial freedom have significantly the effects on the property rights. Turning to the estimates in Table 7, we find that none of countries are significantly different from zero. But, we find that the government spending and the monetary freedom have significantly the effects on the freedom from corruption. Since these intercepts have relatively large standard errors, it is advisable to formally test with Wald test whether they might be all equal, in which case there is no individual heterogeneity. The value of the test statistic F=21.89314 yields a *p-value* of *0.0000* for the property rights and *F= 27.73163* yields a *p-value* of *0.0000* for the freedom from corruption (Table 8); we reject the null hypothesis that the intercept parameters for all individuals are equal. We conclude that there are differences in individual intercepts, and that the data should not be pooled into a single model with a common intercept parameter. The results from applying the fixed effects estimator to the property rights equation and the freedom from corruption equation appear in Table 9 and 10. We find that the fixed effects estimates are identical to the dummy variable estimates. Also, the fixed effects can be tested with Likelihood Ratio. Two versions of the likelihood ratio test appear in Table 8 and 11, an F-test and a X^2 −test. The F-test is identical to the one we considered earlier and gives the same test result. The random effects estimates are given in Table 12 and 13 for the rule of law.

Table 8. Testing the Fixed Effects with Wald Test for Rule of Law

	Wald Test for Property Rights			Wald Test for Freedom from Corruption		
Test Statistic	Value	df	Probability	Value	df	Probability
F-statistic	21.89314	(16, 214)	0.0000	27.73163	(16, 214)	0.0000
Chi-square	350.2902	16	0.0000	443.7060	16	0.0000

Looking at the estimates of the property rights and the freedom from corruption in Table 12 and 13, we find that the business freedom, the monetary freedom and the financial freedom have significantly the effects on the property rights, and that the government spending, the business freedom and the monetary freedom have significantly the effects on the freedom from corruption. Also, we find that there is no difference between the fixed effects estimates and the random effects estimates for the property rights and the freedom from corruption with Hausman test (Table 14 and 15).

Country Specific Fixed and Random Effects Estimates

Table 16 and 17 give results from application of the country and period specific fixed effects estimates. We find that the business freedom and the financial freedom have significantly the effects on the property rights, and that the fiscal freedom, the government spending and the monetary freedom have significantly the effects on the freedom from corruption. Table 18 and 19 show results from application of the country and period specific random effects estimates. We find that the business freedom, the monetary freedom and the financial freedom have significantly the effects on the property rights, and that the government spending, the business freedom and the monetary freedom have significantly the effects on the freedom from corruption.

Finally, the variables which haven't significantly the effects are omitted from the models, and the country and period specific fixed and random effects models are estimated as Table 20, 21, 22 and 23. Looking at the estimates of the property rights and the freedom from corruption in Table 20, 21, 22 and 23, we conclude that the business freedom, the monetary freedom and the financial freedom have an influence on the property rights, and that the fiscal freedom and the government spending have an influence on the freedom from corruption for the country and period specific fixed effects models (Table 20 and 21). Furthermore, we conclude that the business freedom, the monetary freedom and the financial freedom have an influence on the property rights and that the fiscal freedom, the government spending, the business freedom and the monetary freedom have an influence on the freedom from corruption for the country and period specific random effects models (Table 22 and 23). We say that the other variables have a positive impact on the property rights and on the freedom from corruption, while the government spending has a negative effect on the freedom from corruption for the country and period specific fixed and random effects models (see in Table 21 and 23). Furthermore, we reject the null hypothesis according to Likelihood Ratio Test cross-section and period fixed effects for property rights and freedom from corruption (Table 24 and 25). We conclude that the data should not be pooled into a single model with a common intercept parameter.

Table 9. Country Specific Fixed Effects Estimates of Property Rights

		Least Squares Std. Errors			White Period Std. Errors		
Variable	Coefficient	Std. Error	t-Statistic	Prob.	Std. Error	t-Statistic	Prob.
Fiscal freedom	-0.085375	0.057213	-1.492226	0.1371	0.074462	-1.146550	0.2528
Government spending	-0.129761	0.051920	-2.499253	0.0132	0.100363	-1.292915	0.1974
Business freedom	0.389598	0.064400	6.049651	0.0000	0.166298	2.342767	0.0201
Monetary freedom	0.347493	0.091436	3.800378	0.0002	0.153055	2.270376	0.0242
Trade freedom	-0.015064	0.047644	-0.316190	0.7522	0.070796	-0.212786	0.8317
Investment freedom	-0.030514	0.048331	-0.631351	0.5285	0.063548	-0.480176	0.6316
Financial freedom	0.199694	0.062905	3.174513	0.0017	0.065097	3.067638	0.0024
C	1.187680	12.12220	0.097976	0.9220	17.87137	0.066457	0.9471

Table 10. Country Specific Fixed Effects Estimates of Freedom from Corruption

		Least Squares Std. Errors			White Period Std. Errors		
Variable	Coefficient	Std. Error	t-Statistic	Prob.	Std. Error	t-Statistic	Prob.
Fiscal freedom	0.162678	0.068800	2.364510	0.0189	0.128817	1.262857	0.2080
Government spending	-0.250487	0.062435	-4.011980	0.0001	0.096055	-2.607742	0.0098
Business freedom	0.187233	0.077442	2.417713	0.0165	0.101554	1.843691	0.0666
Monetary freedom	0.507235	0.109954	4.613155	0.0000	0.137486	3.689348	0.0003
Trade freedom	0.068928	0.057292	1.203100	0.2303	0.107098	0.643602	0.5205
Investment freedom	0.057739	0.058120	0.993452	0.3216	0.094040	0.613985	0.5399
Financial freedom	0.010433	0.075645	0.137926	0.8904	0.148160	0.070420	0.9439
C	-12.28921	14.57718	-0.843044	0.4001	20.02418	-0.613718	0.5401

Table 11. Likelihood Ratio Test Cross-Section Fixed Effects

	Property Rights			Freedom from Corruption		
Effects Test	Statistic	d.f.	Prob.	Statistic	d.f.	Prob.
Cross-section F	21.893139	(16,214)	0.0000	27.731627	(16,214)	0.0000
Cross-section Chi-square	230.763060	16	0.0000	267.222130	16	0.0000

Table 12. Country Specific Random Effects Estimates of Property Rights

		GLS Std. Errors			White Period Std. Errors		
Variable	Coefficient	Std. Error	t-Statistic	Prob.	Std. Error	t-Statistic	Prob.
Fiscal freedom	-0.066667	0.055013	-1.211837	0.2268	0.062421	-1.068024	0.2866
Government spending	-0.143563	0.050069	-2.867283	0.0045	0.085309	-1.682855	0.0938
Business freedom	0.424241	0.061103	6.943061	0.0000	0.135925	3.121146	0.0020
Monetary freedom	0.406211	0.086511	4.695495	0.0000	0.144149	2.817994	0.0053
Trade freedom	0.009858	0.046161	0.213563	0.8311	0.064816	0.152097	0.8792
Investment freedom	-0.005880	0.046278	-0.127069	0.8990	0.060508	-0.097184	0.9227
Financial freedom	0.234400	0.058306	4.020180	0.0001	0.062137	3.772295	0.0002
C	-10.39868	11.07586	-0.938860	0.3488	13.82960	-0.751915	0.4529

Table 13. Country Specific Random Effects Estimates of Freedom from Corruption

Variable	Coefficient	GLS Std. Errors			White Period Std. Errors		
		Std. Error	t-Statistic	Prob.	Std. Error	t-Statistic	Prob.
Fiscal freedom	0.177646	0.066105	2.687334	0.0077	0.110888	1.602031	0.1105
Government spending	-0.246846	0.060167	-4.102650	0.0001	0.089354	-2.762567	0.0062
Business freedom	0.230632	0.073412	3.141629	0.0019	0.076238	3.025162	0.0028
Monetary freedom	0.567438	0.103943	5.459145	0.0000	0.124823	4.545938	0.0000
Trade freedom	0.096481	0.055480	1.739032	0.0834	0.107923	0.893978	0.3723
Investment freedom	0.076440	0.055610	1.374577	0.1706	0.081800	0.934477	0.3510
Financial freedom	0.033846	0.070028	0.483329	0.6293	0.127846	0.264745	0.7914
C	-24.78743	13.28931	-1.865216	0.0634	16.75805	-1.479136	0.1405

Table 14. Correlated Random Effects - Hausman Test for Property Rights

Test cross-section random effects				
Test Summary		Chi-Sq. Statistic	Chi-Sq. d.f.	Prob.
Cross-section random		11.474953	7	0.1192
Cross-section random effects test comparisons:				
Variable	Fixed	Random	Var(Diff.)	Prob.
Fiscal freedom	-0.085375	-0.066667	0.000247	0.2338
Government spending	-0.129761	-0.143563	0.000189	0.3151
Business freedom	0.389598	0.424241	0.000414	0.0886
Monetary freedom	0.347493	0.406211	0.000877	0.0473
Trade freedom	-0.015064	0.009858	0.000139	0.0346
Investment freedom	-0.030514	-0.005880	0.000194	0.0772
Financial freedom	0.199694	0.234400	0.000557	0.1416

Table 15. Correlated Random Effects - Hausman Test for Freedom from Corruption

Test cross-section random effects				
Test Summary		Chi-Sq. Statistic	Chi-Sq. d.f.	Prob.
Cross-section random		13.443482	7	0.0620
Cross-section random effects test comparisons:				
Variable	Fixed	Random	Var(Diff.)	Prob.
Fiscal freedom	0.162678	0.177646	0.000364	0.4325
Government spending	-0.250487	-0.246846	0.000278	0.8271
Business freedom	0.187233	0.230632	0.000608	0.0784
Monetary freedom	0.507235	0.567438	0.001286	0.0932
Trade freedom	0.068928	0.096481	0.000204	0.0540
Investment freedom	0.057739	0.076440	0.000285	0.2683
Financial freedom	0.010433	0.033846	0.000818	0.4131

Country and Period Specific Fixed and Random Effects Estimates

Table 16. Country and Period Specific Fixed Effects Estimates of Property Right

		Least Squares Std. Errors			White Period Std. Errors		
Variable	Coefficient	Std. Error	t-Statistic	Prob.	Std. Error	t-Statistic	Prob.
Fiscal freedom	0.099643	0.062253	1.600630	0.1110	0.073606	1.353749	0.1773
Government spending	-0.070787	0.049726	-1.423551	0.1561	0.089596	-0.790076	0.4304
Business freedom	0.315801	0.063539	4.970171	0.0000	0.155009	2.037316	0.0429
Monetary freedom	0.253247	0.106047	2.388059	0.0179	0.131206	1.930148	0.0550
Trade freedom	0.051366	0.048160	1.066566	0.2874	0.065513	0.784056	0.4339
Investment freedom	-0.024018	0.045939	-0.522826	0.6017	0.074661	-0.321698	0.7480
Financial freedom	0.169186	0.058408	2.896609	0.0042	0.081674	2.071480	0.0396
C	-9.043054	11.43538	-0.790796	0.4300	19.05676	-0.474532	0.6356

Table 17. Country and Period Specific Fixed Effects Estimates of Freedom from Corruption

		Least Squares Std. Errors			White Period Std. Errors		
Variable	Coefficient	Std. Error	t-Statistic	Prob.	Std. Error	t-Statistic	Prob.
Fiscal freedom	0.375497	0.077983	4.815148	0.0000	0.167168	2.246226	0.0258
Government spending	-0.199559	0.062291	-3.203681	0.0016	0.076375	-2.612890	0.0097
Business freedom	0.147275	0.079594	1.850320	0.0657	0.109464	1.345420	0.1800
Monetary freedom	0.252771	0.132843	1.902773	0.0585	0.121307	2.083728	0.0384
Trade freedom	0.186776	0.060329	3.095954	0.0022	0.132182	1.413018	0.1592
Investment freedom	0.037592	0.057547	0.653238	0.5143	0.106471	0.353071	0.7244
Financial freedom	0.005589	0.073167	0.076387	0.9392	0.134839	0.041449	0.9670
C	-17.46002	14.32485	-1.218862	0.2243	19.31128	-0.904136	0.3670

Table 18. Country and Period Specific Random Effects Estimates of Property Right

		GLS Std. Errors			White Period Std. Errors		
Variable	Coefficient	Std. Error	t-Statistic	Prob.	Std. Error	t-Statistic	Prob.
Fiscal freedom	-0.046819	0.055584	-0.842302	0.4005	0.062126	-0.753617	0.4518
Government spending	-0.134358	0.049895	-2.692810	0.0076	0.087146	-1.541763	0.1245
Business freedom	0.408474	0.061410	6.651596	0.0000	0.138770	2.943531	0.0036
Monetary freedom	0.403257	0.088268	4.568567	0.0000	0.145412	2.773203	0.0060
Trade freedom	0.014678	0.046207	0.317663	0.7510	0.064012	0.229303	0.8188
Investment freedom	-0.003128	0.046054	-0.067931	0.9459	0.060125	-0.052033	0.9585
Financial freedom	0.223684	0.058144	3.847092	0.0002	0.062036	3.605714	0.0004
C	-11.34582	11.17747	-1.015061	0.3111	13.75804	-0.824668	0.4104

Table 19. Country and Period Specific Random Effects Estimates of Freedom from Corruption

		GLS Std. Errors			White Period Std. Errors		
Variable	Coefficient	Std. Error	t-Statistic	Prob.	Std. Error	t-Statistic	Prob.
Fiscal freedom	0.176273	0.066965	2.632300	0.0091	0.111872	1.575671	0.1165
Government spending	-0.247238	0.060934	-4.057471	0.0001	0.089634	-2.758297	0.0063
Business freedom	0.227099	0.074425	3.051362	0.0025	0.077694	2.922998	0.0038
Monetary freedom	0.562837	0.105355	5.342278	0.0000	0.125159	4.496972	0.0000
Trade freedom	0.094067	0.056143	1.675494	0.0952	0.107486	0.875155	0.3824
Investment freedom	0.075098	0.056326	1.333262	0.1838	0.082441	0.910930	0.3633
Financial freedom	0.032611	0.071120	0.458544	0.6470	0.128589	0.253609	0.8000
C	-23.79995	13.56813	-1.754107	0.0807	16.91846	-1.406744	0.1609

Table 20. Country and Period Specific Fixed Effects Estimates of Property Rights

		Least Squares Std. Errors			White Period Std. Errors		
Variable	Coefficient	Std. Error	t-Statistic	Prob.	Std. Error	t-Statistic	Prob.
Business freedom	0.342011	0.062022	5.514391	0.0000	0.167299	2.044317	0.0422
Monetary freedom	0.325994	0.099877	3.263944	0.0013	0.130413	2.499713	0.0132
Financial freedom	0.169809	0.057266	2.965260	0.0034	0.081588	2.081314	0.0386
C	-10.46316	9.263283	-1.129531	0.2600	16.92232	-0.618306	0.5371
$R^2 = 0.90$ $\bar{R}^2 = 0.88$							

Table 21. Country and Period Specific Fixed Effects Estimates of Freedom from Corruption

		Least Squares Std. Errors			White Period Std. Errors		
Variable	Coefficient	Std. Error	t-Statistic	Prob.	Std. Error	t-Statistic	Prob.
Fiscal freedom	0.465498	0.074544	6.244582	0.0000	0.165262	2.816720	0.0053
Government spending	-0.207669	0.063279	-3.281828	0.0012	0.082584	-2.514656	0.0127
C	18.73446	7.854751	2.385112	0.0180	15.59389	1.201398	0.2310
$R^2 = 0.87$ $\bar{R}^2 = 0.85$							

Table 22. Country and Period Specific Random Effects Estimates of Property Rights

		Least Squares Std. Errors			White Period Std. Errors		
Variable	Coefficient	Std. Error	t-Statistic	Prob.	Std. Error	t-Statistic	Prob.
Business freedom	0.383263	0.059218	6.472017	0.0000	0.155468	2.465226	0.0144
Monetary freedom	0.388610	0.090527	4.292744	0.0000	0.144927	2.681416	0.0079
Financial freedom	0.204113	0.053161	3.839494	0.0002	0.065783	3.102808	0.0022
C	-19.37499	8.804509	-2.200575	0.0287	15.10969	-1.282289	0.2010

Table 23. Country and Period Specific Random Effects Estimates of Freedom from Corruption

Variable	Coefficient	Least Squares Std. Errors			White Period Std. Errors		
		Std. Error	t-Statistic	Prob.	Std. Error	t-Statistic	Prob.
Fiscal freedom	0.214841	0.059608	3.604205	0.0004	0.108909	1.972667	0.0497
Government spending	-0.243978	0.060786	-4.013747	0.0001	0.090524	-2.695163	0.0075
Business freedom	0.206472	0.074044	2.788508	0.0057	0.095075	2.171677	0.0309
Monetary freedom	0.481076	0.099713	4.824612	0.0000	0.150846	3.189181	0.0016
C	-8.609187	12.66621	-0.679697	0.4974	20.74140	-0.415073	0.6785

Table 24. Likelihood Ratio Test Cross-Section and Period Fixed Effects for Property Rights

Effects Test	Statistic	d.f.	Prob.
Cross-section F	36.093958	(16,205)	0.0000
Cross-section Chi-square	318.798191	16	0.0000
Period F	4.695177	(13,205)	0.0000
Period Chi-square	62.029119	13	0.0000
Cross-Section/Period F	21.778624	(29,205)	0.0000
Cross-Section/Period Chi-square	334.702326	29	0.0000

Table 25. Likelihood Ratio Test Cross-Section and Period Fixed Effects for Freedom from Corruption

Effects Test	Statistic	d.f.	Prob.
Cross-section F	52.335546	(16,206)	0.0000
Cross-section Chi-square	386.115435	16	0.0000
Period F	3.660892	(13,206)	0.0000
Period Chi-square	49.468039	13	0.0000
Cross-Section/Period F	31.755432	(29,206)	0.0000
Cross-Section/Period Chi-square	404.446798	29	0.0000

CONCLUSION

Our purpose in this paper is to explore the effects of the fiscal freedom, the government spending, the business freedom, the monetary freedom, the trade freedom, the investment freedom and the financial freedom on the rule of law (the property rights and the freedom from corruption) with the linear balanced pooled least squares models, the country specific fixed and random effects models and the country and period specific fixed and random effects models in the Middle East & North Africa from 1999 to 2012. The first finding is that that the business freedom, the monetary freedom and the financial freedom have an influence on the property rights, and that the fiscal freedom and the government spending have an influence on the freedom from corruption for the country and period specific fixed effects models. The second finding is that the business freedom, the monetary freedom and the financial freedom have an influence on the property rights and that the fiscal freedom, the government spending, the business freedom and the monetary freedom have an influence on the freedom from corruption for the country and period specific random effects models. The other finding is that the other variables have a positive impact on the property rights and on the freedom from corruption, while the government spending has a negative effect on the freedom from corruption. Last of all, this empirical research supports the idea that the business freedom, the monetary freedom, the financial freedom, the fiscal freedom and the government spending are the important determinants of rule of law. In the Middle East and North Africa, we suggest that various government policies should be regulated according to these factors again.

REFERENCES

Aidt, T., Dutta, J. and Sena, V. (2008). Governance regimes, corruption and growth: Theory and evidence, *Journal of Comparative Economics,* 36, 195–220.

Apergis, N., Dincer, O. and Payne, J. (2012). Live free or bribe: On the causal dynamics between economic freedom and corruption in U.S. states, *European Journal of Political Economy,* 28, 215–226.

Baltagi, B. (2005). *Econometric analysis of panel data,* (Third Edition). West Sussex, England: John Wiley & Sons.

Baltagi, B. and Chang, Y. (1994). Incomplete panels: A comparative study of alternative estimators for the unbalanced one-way error component regression model," *Journal of Econometrics*, 62, 67-89.

Dawson, A. (2013). The social determinants of the rule of law: A comparison of Jamaica and Barbados, *World Development*, 45, 314–324.

Graeff, P., and Mehlkop, G. (2003). The impact of economic freedom on corruption: different patterns for rich and poor countries, *European Journal of Political Economy*, 19, 605–620.

Haggard, S. and Tiede, L. (2011). The rule of law and economic growth: Where are we?, *World Development*, 39 (5), 673–685.

Hill, R.C., Griffiths, W. E. and Lim, G. C. (2011). *Principles of econometrics* (4th Edition). Wiley, USA.

Hsiao, C. (1986, 2003). *Analysis of panel data* (1st and 2nd Editions). Cambridge, UK: Cambridge University Press.

Licht, A. N., Goldschmidt, C. and Schwartz, S. H. (2007). Culture rules: The foundations of the rule of law and other norms of governance, *Journal of Comparative Economics*, 35, 659–688.

Olsson, O. and Hansson, G. (2011). Country size and the rule of law: Resuscitating montesquieu, *European Economic Review*, 55, 613–629.

Pieroni, L. and d'Agostino, G. (2013). Corruption and the effects of economic freedom, *European Journal of Political Economy,* 29, 54–72.

Robinson, M. (2008). Why the rule of law matters. 11 June 2013, http://www.realizingrights.org/index.php?option=com_content&view=article&id=335&Itemid=134). http://www.heritage.org.

In: Economic and Social Issues …
Editor: Nilgün Çil Yavuz
ISBN: 978-1-62948-152-4

Chapter 9

ARAB SPRING: THE ROCKY ROAD TOWARD DEMOCRACY

Jamaleddine Harakat
Professor of Leadership at the ISCAE

ABSTRACT

The main aim of this study is to investigate the historical, social, economic and political dynamics of the Arab Spring in MENA region. The Arab Spring constitutes perhaps the most far-reaching political transition since the end communism in Europe. Indeed, the year 2011 started with stunning news from North Africa: the overthrows of the regimes of Tunisia and Egypt; Tunisia in a month and Egypt after seventeen days. Such uprisings are an unprecedented event in the Arab word. New aspirations have been developing, with communication among the demonstrators greatly facilitated through social media such as Facebook and Twitter. The Arab people have become so energized and hopeful that they continue bravely making demands despite the sometimes brutal government reprisals. Regardless of the final outcomes, the Arab people want change. The Arab spring rebellions occurred seemingly all at once; this was a social, economic, and political problem just waiting to boil over. It is a watershed even, and the surface stability imposed by repressive governments will never be the same.

1. Introduction

The **Arab Spring** can be considered the most radical change in politics that can be equated to the end of communism in Europe. Indeed, the year 2011 started with spectacular news from North Africa of overthrowing the regimes of Tunisia and Egypt. The Tunisian regime was ousted in a month and the Egyptian in seventeen days. Such uprisings are an unprecedented event in the Arab World. New aspirations have been developing, with communication among the demonstrators greatly facilitated through the social media such as Facebook and Twitter.

The Arab people have become so energized and hopeful that they continue bravely making demands despite sometimes brutal government reprisals. Regardless of the final outcomes, the Arab people want change. The Arab spring rebellions occurred seemingly all at once as there had been social, economic, and political problems just waiting to boil over. It is a watershed even, and the surface stability imposed by repressive governments will never be the same.

The ignition event that sparked the uprising in **Tunisia** was seemingly a routine (but highly significant) event. A poor street vendor in Tunisia (named Bouazizi) was abused by a police officer and, in his despair, set himself on fire in front of a police station. This event shocked the Tunisians and moved them to an unexpected action with very fast outcome: the President Ben Ali fled the country a month after the beginning of the uprising (W. Phares, 2010).

Likewise, a long standing resistance was forming in **Egypt** perpetrated by interactions through Facebook and Twitter. A collective action was initiated after a young man was beaten to death by the police. Again it was a symbolic spark that that brought forth latent outrage. The Egyptians massed in a downtown square (Tahrir Square in Cairo) every day and relentlessly demonstrated until their objective of toppling the regime came to a success seventeen days later (W. Phares, 2010).

In both countries, there is a haunting concern about the continuing presence of many figures from old regimes in their political scenes.

Resistance and demands for political and economic reform caught on virtually everywhere in the Arab world. The ideas took on a depth and momentum that propelled the demonstrators to face violence and overcome fear of their despotic regimes.

The story of **Libya**, the former Jamahiriya, was in a real state of instability. President Qaddafi was lynched and murdered by the insurgents in October 2011, and ever since, attempts for reform have been in place as a government was formed and officials have been trying to mediate among different factions of the opposition. The Eastern part broke away and tried to form its own state but failed in doing so. This had been a natural division as Libya originally constituted of three entities which were united by Italy after the First World War. This unity of Libya was preserved by President Qaddafi and most Libyans wanted to remain as one nation. Potentially, however, a civil war looms (W. Phares, 2010).

In **Bahrain**, a small and wealthy Golf State, the Shiia majority (more than 65 per cent) rebelled against the Sunni government headed by a hereditary King Hamad bin Isa Al Khalifah. The rebellion resulted from an outburst of indignation when the government arrested demonstrators en masse with the help of the Saudi Army. This help was provided because the neighbouring country, Saudi Arabia, also contains its own Shiia minority (W. Phares, 2010).

In **Yemen**, rebellions were met with harsh reprisals. The President Ali Abdullah Saleh, who had been in power for more than two decades, left the country, then returned, then left again in early 2012 for medical care after serious injuries and burns caused by a rocket launched by the insurgents. He promised several times to give up power but recanted. The opposition movement appeared to be faltering due to conflicting tribal interests and lack of organization (W. Phares, 2010).

Finally, **Syria**, the Sham Land, has experienced much turmoil and many civilian casualties, as the highly centralized Assad regime continues to imprison and kill large numbers of the demonstrators and civilians, including woman and children, with no end in sight (W. Phares, 2010). More than 70 thousands have been killed by early 2013 and entire cities are besieged and chaos prevails. To date international sanctions and statements of condemnation have had no effect as protesting and killing still continue.

In other Arab countries, including Morocco, Algeria, Mauritania, and Jordan, spontaneous demands made by demonstrators have led to promises of reform by governments.

In the wealthy Arabian Peninsula states; Saudi Arabia, Kuwait, Qatar, Oman, and the UAE, the rulers have confronted demands, but so far they have been able to buy off or placate the people with stipends and promised economic growth as well as more elected positions in the government (W. Phares, 2010).

The Arab Spring has been effective, as some countries strive to create democratic governments and others are slowly giving in to the demands of their people for more freedom and representation. All leaders have promised economic reforms to ensure higher employment rates and more equitable distribution of wealth. The demands are there but only dormant. This era certainly constitutes a time of transition.

2. Recent History of the Arab World

"We can only lead arab people by religion or by sword"

Ibn Khaldoun in the "MOKADIMA"

The current wave of protests cannot be considered an entirely new phenomenon, resulting partly from the militant activities of dissident activists as well as members of a variety of social and union organizations that have been latently active for years in Tunisia , Algeria , Egypt and others countries in the area.

Revolts have been occurring in the Arab area since the 1800s; but only recently have these revolts been redirected from combating foreign regimes incarnating colonialism to toppling rulers of the Arab states themselves. The revolution in the summer of 2011 marked the end of the old phase of national liberation from colonial rulers and launched a new one of inwardly addressing the problems of Arab society.

Background of the Arab Revolt

The rise of nationalism under the Ottoman Empire dates back to at least 1821. Arab Nationalism has its roots in the Mashriq (The Arab lands east of Egypt). Thus , the Arab Revolt (1916 – 1918) or *Al Thawra Arabiyya* in Arabic or else *Arap Isyani* in Turkish, was initiated by the Sherif Hussein Bin Ali with the aim of securing independence from the ruling of the Ottoman Empire and creating a single unified Arab state spanning from Aleppo in Syria to Aden in Yemen (A. Talmiz, 2006).

European Mandates and Modernization

As of 1920, the British and the French were mandated by the League of Nations to manage the affairs of the former Ottoman provinces of the Levant until they were ready for independence. Britain was to oversee Jordan,

Palestine, Iraq, and Kuwait. It already administered (or had colonized) Egypt and Sudan. France was granted responsibility for Lebanon, Syria, and was already the colonial ruler in North and West Africa. Libya and Eritrea were under Italian control (A. Talmiz, 2006).

As the Western colonial powers controlled and enjoyed the resources of these countries, their civil societies were just being introduced to modern institutions, including secular constitutions and various forms of electoral democracies.

Arab Nationalism or Al Qawmiya Al Arabia

This trend was also known as “Pan Arabism”. The advocates of this political ideology claimed that all the Arabic–speaking people of the region belonged to one nation, *Al Umma Al Arabiya* (the Arab nation).

Pan Arab ideologues wanted to reestablish an “Arab” *Umma* spanning from the Atlantic Ocean to the Gulf. Arab nationalism claimed that Turkish and Persians, let alone Indians (especially Pakistanis) were not Arabs, but were cousins in history and religion.

Although non-Islamist in origin, Pan Arabism kept a number of totalitarian features from the preceding Caliphate rule among which suppression of ethnic minorities and intolerance toward pluralist ideas that can change Arab identity were only a few examples.

Later on, after decolonization, Arab nationalists would change into chauvinistic elites. Movements such as the Baath parties in Syria and Iraq, the followers of the Nasser movement in Egypt, the doctrine of Muammar Qaddafi in Libya, abandoned the original liberalism of intellectuals and replaced it with extreme forms of supremacist nationalism.

Arab nationalism as of the mid-twentieth century had mutated into force that limited or suppressed liberties and military juntas’ crushing democracies across the region (M. Browers, 2009).

Decolonization and the Threat of Democracy

In most regions around the world, the departure of a colonial power signals an immediate advancement toward democracy, or at least a step in that direction. This wasn’t always the case in the Greater Middle East (MENA Area).

It is almost impossible to make global statements about an entire region stretching from Mauritania to Iraq with reference to democracy advancement. Some countries leaped toward multiparty systems and pluralism while others regressed to absolutism and totalitarianism.

The differences, for example, between Turkey and Saudi Arabia, or Lebanon and Libya under Qaddafi's control are enormous. Some, such as Turkey and Lebanon, granted more rights to citizens, including women and the political opposition, than the others countries did. But in the wake of decolonization throughout the region, the dominant political culture retained commune characteristics that resisted the advance of civil societies toward the norms advocated by the international community as the bases of implementing democracy.

Once the colonial powers left the region, gradually and in different ways, the Arab people shifted from living under European colonialism to living under Arab-on-Arab authoritarianism (L. Guazzone, 2009).

It is worth reviewing the main failures in the movement toward freedom, democracy, and recognition of ethnic and religious minorities in the region throughout the twentieth century.

- In **Saudi Arabia**, the Wahhabis seized power in Hejaz (Arabia) as early as the 1920s and formed an absolute monarchy based on Salafism: non-Muslim religions were banned, women's basic rights suppressed, and fundamental political freedoms annulled. By law, no political parties were allowed (P. J. Vatikiotis, 1984).
- In **Egypt**, as the British departed, the constitutional monarchy was removed by the military coup instigated by the Free Officers who installed a quasi-dictatorship under the Pan Arabist leader, Gamal Abdel Nasser, in 1954. Political freedoms were curtailed for all citizens and the rights of the Coptic religious minority suppressed. (P. J. Vatikiotis, 1984).
- in **Libya**, following the withdrawal of the Italians and the British, the constitutional monarchy collapsed in a putsch in 1970. Muammar Qaddafi declared himself the leader of the "revolution" and kept aspiring to become the "Islamic Arab" leader of the whole region. Naturally all freedom perished (P. J. Vatikiotis, 1984).
- in **Iraq**, the withdrawal of the British resulted in the same Pan Arabist officers who bloodily removed the King in 1958. The Baath established a one-party dictatorship in the 1960s seized ultimately in 1979 by Saddam Hussein, one of the most lethal dictators in the

region. Since then all opponents had been oppressed (P. J. Vatikiotis, 1984).

- in **Syria**, a limping multiparty democracy following the departure of the French in 1945 was removed through series of military coups bringing the Baath Arab Socialist Nationalist Party to power in the 1960s. After internal palace coups within the Party, a hard–line faction took over in 1970 under Hafez Assad's control (P. J. Vatikiotis, 1984).
- in **Algeria**, after years of violent struggle against French colonialism, the National Liberation Front (FLN) finally obtained independence in 1962 but only to create a one party regime that banned political freedoms.
- in **Lebanon**, the young state became the most successful multireligious democracy in the Arab world. When it gained its independence from the French in 1943 but domestic and foreign forces shattered its precarious political system.

Pan Arabists in the region, as well as their supporters in the former "Switzerland of the Middle East" feared the spread of the little country's "model" to the region and coalesced to cripple Lebanon's institutions, provoking a ravaging ethnic war in which most rights of all sects and individuals were pulverized. The remaining states of the Arab World, stretching from Morocco and Mauritania to the Gulf, didn't fare better. Unlike the situation in Latin America where democracy had its ups and downs, swinging between military regimes and multiparty elections, the Arab World knew only oppression as a common characteristic for its peoples, albeit perpetrated at different times, in different circumstances, and in the hands of different oppressors, but the twentieth century did not bring peace, freedom, or democracy to the Arab World.

Ideological Thought and Practice in the Arab World

Arab nationalism and Islamism have proven two of the most potent ideological forces in the Arab region over the past century. On the one hand, the two trends would seem to possess a number of natural affinities. Muslims are keenly aware of the central role played by Arabs and Arabic in the development of Islamic civilization.

Similarly, Arab nationalists have acknowledged the special place Islam occupies in Arab civilization. Not only is Islam the religion of the vast majority of Arabs but Islam‘s golden age corresponds with one of the most celebrated periods in Arab history. Baa'th Party founder Michel Aflaq (1910 – 1989) affirmed this relation in claiming that "Islam *...was an Arab movement and its meaning was the renewal and completion of Arabism"*. However, even when Arab nationalists and Islamists have found themselves facing a common enemy – such as corrupted and authoritarian regimes that seek their marginalization or oppression – they have most commonly proven to be each other's worst enemy. Throughout the contemporary era, their relationship has been better characterized as competitive and hostile than as cooperative and complementary (M. Browers, 2009).

Arab leaders, for their part, have often deployed repression and cultivation of one ideology trend at the expense of another in order to diminish the capacity of other trends in acting as a significant oppositional force vis-à-vis the state and to further deepen the lines that divide political groups.

In the 1950s, Jordan's King Hussein viewed Islamists as a strategic ally against his Arab nationalist and socialist critics. In the early 1970s, Egyptian president Anwar al-Sadat bolstered the Muslim Brotherhood in his campaign against leftists and Nasirists. In the early 1980s, Algerian president Chadli Bendjedid facilitated the rise of the Islamist movement as an auxiliary force in his purge of leftists and Boumédiennists. Throughout the 1990s, the Yemeni President Ali Abdullah Salih pitted Islamists against socialists to weaken the political influence of the latter – to cite just a few of many such examples from the region.

3. The Economic and Political Roots of Arab Uprising

"At the Arab land the best way to cross a square is through these three sides"

LAWRENCE of ARABIA in the "The Seven Pillars of Wisdom"

The Modern Pharaoh of Egypt

President Hosni Mubarak came to power in 1981. The economy was characterized by an unhealthy mix of state planning and market regulation in the early 1980s. Mubarak was unwilling to change fundamentally the economic system in order to avoid undermining what was known as “Egypt stability”. Egypt’s basic economic structures continued to deteriorate and the gap with other parts of the developing world widened, but economic and political rent income increased. The major feature of the “Mubarak” era policy concern was shared with the top leadership whose main objective was to stay in power. The regime obsession with power, control and security also explains the design and implementation of all major economic policy measures during the last 30 years.

After the “Bread riots” of January 1977 during President Sadat mandate, security concerns had begun to shape economic policy and often to overrule policy proposals made by external agencies such as the World Bank and the International Monetary Fund (IMF). Due to a massive budget deficit and external debts economic stagnation turned into an acute crisis.

Many reform attempts over the three decades supported by International Financial Institutions (IFIs) failed due to a lack of commitment on the Egyptian side. Egypt, then, has experienced a recurrence of macro-economic problems and a substantial crisis of its domestic economy.

The politico-economic system that produced the recursive economic crises has been conceptualized as a prevailing system. The combination of an authoritarian regime whose political power is based on the monopolization of the economic and political rent income and a national economy in which economic activities are to a large extent either rent – based or rent – oriented. Massive direct and indirect control of economy by the regime has been one of the foundations of its political survival (W. Phares, 2010).

Bureaucracy and Corruption

The numerous corruption scandals uncovered in the last years before the regime’s collapse had usually involved high-level administrators and relatives of office holders in the highest layers of the state apparatus. Cumbersome bureaucracy and excessive corruption remained major reasons for the high share of informal economic activity in Egypt, estimated by some at 50 per cent of the total economy activity (Arab Fund for Economic and Social Development).

Tunisia: The Raptor President

In 1992, Ben Ali married a woman named Leila Trabelsi. Few years later, she embarked on the monumental task of turning the whole country into a version of what she knew best: *the Bazaar*! The Trabelsis soon became what was labeled "the *family*". They seemed to have followed the path of a mafia clan so that it was said that the key to get a top job in the country depended largely on having connections with the "*family*". Thereby the regime of Ben Ali was a victim of the arrogance that grew out of its success. In Tunisia, unlike other Arab countries, the educated citizens expected the well-oiled bureaucracy that ran the country to live up to its historically high standards.

When the global economic crisis struck in 2008, Tunisia was not spared. This occurred when, in a country of just 10 million inhabitants, the number of highly qualified university graduates seeking jobs reached 40,000 a year. The official unemployment rate was 14 per cent. That was not high by contemporary European or American standards. But among recent Tunisian graduates, the rate tripled.

Then came wikileaks cables especially from France such as *Notre ami Ben Ali* and *La regente de Carthage* that detailed extensive corruption among the President's Ben Ali extended family. The ruling elite had grown greedily corrupted and arrogant, just as the strong economic growth on which the loyalty of the masses depended became unsustainable.

The historic Tunisian social contract by which the loyalty of the people was bought rather than earned, became untenable. What the Ben Ali regime had not anticipated was the boiling anger among the growing numbers of the young who were disproportionately unemployed. Many highly educated but unemployed young people started questioning the political censorship that had existed in Tunisia under President Ben Ali. Even Youtube was permanently blocked. Then the global financial crisis struck and, as a result, tourists from hard-hit European countries stayed away in significant numbers. This decline affected not only poor people who made their living on an informal tourism industry accessories, ranging from selling donkey rides to trinkets, but also relatively well-established shopkeepers who depended on foreign visitors (J. P. Tuquoi, 2011). By the same token, foreign investments started to shrink. A poll carried out over the two years before the revolution revealed substantial falls in the number of Tunisians who felt the economy was going in the right direction. The revolution was then at heart against the country's deteriorating economic situation among certain clusters of the population.

Libya: The Jamahirya in Rout

Libya has its own distinct characteristics reflecting its history and the nature of the country's political structure under colonel Qaddafi who had ruled his country since he had become in power in 1969. In his reign, he had always tried to avoid Western institutions of the post-colonial period believing that they might impede the pursuit of his revolutionary ideas, including legal process and civil liberties (P. J. Vatikiotis, 1984).

Qaddafi didn't hold any formal office, except the crucial title of Highest Commander-in-Chief of the Armed Forces. Nevertheless his power was absolute and his legitimacy had solid bases.

Like in Tunisia or Egypt, the Qaddafi family held the power with iron grip. The legitimacy stemmed more from charismatic and authoritarian qualities of the *Leader* (Qaddafi) than from institutions and established laws.

Numerous observers had concluded that Qaddafi was determined to pass power to one of his sons, Saif Al Islam. The latter was given far more opportunities to establish himself in the Libyan political system and to gain experience in the intricacies of domestic politics and foreign relations than Gamal Mubarak, the son of former President Mubarak of Egypt.

Unlike the Syrian and Egyptian examples, the absence of a constitutional structure in Libya opened unlimited opportunities for Saif Al Islam to act beyond any formally administrative or political framework. Importantly, his promotion might have been motivated by the main aim of reviving and even rescuing the regime. Many of Qaddafi‘s economic and social policies generated widespread unrest and opposition. The main origin of such unrest lied in the outcomes Qaddafi‘s policies which resulted in Libya‘s noticeably low economic performance.

An Islamic resistance movement had gained ground since the 1970s, provoked in part by Qaddafi‘s attempts to transform Libyan society and to challenge some important tenets of conservative Islam. While Qaddafi appeared to have well contained military and security forces, the regime faced serious challenges from Islamic groups and from the People‘s Committees, with their strong close power. After a long period of economic, political, and social decline caused by under US pressure and UN sanctions, 1999 marked the beginning of Libya's return to the international system. In a great need of a fresh political face to present to the outside world with a new approach to domestic problems in such difficult times, Qaddafi resorted to his son Saif Al Islam in whom he had complete trust. He had been a major driving force in the forefront attempts to improve Libya's relations with the United States and France.

Like Syria under Assad, and Egypt under Mubarak; Libya's political system was heavily influenced by Qaddafi's immediate family and by tribal networks.

Yemen: The Tribal Republic

Another Arab country in the group of republics considering a dynastic handover of power is Yemen where President Ali Abdallah Saleh has been in power since the unification of North and South Yemen in 1990 (W. Phares, 2010)

Like the leaders of Egypt, Syria, and Libya, Saleh's immediate and extended family had played important roles in helping him to keep power for more than two decades. Saleh's legitimacy was based on his central role in the unification of the two Yemens and on his subsequent efforts to provide stability to the country.

Ali A. Saleh's highly personalized power rested on a range of measures, many of which were delicately balanced compromises and alliances with other powerful forces in the country. His task of maintaining control was particularly difficult, given that his regime lacked economic and military resources to enforce his will in the same way as Syrian, Egyptian, and Libyan regimes did. His target was to arrange for the strategic placement of family members in vital military and political positions throughout his eldest son and heir, Ahmed.

The President son's was a colonel with control of the country's Special Forces and Republican Guards upon whose loyalty and effectiveness, the survival of the regime greatly depended. The intricacy of this political structure reflected the complexity of Yemeni society. Traditionally, it was a deeply divided country, reflecting often expedient alliances based on tribal, social, religious and political ties.

Over the past decade, political Islam had emerged as a serious threat to regime stability. Complicating matters were deteriorating Yemen's economic performance and, as a result, reserves of oil in 2007 contributed to about 85 per cent of Yemen's export income and 33 per cent of GDP, which marked a dramatic decline. It was in this unstable context that President Ali A. Saleh was thought to be attempting to position his son Ahmed as his successor.

The abovementioned rulers were operating in dangerous and divided societies, which had proven fatal to a leader who did not have a sufficient hold on power. All these kinds of regimes had been confronted by challenging opposition and had been willing to employ maximum force to suppress that opposition.

4. The Rising of the Islamist Movements

"Convictions are more dangerous enemies of truth than lies"

NIETZSCHE, German philosopher

Religious rebellion has been around for a long time. Although the religious rebellions of the last two decades of the twentieth century and beginning of the twenty-first have been shaped by modern politics, they inherit a long tradition of religious protest and social change. Religious and political ideas have been intertwined throughout history and around the globe. A number of rebellions against authority, from the Maccabean revolt in ancient Israel to the Taiping Rebellion in China, the Wahhabiya movement in Arabia, and Puritanism in England, have been religious in character. To understand this phenomenon, the religious movements must be considered in the context of the cultures that produced them.

Some social scientists have seen violent political change as eruptions along fault lines in a social system in which pressure has been building for years. This model can be applied to some current cases as well in the Arab world within the framework of the Crane Brintons' theory that confirms that: "*Revolutions occur when rising expectations are thwarted*".

Iran is one of the few places where a religious rebellion has become a revolution and replaced a secular regime. In other locations where religious rule has been established -- such as Afghanistan, Sudan -- the revolutionary regimes have been shaky, and the duration of their political control was brief. Some were toppled while others were transformed.

Whether or not they presented viable political alternatives to established regimes, these movements of Islamists always posed a serious threat of public order. Public security in the last part of the twentieth century became defined as protection against terrorism and political violence whose source was invariably associated with movements of political rebellion with religion agendas. Such a threat became real when two heads of states were assassinated by religious radicals, Anwar al Sadat in Egypt and Mohamed Boudiaf in Algeria, in addition to thousands, on both sides of struggles, who lost their lives.

The goals of these movements are both national and transnational. Even though the desire for a single Islamic nation runs deep in Muslim consciousness, most Islamist movements have been content to settle for an Islamic nationalism limited to respective countries in which they are present. Recently, as Ira Lapidus explains,

> "the capacity of Islamic movements to symbolize social identity has been merged into national feeling."

Egypt's Origin of Islamist Movements

The Muslim Brotherhood (al-*ikhwan al-Muslimeen)* is not only one of the longest surviving but also perhaps the most controversial of all Islamist movements to have emerged in the Arab world. The Brotherhood is a social movement that functions as a political party (Justice and Freedom Party) in some instances. It declares that its ultimate aim is to establish an Islamic state, but asserts its willingness to participate in the democratic process. It broadly rejects the West and Western values, yet is increasingly anxious to be seen in Western, especially in the United States, eyes as a moderate organization that can represent the voice of Muslims in Egypt (S. Akhtar, 2010)

Although the Brotherhood originated in Egypt as a result of a specific set of social and political conditions, its ideology soon spread and branches began to spring up in other countries. Syria and Jordan were perhaps the most important branches in the early days but it was not long before most of the countries in the Middle East had their own branches.

In 1981, Egypt's President Anwar al-Sadat was assassinated by members of an extremist movement, al-Jihad. The al-Jihad movement was at the extreme edge of Egypt's Muslim Brotherhood which was founded in 1928 by Hassan al-Banna. The leaders of this early Islamic political movement were reacting against the transnational modernism that was the legacy of the British Empire, and, prior to it, of the Ottoman Empire. Western culture, political influence, and economic control were the elements of modernity that some of the early nationalists sought to reject. For that reason, Egyptian nationalism grew in both religious and secular directions at the outset. The Muslim Brotherhood represented the Islamic form of Egyptian nationalism, and the

Wafd Party represented its secular side. When King Farouk was overthrown in 1952, it was largely the Wafd vision of a secular Egypt that emerged triumphant.

Yet even after Farouk, Islamic nationalism continued to be a potent force in Egyptian politics. The leader of the revolution, Gamal Abdel Nasser, had once allied with the Muslim Brotherhood, as had his successor, Anwar al-Sadat. By the 1960s, the leaders of the Muslim Brotherhood and Nasser were locked in bitter opposition when they attempted to overthrow his government. Nasser promptly threw them in prison.

Egypt's love-hate relationship between Muslim leaders and secular politicians continued in the 1970s during Sadat's presidency. The movement with which Sadat's assassins were associated made a deep political impact, largely because its ideology was more radical than that of Egypt's moderate Islamist leadership. Despite its aspirations, the radical Islamist movement had yet to be sufficiently united to threaten President Hosni Mubarak with revolution.

The main organization within the movement, the Muslim Brotherhood, has progressively moderated its politics. Though not accepted as a legal party, it is well represented in the legislature. This relatively reasonable position has made the Muslim Brotherhood look quite respectable - especially compared with the strident rhetoric of the extremist. In 1991, during the Gulf War, divisions between moderate and radical factions in the Islamic movement widened.

In the mid-1990 the terrorists' acts of al-Gamaa al-Islamya further alienated it from the Islamist mainstream. In addition to the World Trade Center bombing in New York, tourists were attacked near Luxor and in a café in Cairo, a luxury ship was fired on as it cruised down the Nile, and a bomb was placed in one of the Pyramids. A succession of attacks that began in 2004 on touristic sites in Egyptian resorts along the Red Sea was said to be motivated by radical Islamic opposition to what was regarded as the loose morals of visiting tourists. Three bombs ignited almost simultaneously on a single day in Sharm el-Sheik in 2005 killing eighty-eight people.

Hamas: The Islamic *Intifada*

No other Islamic movement in the Arabic-speaking world has succeeded politically like Hamas since it was formally established in 1987. At first a marginal player in the Palestinian arena, the Hamas has become the major organized force in Palestinian politics having won a decisive victory in the March 2006 Palestinian Legislative Council elections. It then seized control of the Gaza Strip in a military coup. Interestingly enough, these successes came despite the assassination of its founder, Ahmed Yasin, in March 2004, and of his successor Abd al-Aziz Rantisi, a month later (Akhtar, 2010).

The organization was founded in January 1988 and focused primarily on resistance to Israeli rule. Hamas is an acronym for Harakat *al-Muqawama al-Islamiyya* (The Islamic Resistance Movement), which zealously boosts the feeling of resistance against an occupying force in many of its followers.

In August 1988, Hamas, in reaction to a draft "declaration of independence" by PLO leaders, disseminated a charter of its own declaring that the entire Palestine was an Islamic trust land and was an indisputable part of the Muslim world. Needless to say, in the eyes of Hamas, the charter regarded negotiations with Israel and international conferences in pursuit of peace as useless and illegitimate.

From 1989 onward, relations between Hamas and the PLO, particularly Fatah, were fraught with tension. Unlike Arafat, Hamas did not support Saddam Hussein in the first Gulf War when Iraq invaded Kuwait. Instead, the movement called for both Iraqi and U.S. withdrawal.

Consequently, the Gulf States and Saudi Arabia retaliated against the PLO by allocating more funding to Hamas, particularly after Yasin's visit to the area between February and April 1988. With such funds, Hamas was able for the first time to compete with the PLO's welfare infrastructure, particularly since Hamas's institutions were considered more efficient.

Relations between them soured once again when Hamas rejected the Oslo peace process and the Declaration of Principles signed on the White House lawn on September 13, 1993. Hamas joined forces with the rejectionists within the PLO and managed to gain considerable support. The first Hamas suicide bombing in Hadera in April 1994 seemed designed as an attempt to sabotage a deal to create the Palestinian Authority, eventually signed on May 4, 1994. Just as Israel began realizing that Hamas was its major terrorist enemy in the Palestinian arena, Fatah began realizing that Hamas was beginning its bid for ultimate power by attempting to overpower the nationalist camp in the domestic Palestinian arena.

Hamas became so powerful that, by early 2003, Egypt felt it had to negotiate with all the factions to assure both domestic peace and a peace plan. For the first time, Hamas was elevated to equality with Fatah, the PLO, and the PA. Arafat's illness and subsequent death signaled further that the removal of the PLO and Fatah's charismatic leader from the scene lifted another barrier to Hamas's successful challenge.

Other factors, and especially important geostrategic one, made Hamas keep distance from the Muslim Brotherhood as a whole. Hamas's assumption of government through relatively fair elections made most Arab states with authoritarian regimes feel threatened by such a possibility of change from within. That change involving radical Islamic movements paralleling the Muslim Brotherhood that formed the major domestic opposition groups in Egypt, Jordan, and Syria made further crackdowns seem justifiable to their rulers.

The most threatened of all these states was Egypt under Mubarak, particularly after the success of Muslim Brotherhood candidates in Egypt's parliamentary elections in 2005 following Hamas's electoral victory. Since Egypt controls the only crossing at Rafah that connects Gaza to the Arab world, Mubarak used this power to try to weaken Hamas and reduce the attractiveness of its model for his own citizens.

Although "*Hamastan*" in Gaza covered a small area, continuing Hamas rule over the area was widely perceived as having far-reaching regional and even global implications. One of the major questions was related to the struggle between Arab nationalist-ruled states and opposition radical Islamist groups. The Hamas takeover has been linked to an Islamist revolutionary wave that included the Islamist insurgencies in neighbor states.

Syria: The Fierce Struggle

In contrast to its sister organization in Egypt, the Muslim Brotherhood in Syria began by engaging in the politics of parliamentary democracy at the time of the country's independence in 1946. This policy compelled the *Ikhwan* to forego its Islamist agenda and pursue more or less a pragmatic policy. Syrian *Ikhwan* members contested in parliamentary elections, served in cabinets, and engaged in realpolitik. However, the ascension to power of the secular and *Alawi*-dominated *Baath* Party posed a significant threat to the ideology and practice of the Brotherhood, which had already been affected by the political trend set by secular, socialist, and nationalist parties (S. Akhtar, 2010).

In 1964, a Muslim Brotherhood insurgency erupted in Hama, which was swiftly put down by the incumbent regime. Yet, the regime failed to pay attention to the organization's growing underground activity. The insurgency restarted in a disorganized manner in 1976 but soon turned into full-scale urban warfare against the regime and its supporters. The decisive and final showdown took place in Hama in 1982, which was quelled by the regime using disproportionately tremendous force. Since then the regime has pursued a consistent policy toward the outlawed Muslim Brotherhood.

In June 2000, after three decades in power, Assad passed away. His son Bashar took over, hinting broadly at a new era of modernity and reform. Initially, the *Ikhwan* expressed their readiness to make a fresh start with the new ruler in Damascus. Bashar, keeping to the pattern established by his father, released 600 prisoners in November 2000, of whom 380 were *Ikhwan* members. At the same time, the regime reasserted its objection to any form of organized political activity by the Brotherhood.

In May 2001, the *Ikhwan* explicitly signaled their comeback to the political scene by publishing the draft of the Covenant of National Honor for Political Action. The draft started that it contained preliminary ideas for "*dialogue to formulate a covenant of national honor that would regulate the course of political action*."

However the assassination of former Lebanese prime minister Rafiq Hariri in February 2005 sparked mass demonstrators – the so called Cedar Revolution – that compelled Syria to withdraw its troops after three decades from Lebanon. Many Lebanese pointed an accusatory finger to Syrian authorities for assassination. In December 2005, the Vice President Khaddam lashed out at the involvement of the Syrian regime in the Hariri's assassination. The Muslim Brothers decided to work with Khaddam for political transition in Syria with former regime Officials who were ready to commit themselves to democratic change. The regime, through repression, has prevented any formation of a liberal alternative for Baa'thist rule. However, the political preference for an average Syrian was manifested by a growing religious revival in society, symbolized by high attendance of Friday prayer services, high enrollment in religious schools, and widespread wear of the veil. Despite this religious revival being manifested by a growing Islamic sentiment, it should not be equated with a growing support for the Muslim Brotherhood as a specific organization. It is extremely difficult to gauge the extent to which Syrian society supports the *Ikhwan*.

Unless radical changes overtake Syria, the *Ikhwan* movement has little, if any, impact, let alone overthrowing the regime. Even if a Sunni Islamist movement emerged in Syria, it was likely to take a different organizational framework than the traditional Brotherhood group.

Iraq and the Nightmare of Terrorism

Iraq was vulnerable to the rise of Islamist movement following the overthrow of the Saddam Hussein's secular regime in 2003 in part because of the political influence of the close neighborhood. Even if the country had not been invaded by the jihadi activists from neighboring Syria, Jordan, or Saudi Arabia, the Muslim activists within Iraq would have been affected by models of Islamist activism in the Middle East and North Africa. The jihadi elements that came into Iraq in the months following the U.S. military invasion were different from these local insurgents: they were more strident, more expansive in their vision of global religious struggle. They largely contributed to creating religious conflict between the Arab Sunnis and Shi'ites.

Although the sectarian violence in Iraq was often described as Sunni-Shi'a civil war, there was little support for the violence from moderates and mainstream religious leaders on either side. On the Sunni side, the Sunni Association of Muslim Clerics resisted the attempts of the alTawhid jihadis to co-opt into it and the association often played a positive role in helping to moderate violence. On the Shi'a side, the Shi'a dominated Iraq government and pledged to control Muqtada's gangs, and leading clerics such as Ayatollah al-Sistani distanced themselves from Shi'a extremists, and linked to leading Shi'a political Party, the Supreme Council for the Islamic Revolution in Iraq, led by Abdul Aziz al-Hakim.

Tunisia: A Small Country with a Great Revolution

The leader and founder of main Islamist group *Ennahda,* Rachid Ghannouchi emerged more prominently on the Tunisian political scene in 1981 when Bourguiba lessened restrictions on political activity and founded a party he called the Islamic Tendency Movement. The Tendency's ostensible aims, at any rate, sounded even more moderate. By then, however, any mention of Islam was a red line to Bourguiba. In the same year, Ghannouchi was arrested and sentenced to eleven-year jail. In 1984 he was released and resumed his political activity. In 1992 he went into exile in London and was not seen again in Tunisia until the Ben Ali regime had been ousted. The *Ennahda* has no ostensible economic program or even any practical political program. Then how is Tunisia to be governed? Ghannouchi declared:

> "we do not want power to be monopolized by any single party …. . We seek a state in which the executive, legislative, and judicial powers are separate, the rule of law is supreme, and the freedom of conscience, expression, and association are guaranteed."

Ennahda was effective in accomplishing its immediate political aims by muscling in on the Political Reform Committee, the most important of several bodies formed to deal with the democratic transition. The observers confirm that *Ennahda* is highly organized. It has organized mass weddings and raised funds, opened countless offices where political agitation is combined with charity work.

Lack in Civil Society Activism in the Arab Countries

Since the attacks on New York and Washington DC on September 11th 2001, the question of absence of democracy in the Arab world has been at the forefront of both academic discourse and policy-making preoccupation. Within democratic political theory and democratization studies, civil society is always identified as a necessary component for the establishment of democracy. There are a number of approaches to the study of civil society, but they all share the same feature: the assumption that the presence of an active civil society is a sign of positive development. When it comes to the MENA area, the mainstream belief is that the countries in the region crucially lack civil society activism. Thus the main assumption is that civil society dynamism depends largely on its wider institutional context and on the structure of organizations themselves (R. Inglehart, 2002).

5. The Democracy Challenge in the Arab Countries

> "Intolerance is itself a form of violence and an obstacle to the growth of a true democratic spirit"
>
> Mahatma GHANDI

It should be said from the outset that in the Arab world states, there is no fully developed democratic political system; at least in the Western meaning of the term. However, most regimes in the region claim to be democratic. It could be said that all political systems in the region, particularly after falling of secular authoritarianism regimes in countries such as Tunisia, Libya and Egypt, do admit that democracy is the preferable political system and recognize its superiority to other forms of government.

Even though none of these regimes practices what it preaches, it is still important to note that their resistance to democracy is not a matter of principle nor is it based on ideological ground. Rather, as they tend to claim, a matter of practicality, i.e. whether their societies can successfully apply democratic arrangements. Moreover, the Arab regimes tend to argue that societies need to be made ready for democracy, a task that has not been completed in their countries yet. For them, evolving toward democratic policies is a matter of time, assuming time is used in the proper way to prepare their societies for democracy.

Prerequisite conditions are needed to implement the democratic process. Such conditions include social, economic, and cultural dimensions. Democratic reform claimed by the new Islamist ruling elites in many Arab countries should be a process, rather than a buzzword conducive to raising enthusiasm in the crowd. Also, in a process that has a desirable end-goal, societies happen to be on different levels of development and thus may be either far form or close to the point of reaching the desired end-goal. At a certain point in time, different societies could be claimed to have reached different points on the path to the final goal which is democracy. Arab regimes can be classified in terms of how close they are to the end-goal. The basis of this classification is based on three main criteria:

a) The presence of a multi-party system,
b) Levels of respect for human rights,
c) Freedom of expression, especially freedom of the press.

Different countries rank differently on the aforementioned criteria of this composite index. Generally, the overall ranking comes as follows:

Advanced Reformists

This cluster or regimes includes countries that have open multi-party systems, where restrictions on the formation of parties are kept to the minimum. Also in these regimes, periodic and fairly clean elections are held. More importantly, regimes included in this class maintain a reasonable degree of power rotation between the different parties, and therefore there should be no permanent opposition and ruling parties. Regimes of this cluster experience a significant level of respect for human rights. Finally in these regimes a fairly reasonable degree of freedom of the press is guaranteed. Three regimes are included in this category, and can be ranked in descending order as follows: Morocco, Jordan, and Lebanon. (Fattah, 2006).

Crippled Reformists

This class of regimes is characterized by a great deal of political freedom. But at the same time, the government in such countries is presiding over a chaotic situation, where the freedoms available are not fully protected due to the prevalent political instability. Many revolutionary regimes such as those in Egypt, Libya, Tunisia and Yemen are included in this category. In fact, the non-governability of the whole system is partly responsible for both the maintenance of political freedom and the restrictions imposed upon it by the new Islamists rulers (Fattah, 2006).

Stalled Reformists

This category includes countries in which a process of democratization has begun sometime earlier, but was stopped halfway before fulfilling its promises. From a formal point of view, reforms that were introduced earlier onto these regimes are kept in place. However, most of these reforms have been deprived of much of their substance. Although some of the early reforms are still functioning, the overall situation is not very pleasant (Fattah, 2006).

The regime included in this category is Algeria where the country has got to this situation as a result of an attempt at rapid reform that went out of control.

Reform Resistant

This category includes regimes which, by and large, are resistant to introducing any significant reforms to their political systems. However, even in such regimes increasing effort is made to demonstrate their democratic inclinations. Shedding more light on what might seem as democratic practices such as elections and the role of the opposition, remain a cosmetic tactic which such regimes tend to apply. Countries that can be included in this category are Sudan and many countries in the Gulf (Fattah, 2006).

Prague Spring vs. Arab Spring

For a better understanding and appreciation of a democratic development in the Arab world, we have to keep in mind that, contrary to what happened in Eastern Europe and other parts of the world, change wrapped up in continuity is the prevalent mode in the MENA region.

After the collapse of communism, new political systems with new elites have been established in the former communist countries. A development of that kind did not take place in all Arabic countries. On the one hand, old regimes have been demolished in Tunisia, Egypt and Libya. On the other hand old ruling elites remain in power in all the countries in the region. Democratic development in the Arab countries is either a sweeping revolutionary change in many countries or an elite-led change in others (W. Phares, 2010).

Therefore, there is a lot of difficulty in applying the standards emanating from the Eastern European experience to the Arab world. Moreover, the lessons learned from Eastern Europe have been interpreted differently in the Arab world. For many, the main lesson of Eastern Europe has been that failure to reform is a prescription for collapse whereas in the Arab world the main lesson seems to have been that rapid reform is the shortest way to collapse. Therefore, while the collapse of totalitarian regimes of Eastern Europe has usually been interpreted as evidence of the assured failure of non-democratic regimes, it has been interpreted as lack of reforms in the Arab world.

Certain circumstances allowed such in political systems differ from their counterparts in Eastern Europe in one important aspect.

The former communist regimes failed to introduce significant reforms for decades, which contributed to the accumulation of tremendous anger and frustration that led to their fall in the end. However, reform in many Arab countries is an instrument geared to serving the survival of their regimes.

Traditional / Religious and Modern / Secular Dilemma

It could be said, then, that democratic reform in the Arab world is facing a dilemma of some sort: How to design a change that is at the same time responsive to the needs of the ruled and accommodating the survival needs of the rulers. Compromise and gradualism could be the answer to such a dilemma. However, the Arab countries are facing other problems that make this easier-said-than-done recipe. Conflict in the Arab societies is not only between democratic and authoritarian forces. Rather, and more importantly, it is between different conceptualization of the "desired society". Arab policies lack consensus on the definition of the "ought to be society". For some it should be traditional / religious, while for others it should be modern /secular. Along such dichotomy, Arab societies in the Mediterranean tend to be divided. Democratic arrangements would help solving such conflict as they provide for a set of procedural criteria of legitimacy.

However, democracy is not just about procedures. It is also about norms and values, since certain values are more in congruence with democracy than others (M. Fattah, 2006).

No doubt that the procedural democratic rules such as periodic fair and free elections, one man one vote resulting in the rule of a majority, are essential to the success of a democracy. However, democracy is also based on a certain set of values and norms, such as equality, pluralism, tolerance, relativism, and protection of the right of political minorities. It is unfortunate that these very values are disputed and questioned by some important social and political forces in the Arab world. Therefore, the legitimacy crisis many Arab countries are undergoing has roots that go much deeper than just the way through which the rulers are elected. An example of how serious this problem is lies in the case of the Algeria crisis, where the agreed upon democratic procedures failed to secure a peaceful transition when the result threatened to replace the prevalent conception of the desired society with another one. The deep degree of dilemma can be seen in the position taken by some democratic / liberal parties that condemned the army's takeover to prevent the victory of the Islamist party, FIS.

The Lack of Congruence between Fundamentalists and Democracy

The divide between the religious and the secular factions is much deeper than other divides between different views of the desired society. The divide has a lot to do with democracy itself, since the political ideology of the religious, or what is referred to as fundamentalists, is not in the full congruence with democracy in many important aspects. This lack of congruence is derived from the gap between the fundamentalist 'sacred vision' of the world, and the mundane nature of politics and, by extension, of democracy. Although there are some signs of the fundamentalist political thought being reformed in a democratic direction, such reform does not seem convincing enough to the secular democrats to accept the full integration of the fundamentalists into the political system. It has been noticed that the democratic reform adopted by fundamentalists thus far remains at the level of political, or rather procedural, thought, and does not reach deep levels of the theoretical /philosophical premises (M. Kassem, 1999). For many, such partial reform does not exclude the possibility of retreat toward the theoretically better-established totalitarian theocracy.

A cautious attitude prevails among many in the region as whether the fundamentalists would abide by democratic rules if they were to conflict with the sacred. Secular democrats are still concerned about the possibility of “one man one vote one time”. Interestingly, this same concern precludes the inclusion of fundamentalists in the political process. Ironically, however, without such an inclusion, real democracy is unlikely to be implemented because fundamentalists are an essential component of the political communities in the Arab world.

It could be claimed, then, that a viable democratic reform in the Arab world should be designed not only to accommodate the needs of the ruled and the rulers, but also of the contending ideological inclinations. One additional merit of the gradualist approach is to encourage the contending parties to get to a consensus.

The problem of whether and how to include religious fundamentalists into the political systems of the Arab Mediterranean countries after the secular regimes in Tunisia, Egypt and Libya collapsed needs more complex and thought-provoking solutions.

Political Community in the Arab World

Any political system is based on a definition of the political community, which provides the criteria to determine which groups are parts of the community, and consequently integrated into that political system. In Western experience, the definition of the political community went through a number of phases, gradually being expanded and made more inclusive as to accommodate a widest range of social and political forces (A. Talmiz, 2006). Even in these well-defined models, some forces are still excluded from the political community of some Western countries. For example, the New Nazis in Germany tend not to be welcome in its political system. Defining the political community becomes a problem of a bigger magnitude in emerging democracies. Laying the foundations of democratic policies and at the same time being inclusive of a wide range of political, ideological and social forces is a big challenge that cannot be downplayed. In the Arab world, religious fundamentalists have a more advanced thought about the formation of this policy as it remains far from being finalized.

There is no theoretical solution to the problems faced by Arab policies. Building a democracy is a process where early phases lead to subsequent ones. What is needed in the region is a type of leadership that would be highly committed to the democratic principles, and at the same time would be armed with a vision of how to transform its policy to a democracy through a series of consecutive phases of reform. While a lot could be said on the theoretical level in that regard, functioning solutions are country-specific. It would argue that no matter what the definition of the political community is, the very first step toward democracy in the region lies in abiding by whatever in-place rules of the political game.

Even if certain groups are to be excluded from the political process, the rules of process should be fair and strictly observed by all those who are involved in participating. Such a practice should help gain credibility for both democracy and the respective regime, which in turn would allow for the future inclusion of other forces.

CONCLUSION

Do Islamist Movements Challenge the Democracy, or Does Democracy Challenge the Islamist Movements in the Arab World?

One of the widely expressed fears in the West is that current rulers belonging to Islamist Movements in many Arab countries, such as Tunisia, Libya, and Egypt will end up like the Taliban. A tendency toward violence may be the matter that immediately alarms about religiously activists even if not all of them see the Taliban or Iran as the ideal model. Although many Islamist movements tend to be authoritarian, the same is true of some secular nation-states, which, like radical Islamists, uphold ideologies of order and are pledged to maintain society's morals. In most secular societies, however, strong central authority has devolved to systems of authority involving an elected parliament of representatives and independent judiciary system. Most secular nationalists refer to this system whenever they talk about democracy. The question, then, is whether religious nationalism can embrace a democratic system.

The rhetoric of many religious nationalists suggests that they place a high value on democracy. Even those activists most opposed to the secular state affirm the political importance of the democratic spirit (A. Talmiz, 2006).

An international survey conducted by the Pew Foundation in 2006 revealed a surprising correlation between support for Muslim policies and a belief in democracy. In Jordan, Pakistan, and Palestine, the surveyed population confirmed that their countries could and should have a democratic future.

Some of this enthusiasm for democracy tends to be self-serving. If democracy simply means majority rule, then it means letting people have what they want. If the people want a religious society rather than a secular one, then they should have it. This line of reasoning has been used in many countries such as Egypt by the Brotherhood president Morci and his organization to treat democracy process as the legitimization of rule by whichever camp has the preponderance of the population on its side. These arguments equate democracy with the will of the majority.

To a remarkable degree, the Islamist's position on democracy and truth echoed that articulated in Plato's *Republic* where Plato characterized democracy as a "*charming form of government, full of variety and discovery*," which leads naturally to tyranny. Plato feared that if people were allowed to make decisions collectively, they would simply advance their own interest, which would result in policies that were nothing more than the lowest common denominator of individuals' greed and desire for personal security. What was needed, he maintained, was leadership that could rise above self-interest and provide a broad vision for the whole. Fair government was embodied in the philosopher-king (M. Kassem, 1999).

Democratic theory as propounded by John Locke and other eighteenth-century rationalists countered Plato's objections to democracy in two ways. First, proponents of democracy had considerable faith in the ability of individuals to rise above self-interest in their collective decisions and to vote for the welfare of the whole. Second, democratic theorists thought that elected representatives would have a dual role: they would be both mouthpieces of their constituencies and independent judges of what was appropriate for the welfare of the wider community. Many religious nationalists, however, challenge Locke's assumptions, lacking the rationalists' faith that reason alone is sufficient for finding the truth, and unconvinced that unbridled self-interest is an adequate moral basis for a political order. This view puts the religious nationalists back in Plato's position. Religious nationalists have one advantage over Plato: they are clearer than him about where to find truth. The tradition of most religious activists provides a framework of religious law that is considered normative for human activity. According to some activists, the establishment of religious law is the primary goal of religious political movements. Religious leaders in Egypt, for instance, identified main problem with the governments of Anwar al-Sadat and Hosni Mubarak as their elevation of secular law over *shari'a.* Currently, the detractors of the Islamists who rule Egypt blame them for intending to make *shari'a* over the law.

Thereby electoral process, as a means of choosing leaders and making decisions, has become well established internationally, including regions in which religious political activist movements are on the rise. To the degree to which elections are the hallmark of democracy, religious activists are as democratic as any secular politician. However, they break with democratic theorists primarily over two issues. One is whether the democratic system can be legitimate without higher moral authority establishing it: religious politicians deny the possibility. A democratic gang of thieves, they argue, is still a gang of thieves. For the process to be morally valid it must be put to moral purposes. The other issue is the democratic principal of minority right. In many parts of the world, minority communities have watched the rising of religious activism with great apprehension. The question, then, is how religious nationalists should deal with the issue of minority rights when a democratic state is established.

References

J.P. Tuquoi , Notre Ami Ben Ali , ed.La Decouverte. 2011.

Laura Guazzone,ARAB State And Neoliberal Globalization, ed. Ithaca press.2009.

Maye Kassem, In The Guise Of Democracy, ed. Ithaca press. 1999.

Michaell L. Brower's, Political Ideology In The Arab World, ed. Cambridge.2009.

Moataz Fattah, Democratic Values In The Muslim World, ed. Lynne Rienner publishers. 2006.

P.J.Vatikiotis, Arab And Regional Politics In The Middle East, ed. St.Martin's press.1984.

Ronald Inglehart, Islam Gender Culture And Democracy, ed. Sitter Publications.2002.

Shabbir Akhtar, Islam As Political Religion, ed. Routledge. 2010.

Talmiz Ahmad, Reform In The Arab World, ed. India Research Press.2006.
Walid Phares, The Coming Revolution,ed. Threshold.2010.

INDEX

A

B

J

K

L

M

N

O

Q

R

S

T

U

V

W

Y